D1261475

THE ORIGINS OF THE SEDER

The Passover Rite and
Early Rabbinic Judaism

Baruch M. Bokser

UNIVERSITY OF CALIFORNIA PRESS

Berkeley   Los Angeles   London

UNIVERSITY OF CALIFORNIA PRESS
Berkeley and Los Angeles, California

UNIVERSITY OF CALIFORNIA PRESS, LTD.
London, England

Library of Congress Cataloging in Publication Data

Bokser, Baruch M.
  The origins of the seder.

  Bibliography: p. 149
  Includes index.
  1. Seder. 2. Mishnah. Pesahim—Criticism interpretation, etc. 3. Tosefta. Pesahim—Criticism, interpretation, etc. I. Title.
BM695.P35B64   1984   296.4'37'09   83-17932
ISBN 0-520-05006-1

PRINTED IN THE UNITED STATES OF AMERICA

1 2 3 4 5 6 7 8 9

For
    Eugene LeVee
    Rose Levinson
    Miriam Oles
    James Weinberger

CONTENTS

PREFACE AND ACKNOWLEDGMENTS

HOW DID THE SEDER, or Passover eve celebration, become one of the most famous and popular Jewish rituals? The Bible includes extensive discussions of Passover and the Festival of the Unleavened Bread; however, these descriptions do not correspond with later observances of the holiday. In particular, the biblical ritual focuses on the passover sacrifice, which in post-biblical literature no longer holds a central position and is, instead, represented only through a symbol. The present study addresses this transformation in the Passover holiday by analyzing the earliest full account of the Passover evening celebration, in the Mishnah, edited in Palestine around 200 C.E.

To appreciate the meaning of the Mishnah and of the changes in Passover, I must deal with wider historical and literary developments in Judaism between the first and third centuries. The transformation in Passover is part of a larger change in Judaism from a religious life ideally based on a central cult and temple to one structured around the individual home and the synagogue. This development, through which Jews came to perceive their religious activities in their own homes as the highest form of piety, took place gradually and represents one of the major contributions of early rabbinic Judaism.

In the first and second centuries, rabbinic authorities drew upon and adapted earlier teachings while also formulating new insights of their own. They developed ideas and institutions that would enable Jews to practice their religion outside the temple, and they legitimized the new forms as the primary means of religious expression. The Mishnah is the codification of these developments. It incorporates rabbinic teachings as well as the modest heritage of groups that existed before 70 C.E., especially the Pharisees. All these materials are presented through the perspective of the redactor-editor, at the end of the second century. While some of the first-century new developments may actually predate this period and the editing of the Mishnah, they receive new meaning as part of the Mishnah's comprehensive statement. The Mishnah's editor did not include all the teachings enunciated by rabbis in the first and second centuries, and what he did include usually is not presented in its original form and language. Rather the materials have been selected, shaped, and organized into a new whole.

As I indicate in chapter 1, it is this characteristic of the Mishnah that determines my approach and the direction of my investigation. I am interested in what the Mishnah's editor did with the earlier heritage, how he perceived and presented the Passover eve celebration, and how he drew upon the earlier teachings and made them into a new unity. Accordingly, this study takes Mishnah Pesaḥim (= Passover) as its point of departure and also makes frequent use of the Tosefta, the collection of rabbinic teachings edited soon after the Mishnah, which comments upon, complements, and supplements the Mishnah. The Tosefta provides further information and shows an early understanding of the Mishnah, although it has a different thematic and redactional perspective. I also make use of other early rabbinic sources that throw light on our subject. Often these midrashic and talmudic passages analyze the Mishnah and further develop the changes it prescribes in the Passover celebration.

Since this study focuses on Mishnah Pesaḥim 10 and draws heavily upon Tosefta Pisha (= Passover) 10, I present translations of these texts in chapter 3 of the present study. Both are necessarily fresh translations. Since a critical edition of the Mishnah is not available, the translation of the Mishnah is based upon available manuscripts. For the Tosefta I have used Saul Lieberman's critical edition. Appendix B presents the Hebrew text of these two works. Critical editions are essential in working with rabbinic texts, which over the centuries have become contaminated by numerous interpolations and corruptions. This applies especially to Passover materials since they have frequently been revised to make them conform to changes in the seder and haggadah.

* * *

My focus upon the Mishnah and its perception of the evening celebration has enabled me to provide a new and, I believe, significant contribution to research on Passover and the seder while making use of the extensive earlier scholarship on the subject. In chapter 1 and at appropriate points throughout the study, I discuss in some detail the approaches of these earlier works. Generally, what distinguishes them from the present monograph are the following: Some works explain individual passages from biblical, rabbinic, or medieval sources. Most trace the history of the Passover holiday, or of selected elements of its celebration, through many periods. They frequently weave their arguments with references deriving from diverse contexts and times. The benefit of these works lies in their in-depth analysis and diachronic perspective. The present study provides a complementary perspective; and although I am sensitive to antecedent and later developments, my point of departure remains the Mishnah, specifically Mishnah Pesaḥim 10. I examine this work as a unit and attempt to see its parts in relation to the document as a whole.

Study of the Passover evening celebration may shed light on complex and important issues in the history of Judaism. One such issue, discussed in chapter 1, is the formation and nature of rabbinic Judaism. Since the time of the Mishnah, if not earlier, the Passover evening celebration has been a home ritual in which people strengthen their bonds of fellowship. The participants engage in practices and employ symbols laden with cultic meaning, an observance that quintessentially represents rabbinic Judaism's program for a religious life without a central cultic temple. Already in the Bible, as in Exodus 12, the Passover evening celebration is described as a decentralized celebration organized in the home. Apparently, even when the cult became centralized in Jerusalem, the family meal continued. Thus, the evening celebration provided a prototype for later rabbinic rituals and observances indicating how one could be religiously involved without being in the temple.

A second major issue taken up in chapter 1 has to do with the pre-70, prerabbinic heritage and the wider Hellenistic, Roman, and Christian contexts—especially their use of banquets and fraternal meals and their understanding of sacrifices. It is not novel to assert that these antecedents and the wider context may have influenced the character and direction of developments in Judaism. The relative roles of the antecedents and the wider context, however, are not always clear. The present study focuses on the impact of these factors and evaluates the degree to which each may have played a significant role.

Chapter 2 reviews the earlier Jewish accounts and regulations of the holiday and touches upon their relationship to the Mishnah's projected ritual. Chapter 3 presents the continuous text of the Mishnah and the Tosefta, enabling the reader to discern immediately that they differ stylistically and substantively from the earlier materials. Chapter 4 closely examines the Mishnah's description of the pre-70 observances, demonstrating how that portrayal is biased by the Mishnah's interests and how it forms part of a tacit argument that the essential elements of the ritual are still viable post-70. This argument constitutes the Mishnah's response to the contemporary challenge of the loss of the temple and sacrificial order.

In an attempt to evaluate the Mishnah's response to the challenges facing

Judaism in the first and second centuries, chapter 5 is devoted to an examination of communal meals, banquets, and symposia in antiquity, especially in Judaism. Comparing several examples of meals and of rituals or intellectual discussions held around a meal, it evaluates the claim, made by certain scholars, that the Passover celebration is a "Jewish symposium," and rejects the thesis that the influence of the symposia literature *caused* the expansion of the Passover rite. Though these scholars have noticed many symposiatic elements in the seder, I maintain that those elements do not determine the meaning and character of the celebration as portrayed in the Mishnah. Indeed, the Mishnah takes pains to differentiate the seder from a symposium; it also contains elements that reflect the distinctive world view of early rabbinic Judaism. Chapter 6 reviews this dimension of the Mishnah.

Chapter 7 presents the conclusions of the study and discusses their implications. It examines how the Mishnah's restructuring of the Passover rite affected both the ideological meaning of the festival and the projected experience of the celebrants. By analyzing the significance of the particular form that the Mishnah chose to convey its message, chapter 7 articulates the need of early rabbinic Judaism to show continuity with the past, which leads into a discussion of the nature of change and development in rabbinic Judaism.

Several scholars have suggested that Jews actually continued to offer a paschal sacrifice even after the temple was destroyed in 70. Such a claim might seem to invalidate my thesis since in that case Jews would not have had the loss of the paschal sacrifice to respond to nor the inability to partake of it in the evening celebration. In Appendix A, after examining the evidence that scholars have assembled to support this proposition, I argue that they have not necessarily proven their case. Even if some Jews did offer a paschal sacrifice after 70 (as the Samaritans have until the present day), scholars agree that they would have discontinued the rite in the second century. Accordingly, from the perspective of the Mishnah, edited about 200, the crisis surely would have existed.

A glossary at the end of the book defines technical terms and phrases.

In the notes, references to primary and secondary works follow the standard sequence and chronology of sources, except where they appear in order of importance. To facilitate citation of references, I have employed a system of abbreviations. A rabbinic work is denoted by its title and, where appropriate, edition and date. Other works, including medieval and modern studies, are denoted by the name of the author and, where necessary to differentiate among several works by the same person, the date of publication or an abbreviated title. A comprehensive list of these works appears in the Abbreviations and

Bibliography. I have transliterated the titles of foreign works except where they supply an English translation.

Several works have proved formative in my thinking and may be said to have provided the foundation for this book. These include: Meir Friedmann, *Meir ʿAyin ʿal Seder VeHaggadah Shel Lele Pesaḥ* (Vienna, 1895; reprint ed., Jerusalem, 1971); Siegfried Stein, "The Influence of Symposia Literature on the Literary Form of the Pesah Haggadah," *Journal of Jewish Studies* 7 (1957):13–44; E. D. Goldschmidt, *The Passover Haggadah, Its Sources and History* [Hebrew] (Jerusalem, 1960); Saul Lieberman's comprehensive commentary on the Tosefta, *Tosefta Ki-Fshuṭah, to Moʿed* (New York, 1962); J. B. Segal, *The Hebrew Passover, From the Earliest Times to A.D. 70*, London Oriental Series, vol. 12 (Oxford, 1963); Menachem M. Kasher, *Hagadah Shelemah, The Complete Passover Hagadah* [Hebrew], ed. Shmuel Ashknage (Jerusalem, 1967); and Joseph Tabory, "The History of the Order of the Passover Eve" (Ph.D. diss., Bar Ilan University, 1977). In addition, Professors David Weiss Halivni and Jacob Neusner have contributed significantly to this study, through their written publications as well as oral communications, and I appreciate their continued interest in my research.

I am also indebted to colleagues who heard earlier versions of this study at the Annual Meeting of the Society of Biblical Literature, October 28, 1976, St. Louis, Missouri; at a meeting of the Group in Ancient History, University of California, Berkeley, February 23, 1977; at the Center for Hermeneutical Studies in Hellenistic and Modern Culture, the Graduate Theological Union and the University of California, Berkeley, June 5, 1977 (the paper and the discussion of which were published as *Protocol of the Thirtieth Colloquy: Philo's Description of Jewish Practices*, ed. Wilhelm Wuellner); and at the Seventh World Congress of Jewish Studies, Jerusalem, August 1977. I have gained valuable insight from the challenging questions, constructive criticism, and suggestions of my colleagues.

I also want to thank the following individuals who answered questions on specific topics: Professors Guitty Azarpay, Anne D. Kilmer, Jacob Milgrom, and Martin Schwartz, University of California, Berkeley; Gary G. Porton, University of Illinois, Champaign-Urbana; and Menachem Schmelzer, Jewish Theological Seminary of America. I am grateful as well to those who read earlier versions of this study and offered many critical observations and useful suggestions: Professors Ben Zion Bokser, Queens College; Joel Gereboff, Arizona State University; William S. Green, University of Rochester; Baruch

Levine, New York University; Jacob Neusner, Brown University; Joseph Tabory, Bar-Ilan University, Israel; Shemaryahu Talmon, Hebrew University, Israel; David Winston and Wilhelm Wuellner, Graduate Theological Union, Berkeley; Tzvee Zahavy, University of Minnesota; and the readers for the University of California Press.

I gratefully acknowledge my debt to the Library of the Jewish Theological Seminary of America, the Jewish Museum, New York, and the Hungarian Academy of Science, Budapest, for providing me with illustrations and granting me permission to reprint them. I also thank the late Professor Saul Lieberman and the Jewish Theological Seminary of America for permission to reprint Tosefta Pisha 10 from *The Tosefta*, vol. 2, New York, 1962.

I am grateful as well to the University of California, Berkeley, for providing funds for typing and other expenses and for awarding me a Career Development Summer Research Grant in 1977, when a significant portion of this study was researched.

To Ms. Linda Hess and Dr. Nina Morris-Farber, who offered many editorial improvements, Mss. Helen Green and Florence Myer, who typed several versions of the manuscript, and to the editorial staff of the University of California Press, in particular Dr. John R. Miles, my sincere thanks.

It is my pleasure to also thank my wife, Ms. Ann F. Wimpfheimer, who entered my life when this study was near completion and who has enriched my work in innumerable ways. She has shown me the meaning not only of Proverbs 18:22, "He who finds a wife has found happiness," but also of the rabbinic comment, "And if she is a good woman, there is no end to her goodness" (Midrash Tehillim 59). Finally, I remain indebted to Mr. Eugene LeVee, Ms. Rose Levinson, Ms. Miriam Oles, and Dr. James Weinberger who taught me true friendship and who gave me much support while this study was being researched and written.

March 1, 1984
1 Adar 27, 5744
the end of the sheloshim, thirty-day period of mourning,
for my father, Rabbi Ben Zion Bokser,
may his memory be for a blessing

TRANSLITERATIONS AND TRANSCRIPTIONS

TO TRANSLITERATE, I REPRODUCE the consonants of the Semitic words by using capital letters of the Roman alphabet. The following symbols are used:

א	= '	מ ם	= M	
ב	= B	נ ן	= N	
ג	= G	ס	= S	
ד	= D	ע	= '	
ה	= H	פ ף	= P	
ו	= W	צ ץ	= Ṣ	
ז	= Z	ק	= Q	
ח	= Ḥ	ר	= R	
ט	= Ṭ	שׁ	= Š	
י	= Y	שׂ	= Ś	
כ ך	= K	ת	= T	
ל	= L			

I also make use of a second system, transcription, which attempts to reproduce the vowel structure as well as the consonants. I use most of the same symbols as in the transliteration system, except that they appear as lower case letters in italics. There are, however, several different and additional symbols. In transcription I use *v* for W and *sh* for Š, and *v*, *kh*, and *f* for spirants B, K, and P, respectively. Furthermore, I am not consistent in the indication of *alef* at the beginning of words.

Where a name has a fixed or standard rendering in English, I generally have used the English equivalent. Elsewhere, I have tried to reproduce the Hebrew; but I am not fully consistent in this matter.

Illustration 1.
Passover plate with symbolic objects: the unleavened bread on top, bitter herbs on the bottom, and the passover lamb in the middle flanked by two symbolic substitutes, the egg and shankbone. The Jewish Museum/EPA F2255 Seder Plate, pewter, 1770 diameter 14½".

Illustration 2.
The biblical rite: eating the passover sacrifice. Participants are standing, with loins girded and staff in hand, eating the passover sacrifice in haste. Haggadah with German translation. Venice, 1663. Courtesy of the Library of the Jewish Theological Seminary of America.

Illustration 3.
A rabbinic seder: without the sacrifice. The family participates in a meal with ritual objects at hand. Haggadah. Augsburg, Germany, 1534. Courtesy of the Library of the Jewish Theological Seminary of America.

1

DEFINING THE PROBLEM

INTRODUCTION

P EOPLE USUALLY DEFINE THE meaning of Passover in terms of freedom and often describe the festival by recounting the ritual of the evening celebration, the seder. While the roots for the idea of freedom can be found in the Bible, the foundation for the evening rite is difficult to uncover. In fact, the structure of the Passover seder is based upon the description in Mishnah Pesaḥim 10.[1] Surprisingly, although this account diverges significantly from that of the Bible, the Mishnah writes as if the elements of the celebration had not changed since temple days. What is the significance of this anomaly?

An analysis of the Mishnah indicates that this anomaly is intentional and that it reflects the overall purpose of the Mishnah, which is to create a precedent for the observance of the celebration without the temple and the passover sacrifice. What Jews could do after 70 C.E., without the sacrificial order, is very close to what Jews did before 70, when they were without access to the temple. The Mishnah wants us to believe that the paschal sacrifice was important, but not crucial, and that one could manage without the sacrifice because other important elements remained viable nonetheless.

When a temple-based religion finds its foundation destroyed, several responses are possible. Early rabbinic Judaism chose to lay out a system in which one could serve God and enact the highest forms of piety without a temple. The rabbis extended the Pharisaic notion that God could be experienced outside the temple as well as inside, the implication being that the experience of God was not contingent upon the temple. The rabbis also made use of whatever biblical antecedents existed for extratemple practices and made them part of a mandated system. Instead of the pious acts of inspired individuals, these practices became the public cult. While early rabbinic authorities worked out these developments, they also had to correlate the new foundations for religious life with the old structure and to demonstrate that any new means of piety were as effective as the earlier ones.

1

As the Mishnah applies this mandate to Passover, it is paradigmatic of the larger process and therefore significant in respect to the formation of early rabbinic Judaism. Passover also provides an especially interesting comparative example, because already in the Bible the rite has qualities of a home ritual with cultic overtones and as such lent itself to the new perspective of rabbinic Judaism; in numerous ways its account in the Mishnah reflects the transformation in Judaism.

THE CHARACTER OF THE MISHNAH

As a literary document deriving from a particular historical context, the Mishnah can be analyzed in terms of the aims and images that its editor wished to project. In the Mishnah, earlier traditions were shaped into a new unity by the process of redaction, which makes the sources and contents of a work subservient to their context. Therefore, even though elements of the Mishnah may have a prehistory or a precedent in earlier literature, what the editor-redactor of the Mishnah has done with the earlier heritage constitutes something new and historically significant.[2]

The point of the Mishnah is not always immediately discernible. Its arguments are oblique, and not explicit, because it took shape during a time when Jews could not openly or consciously accept discontinuity with the earlier period. The Mishnah wants us to believe that nothing has changed. Indeed, the force of its argument lies in portraying the old in light of the new and the new in light of the old.[3] In psychological language, this response to the temple's destruction represents "resisting the trauma." In the words of Mortimer Ostow:

> To those who are committed to a religious life, the existence of a crisis makes observance even more necessary. It is vital to retain the forms of observance and worship that have signified continuity with the past and that protect against discontinuity. Maintaining one's way of life under hostile attack serves also to sustain one's self-esteem, which is always at risk under pressure.[4]

In postmishnaic times, Jews drew upon certain earlier trends and "worked through" the traumatic disruption to find a new basis for religious life. Eventually they came to take these new forms for granted, no longer needing to see them purely in terms of old cultic notions and institutions. At this point, they could acknowledge that the earlier form of the evening rite had undergone changes. While a comprehensive analysis of these developments falls outside the purview of this study,[5] I occasionally refer to sources that reflect this perspective, for they shed light on the issues with which the Mishnah grappled, and often clarify what the Mishnah only implied.

The structure and purpose of the present study distinguish it from earlier works about Passover, most of which trace the history of the haggadah, the Passover holiday, or the seder, through significant periods of Judaism. The best and most comprehensive of these studies are the works of Goldschmidt, Segal, Kasher, and Tabory.[6] They often choose, as their point of departure, the whole haggadah rather than a specific ancient text, so that the reader is exposed to a rich panorama of rituals and prayers from diverse periods. These works treat the various factors that may have shaped the holiday or its depiction in literature. Some emphasize the seder's continuity or discontinuity with biblical accounts, others stress the ways in which the Hellenistic context influenced the seder. Siegfried Stein, in particular, has made an important contribution in this regard. He provides a stunning picture of the symposiac elements of the seder, pointing to similarities between the haggadah and the symposia in table manners, dietary habits, and the role of philosophical discussions around a meal. He suggests that symposium literature provided the impetus for the formation of the haggadah's elaborate ritual, and that while some seder elements may be found in the Bible and in first-century traditions, the developed form of the "fixed seder ritual" comes from the second century.[7]

Certain scholars interested in the background of the Last Supper have also sought illuminating information in the Jewish Passover,[8] while others, such as Alon and Safrai,[9] have pointed to elements of the holiday, in particular the teaching attributed to Rabban Gamaliel, that apparently seek to overcome the loss of the temple and to provide a new basis for the evening celebration. Safrai suggests that the developed haggadah, with its emphasis on study and exposition, supplemented the earlier sacrificial ritual meal, which had included only unleavened bread, singing of praises to God, and the drinking of wine. In contrast to the other scholars, Safrai examines the Mishnah in its own right, as do several commentaries to Mishnah Pesaḥim.[10] Both Safrai and the commentaries try to place the individual teachings of the Mishnah in their historical context and to trace their development. But they do not draw upon all the evidence in the Mishnah, nor do they sufficiently appreciate the tendency of the Mishnah to portray the new as if it were the old protocol of temple days. Nevertheless, all of these studies enrich our understanding of the many factors affecting the history of the seder.

My own position is that the Mishnah should be understood in its own terms and that an analysis of the Mishnah indicates that the essential factor in its description of the evening ritual is the need to overcome the loss of the temple.

Based on these positions, I propose that the history of the Passover celebration is not an isolated phenomenon but instead illustrates the general early rabbinic reinterpretation of cultic rites and legitimization of extratemple means of religious expression.

Though the Passover evening celebration has roots in the Bible, the seder departs from biblical accounts of the holiday in essential ways. The Bible is not a monolith; other developments had occurred, so it is important for us to understand the relationship of the Mishnah and early rabbinic Judaism to antecedent trends in Judaism. Therefore, we must consider the roles of the temple and of extratemple rites in the Bible and Second Temple Judaism and in particular the possibility that the extratemple rites served as precedents for rabbinic practices. If alternatives to the temple already existed, why did the temple's destruction raise a problem to which the Mishnah had to respond?

At the outset, it will be necessary to clarify how the Bible presents the temple and the cult as one of several models of religious piety.[11]

First, the book of Leviticus gives the perspective of the temple cult and declares that people's actions affect the cult and the presence of God in the temple. Individuals are to conduct themselves according to the precepts of Leviticus in order to be holy. This model would have been popular among those who had access to the temple and for whom temple practices proved religiously fulfilling.

Second, the book of Deuteronomy both centralizes the cult and holds human wisdom in great esteem. It rationalizes many "sacro-cultic" institutions, interpreting laws and notions in terms of their impact not upon the cult but upon people, especially the community of Israel. It also assumes that people are intrinsically holy and that their holiness imposes upon them a responsibility to conduct their lives properly. While Deuteronomy assigns important roles to the cult and sacrifices, it gives prominence to religious practices that do not depend upon the sacrificial order. Its ideology would be appropriate for those who want to see the cult in noncultic terms and to justify the temple on the basis of its benefit to society, as exemplified in 1 Kings 8—9. Moreover, those interested in nontemple practices could find precedents in it.

Third, Psalms, a collection of religious poetry, expresses the stirrings of the individual. These compositions could be drawn on by musical guilds, later religious poets, and those developing a verbal liturgy.

Fourth, the prophets provide guidance concerning the issues of the day.

While they do not precisely offer a separate type of piety, they do provide a model of individuals with distinctive personality traits who expound an uncompromising religious and moral message. Although the specifics of their message may differ, they all intercede with God on Israel's behalf, criticize the people's social and religious practices, and remind them that they can improve themselves and that the future will bring the full realization of divine promises. The motifs of these prophecies became popular among apocalyptic writers, and the oracles served preachers as they criticized or attempted to encourage the community.

During the Second Temple period, people drew upon one or more of these four models. Numerous sources stress the importance of a central temple but also mention alternatives to it and its ritual. For example, Aristeas, Ezekiel the Epic Poet, and Philo of Alexandria glorify Jerusalem and its temple. Philo describes the temple's unique role in these terms:

> The highest, and in the truest sense the holy, temple of God is, as we must believe, the whole universe, . . . There is also the temple made by hands; for it was right that no check should be given to the forwardness of those who pay their tribute to piety and desire by means of sacrifices either to give thanks for the blessings that befall them or to ask for pardon and forgiveness for their sins. But he provided that there should not be temples built either in many places or many in the same place, for he judged that since God is one, there should be also only one temple. Further, he does not consent to those who wish to perform the sacred rites in their houses, but bids them rise up from the ends of the earth and come to this temple. In this way he also applies the severest test to their dispositions. For one who is not going to sacrifice in a religious spirit would never bring himself to leave his country and friends and kinsfolk and sojourn in a strange land, but clearly it must be the stronger attraction of piety which leads him to endure separation from his most familiar and dearest friends who form as it were a single whole with himself. [12]

By contrast Philo and other sources indicate that the temple did not constitute the only religious institution and that religious life also had undergone some decentralization. Many scholars have relied upon such references to claim that certain Jews periodically gathered in Palestine, perhaps in regional assemblies during periods when they sent offerings to the Jerusalem Temple. Moreover, while synagogues probably had not yet taken shape as a full-fledged institution, recitation of prayers had become popular in some circles. Archaeological and epigraphic evidence indicates that prayer houses or places for reading of the Torah and instruction in the Commandments did exist before the temple's destruction; in fact, Philo even refers to a synagogue in Alexandria. But, as archaeologists also note, the prayer houses in Palestine were quite plain and, in comparison, were architecturally overshadowed by the magnificent Jerusalem Temple. It is also not clear to what degree these institutions were more than community centers or places for personal prayer.[13] Nevertheless, they do attest to some kind of decentralization or democratization, which would indicate a response to people's need for meaningful religious experiences and accessible ways of participating in them.

To relate this trend to the concurrent elevated significance of the temple, consideration must be given to how such practices interacted with the role of the temple in the lives of people. Did people regard the extratemple activities as mere personal devotion or as part of the official cult? Were more personal practices undertaken in conjunction with the official sacrificial cult or independently of the temple?[14]

While we do not yet have comprehensive answers to these questions, the research of Nahum Sarna and other scholars who have examined the biblical materials is quite suggestive. Sarna proposes that the developing role of recitation of Psalms and the offering of incense independent of animal sacrifices filled a gap in the time of the first temple, when the centralization of the cult brought an end to sacrifices at local shrines:

> The closing down of the cult centers, whether by force of the deuteronomistic movement or by enemy action, obviously left in its wake a spiritual void that had to be filled. It is absurd to believe that the designation of Jerusalem as the exclusive cult center was either intended to, or could actually succeed in depriving all votaries of the national religion not within easy reach of Jerusalem of all form of self-expression. The one constituent of the cult that was independent of both edifice and priesthood was psalmody and it must have filled the breach.[15]

Whether prayer existed in biblical times is not an issue. The act of prayer arises from an ancient human impulse by an individual to express yearning, awe, joy, thanksgiving, or grief.[16] By contrast, a public cult is a regular group experience which binds individuals together. Through it individuals are identified with a community and are permanently and continually tied to their God and the divine realm. It is from the perspective of the main cult that members orient their religious life and their understanding of the world. Private prayer is distinct from the community cult; for even where private prayer is synchronized with the sacrificial order, it only supplements that order.[17]

Because of the above distinction, Joseph Heinemann has argued that rabbinic prayer is not merely the continuation of biblical prayer,[18] but rather that rabbinic prayer supersedes the public cult and becomes part of a mandated system. Other areas of religious and cultic life also experienced a similar type of transformation.

This distinction enables us to recognize developments in the realm of personal religion and extratemple practices without minimizing the dominant role of the temple in people's consciousness. Early break-off groups continued to perceive reality through a temple. So it is not surprising that the notion of a temple remained central for many Jewish groups from the Second Temple period, for as Talmon observes,

> These splinter groups, the earliest Jewish sectarians, demonstrated their deviation from the main community not by introducing new forms of devotion, but rather by transferring to independent sanctuaries the sacrificial service as it had been developed in Jerusalem.[19]

Two examples would be the Elephantine community in Egypt which maintained its own temple and the Samaritans, a splinter group that claimed the true temple was located on Mount Gerizim.

Later groups interpreted the notion of the temple in a new way. While for diverse reasons they were not able or willing to establish a substitute sacrificial cult, they still kept the temple as their central concept. Examples of this can be seen in the Qumran community, and in the circles that composed the Temple Scroll, and also in significant portions of the early Christian community. Each of these communities described their group of believers in terms of the temple and apparently saw themselves as the new temple. Since the actual temple in Jerusalem had become polluted, God was to be found only in their midst. Understandably, therefore, they described many of their activities and institutions in cultic language.[20]

The Pharisees, the pre-70 group seen by the rabbis as their own forerunners, claimed that the individual could experience God's presence outside the actual temple. Yet even in this claim the Pharisees showed their belief in the temple's centrality. In effect they adopted the biblical notion that Israel was to be a nation of priests, all of whom were to act in their daily lives as priests act in the temple and to eat their meals at home in the manner that priests ate consecrated food in the temple. However, since the Pharisees extended the laws of the Book of Leviticus to the physical area outside the temple (relating extratemple life to the temple), their system, in contrast to the Qumran and the early Christian systems, would have been shaken by the destruction of the Jerusalem Temple.[21]

The temple, then, was the sacred source for Jews of diverse backgrounds, providing imagery that imparted meaning to a large spectrum of religious activities. The practical facts of the Diaspora also contributed to the temple's transcendent role; for it was through the temple that widely dispersed groups of Jews maintained their sense of unity and identity. As E. Mary Smallwood points out, the role of the temple in the Jewish community had an economic as well as an emotional dimension:

> For the Diaspora communities, as for Palestinian Jews at a distance from Jerusalem, the synagogue was the local centre. But it was of purely local significance. Jerusalem was the religious focus for all Jews, wherever they lived, and though for the vast majority of the Diaspora a pilgrimage there was out of the question, they could, and were required to, contribute to the upkeep of the Temple and the cost of sacrifices. From the very early days numerous dues had been levied, many of them in kind, for the support of the priests and the maintenance of the Temple cult. The payment of dues in kind was obviously a practical impossibility for Jews living at any distance from Jerusalem. But the money-tax of half a *shekel* (2 denarii in Roman currency or 2 drachmae in Greek, whence the term *didrachmon*), paid at least from the late Hellenistic period by all adult male Jews between the ages of twenty and fifty, including freed slaves and proselytes, for the upkeep of the Temple, could be levied anywhere. There is abundant evidence that it was paid by the Diaspora communities in the Roman period, when it was collected locally and conveyed to Jerusalem by "sacred envoys."[22]

Clearly Jews of diverse persuasions, along with temple personnel and inhabitants of Jerusalem, experienced trauma when the temple was destroyed. People coped with their disorientation in different ways. An apocalyptic work like 4 Ezra, for example, calls for divine intervention to restore the actual temple. Early rabbinic authorities, by contrast, faced reality more directly and offered a more lasting solution. They evolved a system that made it possible to live without the temple, though as we have already seen, they could do so only gradually, as Jews learned consciously to accept discontinuity with the past.[23]

PASSOVER AS A PARADIGM

The Biblical Heritage

Passover serves as a paradigm of the overall crisis and challenge. With the destruction of the temple, several key elements of the Passover evening celebration became defunct. No longer could Jews offer the paschal sacrifice and eat portions of it in the evening meal; nor could they put its blood on the doorposts. And what of the unleavened bread and bitter herbs, which originally were mere accompaniments of the sacrifice?

For Jews seeking to continue the ancient practices in viable ways, the Bible offered certain precedents for an observance of Passover without the temple. Exodus 12's portrayal of a home gathering with cultic overtones provides a general model of how to perform rituals and pious activities outside of a temple. Several practices elsewhere consigned exclusively to priests in the temple are in this passage applied to Jews at large. For example: lay people are to bring the sacrifice, the participants are to consume the meat of the passover lamb before the end of the night, and they are warned against breaking the animal's bone. As Philo later observes, it seems that individual Jews are acting as priests:

> In this festival [= Passover] many myriads of victims from noon till eventide are offered by the whole people, old and young alike, raised for that particular day to the dignity of the priesthood. For at other times the priests according to the ordinance of the law carry out both the public sacrifices and those offered by private individuals. But on this occasion the whole nation performs the sacred rites and acts as priests with pure hands and complete immunity. The reason for this is as follows: . . . So exceedingly joyful were they [for their exodus] that in their vast enthusiasm and impatient eagerness, they naturally enough sacrificed without waiting for their priests. This practice . . . was sanctioned by the law once in every year to remind them of their duty of thanksgiving. . . . On this day every dwelling-house is invested with the outward semblance and dignity of a temple. The victim is then slaughtered and dressed for the festal meal which befits the occasion.[24]

Philo's interpretation of the Passover practices provides an example of how the biblical text may be adapted so that the festival may be seen to comprise more than the offering of the passover sacrifice in the temple. Earlier Second Temple Palestinian sources, such as the Books of Chronicles and Jubilees, also emphasize the festive nature of the evening and mention the singing of praises to God by the Levites and the offering of extra sacrifices so as to ensure an abundant supply of meat.[25]

Another element of the Passover evening celebration that the Pentateuch mentions is unleavened bread, *maṣṣot*, both in conjunction with the sacrifice and separately, as part of the prescription to eat unleavened bread and to avoid leavened bread for seven days. It also refers to bitter herbs, though only in the context of the sacrifice.[26]

In addition to various elements of observance, the message of Passover remained viable and relevant as well. Within the biblical period the memory of the exodus gave people hope that their imperfect present situation would end and a new liberation would occur, a message that also fit the situation of the Jews under Roman domination.[27] As reflected in Philo and other sources, this message of thanksgiving and hope for future protection or redemption was often tied to the offering of the paschal sacrifice.

In studying the history of Passover, one is thus faced with issues of change and continuity. Hence, the relation of the pre-70 heritage of both temple and nontemple (primarily private) rites to the Passover celebration must first be clarified, and then, second, how those pre-70 institutions would have been affected by the loss of the temple. Chapter 2 treats these prerabbinic materials in detail. Let me now, however, illustrate the complexity of the problem by briefly discussing the meal aspect of the celebration since it has affinities with both the pre-70 sacrificial meal as well as other ancient forms of meals.

The Meal

A large body of scholarship has developed that deals with the nature of meals during the period with which we are concerned. Some writers connect the Passover meal to Jesus' Last Supper, while others interpret it in terms of the Hellenistic and Greco-Roman symposia and banquets. In chapter 5 I will argue that, despite certain similarities, the seder, as described in the Mishnah, differs essentially from Hellenistic meals. For the present discussion, however, the general question of cross-cultural influences will be considered.

As ancient and modern writers have noted, a meal provides a context for close interpersonal contact, creating and reinforcing the bonds of friendship.[28] The meal may have special uses as well. Mary Douglas suggests a connection between a dining table and a cultic altar: "the meal and sacrificial victim, the table and the altar. . . [may] stand for one another." Further, "the ordered system which is a meal represents all the ordered systems associated with it."[29] Members of an intimate group often find the meal a natural setting in which to share religious activities. While bonds of friendship are strengthened by common experiences at a central temple or local shrine, they will be more personal in small groups.[30]

Scholars have traced three stages in the development of the symposium, the Greco-Roman banquet and drinking party, noting the roles that the meal and its etiquette play in each stage. Plato's *Symposium* provides an early example of a symposium in which the participants have intellectual interchange around a festive banquet. In a later phase, the symposium becomes a literary genre which writers use to discuss specific topics.[31]

In the Bible, the meal and banquet are not uniquely associated with Passover. For example, the Books of Esther and Daniel refer to such gatherings. Leviticus and Deuteronomy prescribe how priests and Israelites should eat of their sacrifices, and 1 Samuel 9:13, 22−25 depicts one such communal meal. The Letter of Aristeas (from the biblical Apocrypha) describes an intellectual discussion at a banquet. And as we have already seen, Exodus 12 describes the eating of the paschal lamb as a family meal.[32]

In the first centuries before and after the Common Era, the meal assumes a prominent role in the writings of several groups. Qumranite texts set forth a special etiquette, including procedures for study and praising God at a group meal. The Therapeutae, described by Philo in *On the Contemplative Life*, likewise turn the meal into a special occasion with numerous cultic overtones. For members of the early church, gathering at a meal became an opportunity to remember and experience Jesus. Even the activities of the Pharisees apparently were centered on a table fellowship. Meals enabled them to express their piety and belief that God's presence was not limited to the temple but could be experienced in one's home. Therefore the Pharisees taught that people should prepare and eat a regular meal as priests prepare and eat consecrated food.[33]

It is noteworthy that the groups who make use of the meal are those for whom the Jerusalem Temple did not prove completely satisfying religiously. Since the Mishnah also reflects the perspective of a religion without a temple, its description of the Passover meal may be seen as another variation on the extratemple gathering, albeit with a precedent in Exodus 12. Nevertheless, close attention to the rabbinic materials reveals that the Passover meal differs from these other instances. For example, the Mishnah stresses that the special meal is not just for a special class of Jews or the elite members of the group; but that everyone should participate, even the poor.[34] This accords with a general shift in the role of a meal in early rabbinic Judaism. Many of the Pharisaic teachings preserved in the Mishnah pertain to the protocol at a meal, including the sequence and formula of the Sabbath or holiday Sanctification over wine to usher in the day and the Havdalah ceremony over wine to escort it out. These benedictions originally may have taken place at meals. Early rabbinic Judaism adapted and extended the Pharisaic program, claiming all people could experience the divine not only outside the temple but also entirely without the temple, and they presented this program to all of Israel rather than to a small intellectual circle. Moreover, as the liturgy was gradually standardized, the benedictions of Sanctification and Havdalah became part of prayer services. As the context of a meal became secondary, a question arose concerning the proper and preferred location at which to recite these blessings.[35] The meal no longer had the character of a closed fellowship but became a gathering that anyone could organize or participate in.

To what degree, then, does the use of the meal at the Passover evening celebration continue a biblical practice? To what degree does it draw upon and extend sectarian or upper class use of a meal? To what degree does it take over the traits of Hellenistic banquets? We do not necessarily approach an answer when we notice the analogues between the developed form of the seder and the symposium, for these similarities simply give rise to further questions. For example, did the shapers of the seder rely on Greek models for the techniques of intellectual discussion? After all, the Bible also introduces a didactic element into the holiday: in three passages the festival and its events are explained by the model of a parent instructing a child. However, the biblical reference to a child's question regarding the evening celebration responds to a feature of the rite dependent upon the sacrifice, namely, the placing of blood on the doorposts and lintel! So clearly, the seder's intellectual dimension does not have a simple linear relation to the Bible or to the symposia. Henry Fischel suggests that the contemporary culture stimulated the Jews creatively to adapt the indigenous institution of the meal and to attribute new meaning to it.[36] It will be seen that the composers of the Mishnah treated the practices of the symposia in both positive and negative ways, because they were not merely imitating the symposia but responding to the crisis of the temple's destruction and laying a new foundation for an evening celebration.

CONCLUSIONS

While the history of every aspect of the developed seder is beyond complete explanation, this chapter has isolated the different roles that three distinct forces took in shaping the passover seder and the formation of early rabbinic Judaism in general. The first force was the Bible, which presented several models that could be drawn upon. The second was the historical situation which meant that Jews in general and early rabbinic authorities in particular had to adjust to the end of the temple cult while maintaining a sense of continuity with the past and a faith in the viability of essential cultic elements. That events made them vulnerable in this regard is reflected in the fact that Christians who attacked the authenticity of Judaism frequently asserted that the lack of a paschal lamb proved that Passover (and Judaism) had become passé. The third force was that Jews naturally participated in the wider culture, employing and adapting various Hellenistic forms, which to them may not have seemed foreign. However, in doing so, at least initially, they took steps to distinguish their rites from the manners of their non-Jewish neighbors. What makes this case particularly interesting is that in the Bible the Passover meal was already a home ceremony with cultic overtones and therefore analogous to later rabbinic practices.

Although Jews' understanding of institutions and events had been shaped by the temple cult, those of the late second century, including the composers of the

Mishnah, struggled to distance themselves from cultic notions. Evidence of this distancing may be discerned within the Mishnah and abounds among Jews of the third century. The new trends in the Passover material that appear embryonically in the Mishnah are fully developed in later rabbinic sources.[37] In seeking to understand the Mishnah in its own terms and context, the present work explores the initial stages of readjustment to cultic institutions and the beginnings of distancing. Characteristic of this early stage is the denial that change has occurred, but a review of prerabbinic evidence in chapter 2 will reveal the Mishnah's actual discontinuity with the earlier heritage. Once the specifics of the Mishnah's restructuring of the rite have been examined (chapters 3 through 6), the significance of the Mishnah's effort can be appreciated from a wider historical perspective.

2

PRERABBINIC DESCRIPTIONS OF THE PASSOVER EVE RITUAL: THE CENTRALITY OF THE PASSOVER SACRIFICE

P RERABBINIC ACCOUNTS OF THE evening celebration are not all alike; they do, however, share in assuming the centrality of the passover sacrifice. Moreover, all extant expressions of first-century Jews characterize the festival in terms of the sacrifice and the temple. This explains why the author of the Mishnah had to correlate his version of the holiday with the earlier accounts. However, in addition to drawing upon earlier features of the celebration, the Mishnah provided them with a new context and a basis independent of the paschal sacrifice. To appreciate the Mishnah's relationship to the earlier heritage, I will review the previous accounts and note the developments in the history of Passover, especially as they relate to the evening rite.

BIBLICAL ACCOUNTS

The Bible associates the holiday of the paschal lamb and the Festival of the Unleavened Bread (*maṣṣot*) with the Israelites' exodus from Egypt. The various biblical descriptions have led scholars to hypothesize the existence of two separate holidays that may have existed even before the exodus from Egypt, to trace their independent origins, and to suggest how they were later combined in the Bible.[1]

The passover sacrifice always sets the tone for Passover eve regulations and the communal meal and frequently is associated with the participants' protection and blessing of bounty. Chapters 12 and 13 of Exodus describe what the Israelites did in Egypt and what they were told to do later in remembrance of their experience. This biblical account had a significant impact on later descriptions. Exodus 12:1−20 presents God's command to Moses and Aaron on the eve of the exodus:

> Speak to the whole assembly of Israel . . . each of them shall take a lamb to a family, a lamb to a household. . . . You shall apportion the lamb according to what each person should eat. . . . and all the aggregate community of the *Israelites shall slaughter it* at twilight [of the fourteenth day of the month]. They shall take some of the *blood* and put it *on the two doorposts and the lintel* of the houses in which they are to eat. They shall *eat the flesh that same night*; they shall eat it roasted over the fire, *with unleavened bread and with bitter herbs.* . . . You shall not leave any of it over until morning; whatever is left of it [WHNTR] until morning you shall burn. This is how you shall eat of it: your *loins girded*, your sandals on your feet, and your staff in your hand; and you shall eat it hurriedly: it is a passover offering to the LORD. For that night I will go through the land of Egypt and strike down every first-born in the land of Egypt, both man and beast. . . . And *the blood* on the houses in which you dwell *shall be a sign for you*; when I see the blood I will pass over you, so that no plague will destroy you when I strike the land of Egypt. This day shall be to you one of remembrance; you shall celebrate it as an institution for all time. Seven days you shall eat unleavened bread; on the very first day you shall remove leaven from your houses. . . . You shall observe the [Feast] of Unleavened Bread, for on this very day I brought your ranks out of the land of Egypt; you shall observe this day throughout the generations as an institution for all time. In the first month, from the fourteenth day of the month at evening, you shall eat unleavened bread until the twenty-first day of the month at evening.

The text explicitly requires individual or combined households to slaughter a lamb, to put its blood on doorposts and lintel, and, with girded loins, to eat the animal. The blood has an apotropaic function, for when God sees the blood, He will protect that household. This section of the text closes with the holiday of Unleavened Bread.

In Exodus 12:21−27 Moses conveys God's instructions to the people, enjoining them to establish the rite as a permanent institution. The passage makes it clear that these procedures are the ones that will elicit a child's inquiry:

> And when your children ask you, "What do you mean by this rite?" you shall say, "It is the passover sacrifice to the LORD, because He passed over the houses of the Israelites in Egypt when He smote the Egyptians, but saved our houses." (vs. 26−27)

Following an account of the actual exodus, Exodus 12:43−50 deals with those people who in the future will be eligible to partake of the paschal sacrifice. Verse 46 comments on how the sacrifice must be treated:

It shall be eaten in one house; you shall not take any of the flesh outside the house; *nor shall you break a bone of it.*

The ban on breaking the animal's bone and the several regulations concerning the blood have been seen by some critics as remnants of an earlier apotropaic rite such as one for the protection of flocks of sheep and goats.[2] As we shall see, several texts, though in different ways, associate rites of Passover and Unleavened Bread with divine favor, protection, or bounty.

Exodus 13:1−16 presents additional methods on how one is to remember the exodus experience. Verses 6−8 prescribe the eating of unleavened bread for seven days. In the form of an instruction to a child, verse 8 specifics the reason:

And you shall explain to your son on that day, "It is because of what the LORD did for me when I went free from Egypt."

Verses 11−15 require the dedication or redemption of firstborn humans and animals. A third explanation to a child supplies the reason:

And when, in time to come, your son asks you, saying, "What does this mean?" you shall say to him, "It was with a mighty hand that the LORD brought us out from Egypt, the house of bondage. When Pharaoh stubbornly refused to let us go, the LORD slew every first-born in the land of Egypt, the first-born of both man and beast."

Exodus 34:18−21 deals with the holiday of Unleavened Bread and the law of the firstborn but does not mention the passover offering.

Leviticus 23:4−8, in a list of holidays, mentions the passover offering on the fourteenth of the month and then the seven-day Feast of Unleavened Bread. The chapter's next section, verses 9−14, deals with bringing the first sheaf of the harvest before the Lord and to the priest, and with the day's special sacrifice and libation, all of which presumably occurs during the holiday. From then on people are permitted to make use of the new produce and eat the "bread, and parched grain, and fresh ears." The festival is thus associated in this passage with the proper use of divine bounty.[3]

The first of two relevant passages in the Book of Numbers, 28:16−25, lists sacrifices for holidays and mentions the passover offering and the seven-day Feast of Unleavened Bread. The second pertinent passage, Numbers 9:1−15, has a novel element, namely, the implication that people cannot or may not celebrate the holiday without the paschal offering. If, as scholars suggest, the

Feast of the Passover Offering was still distinct from the Feast of Unleavened Bread, the critical role of the sacrifice is not surprising. The text presents God's command to the Israelites, in the second year following the exodus, to offer the passover sacrifice "in accordance with all its rules and rites." In addition, it designates what people are to do when they are unable to participate because of ritual impurity or physical distance. In such cases, the text instructs these individuals to bring their offering one month later. Verses 11−12 are noteworthy, again because the passover offering is the center of attention:

> they shall offer it . . . at twilight. *They shall eat it with unleavened bread and bitter herbs*, and they shall not leave any of it over until morning. They shall not break a bone of it. They shall offer it in strict accord with the law of the passover sacrifice.

As part of a review of the three seasonal festivals, Deuteronomy 16:1−8 locates the Passover rite in the sanctuary which "God will choose." It therefore changes the character of the celebration, which is no longer to be a domestic rite but instead part of a national gathering—though families might celebrate together in that central location. The text mentions that one could leave to go home only in the morning, and that one should eat unleavened bread both with the sacrifice and on the following days:

> You shall not eat anything leavened with it; for seven days thereafter you shall eat unleavened bread, bread of distress − for you departed from the land of Egypt hurriedly.

Verse 6 specifies that the sacrificial animal should be slaughtered at sundown. Moshe Weinfeld suggests that the failure to mention the blood on the doorposts and the ban on breaking the bone represents an intentional deletion of an apotropaic element.

Joshua 5:10−11 describes the first Passover on the western side of the Jordan River. After the Israelites circumcise themselves, they are eligible to partake of the passover offering. The text specifies that the sacrifice was carried out toward evening and mentions the eating of unleavened bread and the cessation of manna, after which the land provided them with bountiful produce. Hence eating of the land's bounty is associated with offering the passover sacrifice and eating unleavened bread.

2 Kings 23:21−24 describes Josiah's reform of the cult, a reinstatement of the passover sacrifice, which had not been performed, or rather not performed properly, for generations. Ezekiel 45:21, referring to the festival, prophesies how, at some time in the future, the temple will be purified, the passover sacrifice offered, and the seven-day Festival of Unleavened Bread observed.

Before turning to the later biblical books, it should be noted that the passover offering has consistently dominated the earlier accounts. Unleavened bread is mentioned either as part of a separate holiday or as an accompaniment to the sacrifice, and bitter herbs are mentioned only as an accompaniment. Several sources also suggest the beneficial, if not apotropaic, effect of the sacrifice.

The three accounts of the festival in Chronicles and Ezra include several novel elements.[4] Ezra 6:19–22 makes brief mention of the passover and the Feast of Unleavened Bread of those who had returned to Israel from exile. According to the text, the priests and Levites purified themselves, and then the Levites slaughtered the sacrifices for the rest of the returnees, including those who had separated themselves "to seek (LDRŠ) the LORD." All of this occurs as part of a national celebration at the dedication of the reconstructed temple.

The two sections in Chronicles are longer and provide additional information. 2 Chronicles 30:1–27 describes Hezekiah's passover (according to the author, delayed by one month) in which the king invited Israelites from all over the country to gather in Jerusalem to offer the passover sacrifice and thereby cause God to turn aside from his anger. Not all Israelites came but many did, bringing the passover offering along with additional sacrifices. Even those who had not purified themselves ate of the passover offering. In addition, those who came to Jerusalem also observed the Festival of Unleavened Bread for seven days. Note the language in verse 21:

> And the Israelites that were present at Jerusalem kept the Feast of Unleavened Bread seven days *with great gladness, the Levites and the priests praising the LORD daily* with powerful instruments for the LORD.

The text emphasizes the abundance of additional sacrifices and rejoicing.

In the Chronicler's version of Josiah's passover, the additional sacrifices and great rejoicing are also mentioned. 2 Chronicles 35:1–19 goes on to specify the eating of the passover sacrifice by kinship groups and the role of Levites and other experts in singing. It should be noted that this reference in 2 Chronicles mentions as well the passover offering together with the seven-day Festival of Unleavened Bread.

Both of the 2 Chronicles' accounts of royally sponsored festivities, as well as the briefer account in 2 Kings, highlight the celebratory quality of the events, reflecting the character of the national holiday which was now centralized in Jerusalem—or, at least, assumed to be centralized there. It is unclear whether the two occasions referred to in the texts were exceptional or whether Passover was chosen for the special celebration because it inherently lent itself to joyous festivity. In any event, the text adds the elements of extra sacrifices, rejoicing, and praises to God. As Israel's song at the sea indicates, in Exodus 15, it is not inappropriate for people to sing and praise God in response to an act of divine redemption. It will be seen later that other prerabbinic sources likewise mention this feature.[5]

The nonbiblical Second Temple sources follow the perspective of the biblical accounts, especially in regard to the centrality of the communal sacrificial meal, but they also supplement the biblical account with several new developments.

Jubilees, written in second-century B.C.E. Palestine, devotes a long section to Passover. Chapter 49, based on Exodus 12 and drawing on other biblical passages, combines the account of the exodus with the rules for the later holiday.[6] The author, however, does not mention bitter herbs or unleavened bread, though at the close of the chapter he does refer to the seven-day Feast of Unleavened Bread, emphasizing the slaughter of the offering and the people's joy, as they eat, drink wine, and praise God. While singing and praising God were already mentioned in Chronicles, wine appears in Jubilees for the first time.

> They should eat it . . . from the time of the setting of the sun. For on this night—the beginning of the festival and the beginning of the joy—yea were eating of the passover in Egypt, when all the powers of Mastema had been let loose to slay all the firstborn in the land of Egypt. . . . And all Israel was eating the flesh of the paschal lamb, and *drinking the wine, and was lauding and blessing, and giving thanks to the LORD* God of their fathers, and was ready to go forth from under the yoke of Egypt, and from evil bondage. . . . And the man who . . . does not come to observe it . . . and *to eat and to drink* before the LORD on the day of its festival.

The last point corresponds with the Deuteronomic version, which centralizes the rite. This is made clear in verses 16–21, which prescribe that the offering should be slain and eaten only in the sanctuary and not "in their cities, nor in any place save before the tabernacle of the LORD." Like Exodus, Jubilees specifically mentions the proper time to slaughter and eat the sacrifice, along with the ban on leaving its flesh until morning, and the prohibition against breaking the animal's bone. Unlike in Exodus, however, the reference in Jubilees to leaving the animal's bone unbroken is expanded. This is one of two places in which we find an added emphasis on the apotropaic effect of the celebration:

> and not break any bone thereof; for *of the children of Israel no bone shall be crushed* (13) . . . . And do thou command the children of Israel to observe the passover throughout their days, every year. . . and it shall come for a memorial well pleasing before the LORD, *and no plague shall come upon them* to slay or to smite in that year in which they celebrate the passover in its season in every respect according to His command (15).

The promise of a year free from plagues makes the festival a kind of preventive health measure, in effect, apparently, until the end of the fiftieth Jubilee, the Jubilee of Jubilees, when complete redemption will come about.

The epic Greek poet Ezekiel, a second-century B.C.E. non-Palestinian, vividly describes the preparations of the night before the exodus. In his reiteration and expansion of Exodus 12 and 13, Ezekiel mentions the time in the evening to slaughter and eat the offering, and the accompanying preparations: girded loins, sandaled feet, staff in hand, and blood on the doorposts. These procedures, he says, provide a release from evils and death. A recent analysis of the text by Howard Jacobson sheds additional light on Ezekiel's narrative. Jacobson argues that the account of the Passover regulations consists of three parts. The first and third parts lay out the preparations for the departure: God commands Moses, and Moses expands these instructions for the people. The second part presents two sets of instructions for the future: eating unleavened bread for seven days in memory of the seven-day journey from Egypt to the Sea of Reeds where the Israelites attained final liberation; and offering firstborn animals to recall God's deliverance of the Israelite firstborn in Egypt. If Jacobson is correct, then Ezekiel assumes that his non-Palestinian audience will be interested in the details of the preparation and eating of the passover offering only as an account of the past and not as guidelines for the present. Presumably Ezekiel's audience would celebrate the holiday by eating unleavened bread.[7]

The three Jewish communities that had temples of their own outside Jerusalem supply additional information concerning Passover in this period. One community is the Elephantine Egyptian Jewish garrison whose temple was destroyed in 411 B.C.E. Scholars differ over whether they offered a passover sacrifice. Two inscribed Aramaic potsherds (*ostraca*) mention passover, *pasha*, though it is unclear if the meaning is to "perform" something on Passover or to "offer" the passover sacrifice. One of the potsherds seems to mean to "perform" something on Passover. A third ostracon, which may refer to Passover, speaks of when one must stop eating bread before the holiday. A papyrus dated to 419 B.C.E. mentions the eating of unleavened bread and the ban on leaven and beer for seven days. Nothing, however, is said about an evening celebration.[8]

The second Jewish community with its own temple, the Samaritans, have offered a passover sacrifice on Mount Gerizim since Second Temple times. The history of their religious practices, however, is difficult to trace because the earliest sources on these matters were composed in late antiquity, if not later, and their procedures reflect a literal understanding of the Pentateuch. Samaritans follow the practices detailed in Exodus 12, adapted to Deuteronomic centralization, which they believe refers to Mount Gerizim. They slaughter the animal in the evening, and while the meat roasts, they gird their loins, put on heavy shoes, and take up staffs. At midnight each family group eats the meat while making sure not to break any bones, and then burns the leftover meat and bones before morning. During the slaughter of the animal and afterwards the Samaritans engage in prayer and praise of God. They also observe a seven-day period of eating unleavened bread.[9]

Some scholars have suggested that the Samaritan religion may closely resemble biblical religion before rabbinic Judaism reshaped it.[10] If so, it unmistakably illustrates the sacrificial nature of the Passover evening rite and, at the least, it attests to the centrality of the passover offering for one Second Temple group.

The third Jewish community with its own temple was located at Qumran. This community's written documents and archaeological remains do not contribute any new information, although some of the numerous fragments of biblical texts and references to biblical verses uncovered there are related to Passover. The group's apocryphal and sectarian texts, however, do not treat Passover.[11] Collections of animal bones, buried without flesh attached and either charred or uncharred, have been uncovered, and some scholars have suggested that they may be remnants of a paschal sacrifice. But since no altar has been discovered and since the Qumran literature indicates that at that time the group believed no sacrifices could be offered, the sacrificial identification has not received wide acceptance. At most, scholars agree that the bones are the remains of meals.[12] If the passover interpretation is correct, we would have evidence that the community considered the passover sacrifice special— one that should be offered despite the fact that they did not otherwise offer sacrifices.

The Temple Scroll, found at Qumran but possibly written by someone outside the community, mentions the passover sacrifice (17:6−9) and the Feast of Unleavened Bread (17:10−16). The former reference draws upon Leviticus 23:4, Deuteronomy 16:1−7, and other verses, and in addition to other descriptions, further defines the time of the offering and specifies that it should be eaten within the temple courtyards. This latter regulation would make a multiple-course family dinner quite difficult and seems to preclude a celebration consisting of significantly more than eating the sacrifice. Therefore it is not surprising that the author fails to mention a passover celebration.[13]

Before turning to those sources most contemporaneous with the rabbinic materials, and after having examined biblical and nonbiblical sources that derive from diverse individuals, communities, situations, and centuries, one overall observation may be made. While some works connect new practices with the existing Passover rite, none assumes that a nonsacrificial celebration occurs.

In trying to understand the wider context and heritage that would have influenced the rabbinic understanding of Passover, I will now examine the Wisdom of Solomon, Philo, and Josephus. As with other nonbiblical Second Temple works, one cannot know if rabbis actually knew these materials, though we do know they represent several readings of the Bible nearly contemporaneous with early rabbinic Judaism. As shall be seen, these nonbiblical works also assume the centrality of the passover offering despite their disparate socioreligious orientations.

The Wisdom of Solomon, probably written around 37—41 C.E., attempts to demonstrate that divine wisdom and justice were at work during the exodus. Wisdom, 18:2—25, for instance, points out the striking antithetical details associated with the destruction of the Egyptian firstborn and the protection and glorification of the Israelites in Egypt. God punishes one and correspondingly rewards the other. Wisdom 18:9 mentions the offering of the sacrifice and apparently on the basis of the later custom of praising God portrays, as in Jubilees, the Israelites raising "a chant of praises of the fathers."[14] As mentioned before, when considering passages such as Exodus 15, it is not unreasonable to assume that the Israelites would have expressed thanksgiving in some way.

Philo, the Greek Jewish thinker from first-century Egypt, is shaped by a philosophical approach to the world and an allegorical reading of the Bible similar to that of Wisdom. In some ways Philo resembles the rabbis, but in others he differs greatly from them. Though he respected and glorified the temple, which still existed in his day, Philo addressed an audience that would have had no ready access to it. Moreover, because he interprets the biblical heritage in terms of Greek philosophy, he cannot be satisfied with the literal version of Passover or its regulations. While his treatment of the holiday, primarily based on Exodus 12, reflects ideas that he develops throughout his writings, it nevertheless continues to assume the centrality of the passover offering.[15]

Philo asserts that all of the Israelites were in a state of purification before their departure from Egypt and were therefore able to slaughter and offer the paschal sacrifice. All of the people of Israel were therefore elevated to the spiritual status of priests.[16] Furthermore, the houses of the Israelites resembled temples:

> On this very day every *dwelling-house is invested with the outward semblance and dignity of a temple*. The victim is then slaughtered and dressed for the festal meal which befits the occasion. The guests assembled for the banquet have been cleansed by purificatory lustrations, and are there *not as in other festive gatherings*, to indulge the belly with wine and viands, but to fulfil with *prayers* and hymns the custom handed down by their fathers.[17]

In this passage Philo also contrasts the "higher" Jewish feasts with non-Jewish ones. These "higher" feasts, such as the offering of the passover sacrifice, are designed to thank God for the migration from Egypt.[18] They are, as such, spiritual meals rather than banquets in which people merely indulge their passions. Philo makes this contrast between a higher and a baser celebration in several contexts;[19] accordingly, he makes no mention of wine in connection with the spiritual meals. If wine had become a common indulgence in Philo's community, it is understandable why he would consider it unfit for the special occasion of Passover and therefore omit any mention of it (Wisdom similarly fails to note it), though Philo does mention the singing of prayers and hymns. The Chronicler and Jubilees, by contrast, stress both the singing and the physical enjoyment. Specifically, the Chronicler mentions eating the meat of the sacrifice, while Jubilees adds the drinking of wine.

Philo uses the Greek notion of perfecting the soul to explain not only the higher purpose of Passover but also the use of unleavened bread and numerous details of the account in Exodus 12.[20]

Although Philo's presentation of the law closely follows the biblical record and does not add any local extratemple practices, his comments on Numbers 9 provide an interesting reflection of his Diaspora perspective. He states that, among the multitudes who make a pilgrimage to Jerusalem, those who are too far away to reach Jerusalem on time are given the dispensation to come a month later:

> The same permission also must be given to those who are prevented from joining the whole nation in worship not by mourning but by absence in a

distant country. For settlers abroad and inhabitants of other regions are not wrongdoers who deserve to be deprived of equal privileges, particularly if the nation has grown so populous that a single country cannot contain it and has sent out colonies in all directions.[21]

While assuming the truth of the biblical record, Philo also uses allegory to uncover for himself and his projected audience the hidden, deeper meanings of the biblical text. The early rabbinic authorities represented in the Mishnah are at a different stage in their relationship to the biblical heritage, so they do not adopt an alternative value system that provides deeper meanings. By transferring cultic notions to the Passover evening celebration the Mishnah describes a meal somewhat analogous to Philo's, but it rearranges the elements, while Philo's Passover meal remains basically tied to the biblical rendition and to a celebration structured around the paschal sacrifice. Moreover, the Mishnah's reinterpretation takes the form of a subtle recasting of the biblical materials while, as we have just seen, Philo develops his ideas explicitly based upon the biblical record. Only when rabbinic authorities openly adopt a new basis for religious life, untied to the temple cult, do they freely reinterpret the biblical institutions, and at that stage their comments may find more specific similarity to Philo's.[22]

Josephus, the first-century C.E. Jewish historian who wrote in Greek but lived first in Palestine and then in Rome, frequently mentions Passover but adds little that differs structurally from what has been encountered in other sources. He links Passover with the Feast of Unleavened Bread and sees the festival as a thanksgiving for the deliverance from Egypt. In *Antiquities* he paraphrases the accounts in Exodus and Leviticus as well as the celebrations of the returnees from Ezra 6 and of Hezekiah and Josiah. He mentions the eating of the sacrifice in fraternities, the multitude of participants who came on pilgrimage to Jerusalem, and also the great number of sacrifices. In addition, he refers to the singing of the Levites, mentioned in Chronicles, and goes on to note their use of musical instruments. In *Wars* and the parallel sections of *Antiquities*, Josephus describes several first-century instances of the celebration. He too emphasizes the huge number of pilgrims, many of whom came from abroad, as well as the joy the participants experienced.[23] Therefore, like Wisdom and Philo, Josephus sees the holiday as structured around the passover sacrifice. *Wars* 6: 423–424 epitomizes this concept:

Accordingly, on the occasion of the feast called Passover, at which they sacrifice from the ninth to the eleventh hour, and a *little fraternity*, as it were, *gathers round each sacrifice*, of not fewer than ten persons (*feasting alone not being permitted*), while the companies often include as many as twenty, the victims were counted and amounted to two hundred and fifty-five thousand six hundred; allowing an average of ten diners to each victim, we obtain a total of two million seven hundred thousand, *all pure and holy.*[24]

<h2 style="text-align:center">EARLY CHRISTIAN LITERATURE</h2>

Early Christian literature adds to our body of evidence concerning the significance of the passover offering, and points to the historical crisis that Jews faced post-70 when they could no longer bring a passover offering to the Jerusalem Temple. This perspective emerges through three aspects of the Christian tradition: references to a Passover meal, especially in regard to the Last Supper; the interpretation of Jesus as a paschal lamb; and the attacks on Judaism for the lack of a passover sacrifice.[25]

The first Christian records that throw light on the Passover meal are the actual references to Passover as a feast. The New Testament passion narratives, such as Luke 2:41, along with other passages mention that Jews would go up to Jerusalem to participate in the Passover feast and to eat from the passover sacrifice. Descriptions of the Last Supper depict the actual preparation and eating of the sacrifice in groups and attest to the significance of the meal. Scholars do not agree, however, on whether the Last Supper originally consisted of a Passover gathering. The narratives are inconsistent: the Synoptic gospels assign the Supper to Passover eve while the gospel of John apparently dates it to the preceding day.[26]

Those who accept the identification of the two meals point to the supposed parallels with a Passover meal or seder: a sacrifice, which is prepared in advance and which Jesus and a group of his disciples eat in Jerusalem; an opening blessing; dipping and didactic elements; and a closing hymn. If the Supper originally was a Passover meal, this would help to explain how that event and Jesus' passion bring redemption.[27]

Scholars who claim that this is ''not the earliest interpretation of the death of Christ and the sacrament'' point to John's dating and to various problems in the text of the other accounts.[28] They also argue that the parallels between the Last Supper and the Passover meal are inconclusive, since the features of the Last Supper are not unique to a Passover meal. They claim that one must distinguish between a Passover meal in remembrance of the exodus, a fraternal meal designed to satisfy hunger, and a sacramental meal to recall Jesus' death and to partake of those things promising salvation. At one point, perhaps even in the earliest stage, the latter two types of meals—but not the first—became superimposed upon each other and elements of the two became combined.[29]

The current state of scholarship tends to argue against the identification of the Last Supper as a seder.[30] Whatever the outcome of the debate, three important points emerge. First, the comparison between the meals reminds us of the features held in common in ancient meals and the ways in which the meal may be adapted to fit diverse purposes. Second, regardless of when the Last Supper was first interpreted as a passover meal, that interpretation nonetheless affirms that the Passover gathering could be perceived in cultic and salvific terms. Third, the narratives assume that both the Last Supper and the Passover meal are structured around a passover offering, although the eating of the sacrifice might be supplemented with other elements relevant to the purpose of each meal, including didactic instruction concerning the specific significance of each gathering.

Christians also used the paschal sacrifice motif to interpret the nature of Jesus. Some early Christian writers, especially the authors of John, the Letter to the Hebrews, and the Letters of Paul, saw the crucified Jesus as a sacrifice that atoned for the sins of the believers; some identified this sacrifice as a paschal offering. This interpretation, which occurs as early as 1 Corinthians 5:7−8, could subtly contrast the literal passover offering with the ultimate one, namely, Jesus because of the analogous features of the Last Supper and the Passover meal. Melito of Sardis, a second-century writer, deftly develops this theme in his Passover Homily, in which Jesus becomes the paschal lamb who insures redemption and salvation.[31]

Melito's sermon provides specific information about the practices and the ideas of Passover. Several scholars have pointed to passages that seem to echo elements of the rabbinic Passover evening celebration. These include the review of past history from "disgrace to glory"; the expounding of Deuteronomy 26:5−9; the declaration and exposition of the three essential elements of the holiday and the requirement to praise God; the use of bitter herbs and music; the reclining posture; and the meaning of the term *afiqimon*. These elements likewise provide striking parallels with the Mishnah's order for the evening. But it is the motif of the passover sacrifice embodied and surpassed in the role of Jesus that constitutes the central structure of the Last Supper and the critical distinction between the ceremonies. The Mishnah, by contrast, plays down the sacrifice and emphasizes the other elements.[32]

In fact, Melito's sermon is basically an adaptation of Exodus 12. Jesus is the true sheep:

> The scripture from the Hebrew Exodus has been read and the words of the mystery have been plainly stated, how the sheep is sacrificed and how the people are saved and how Pharaoh is scourged through the mystery. . . .[33]

It is clear that your respect was won when you saw the mystery of the Lord occurring in the sheep, the life of the Lord in the slaughter of the lamb, the model of the Lord in the death of the sheep; that is why you did not strike Israel, but made only Egypt childless.[34]

⌐ The model of the sheep that suffers and dies is fulfilled in Jesus, just as the Old Testament and Judaism are fulfilled in the Gospel.

Once, the slaying of the sheep was precious, but it is worthless now because of the life of the Lord; the death of the sheep was precious, but it is worthless now because of the salvation of the Lord; the blood of the sheep was precious, but it is worthless now because of the Spirit of the Lord; a speechless lamb was precious, but it is worthless now because of the spotless Son; the temple below was precious, but it is worthless now because of the Christ above. . . .

You have now heard the account of the model and what corresponds to it; listen also to the constitution of the mystery. What is the Pascha? It gets its name from its characteristic: from *suffer* (*pathein*) comes *suffering* (*páschein*). Learn therefore who is the suffering one, and who shares the suffering of the suffering one, and why the Lord is present on the earth to clothe himself with the suffering one, and carry him off to the heights of heaven.[35]

Justin Martyr, in the *Dialogue with Trypho*, expresses a similar sentiment, articulated in a manner that illustrates the third point of early Christian references to Passover, the attack on Judaism for its lack of a passover offering.

"The mystery of the lamb which God ordered you to sacrifice as the Passover was truly a type of Christ, with whose Blood the believers, in proportion to the strength of their faith, anoint their homes, that is, themselves. You are all aware that Adam, the result of God's creative act, was the abode of His inspiration. In the following fashion I can show that God's precept concerning the paschal lamb was only temporary. God does not allow the paschal lamb to be sacrificed in any other place than where His name is invoked (that is, in the Temple at Jerusalem), for He knew that there would come a time, after Christ's Passion, when the place in Jerusalem (where you sacrificed the paschal lamb) would be taken from you by your enemies, and then all sacrifices would be stopped. Moreover, that lamb which you were ordered to roast whole was a symbol of Christ's Passion on the Cross. Indeed, the lamb, while being roasted, resembles the figure of the cross, for one spit transfixes it horizontally from the lower parts up to the head, and another pierces it across the back, and holds up its forelegs."[36]

Justin's polemical implication is that Jews can no longer partake of the passover offering though Christians can, through the body of Christ. He therefore refers denigratingly to the Jerusalem Temple as the "place in Jerusalem." Melito may also be making the same sort of statement in saying "the temple below was precious, but it is worthless now because of the Christ above."[37] These attacks strike Jews where they are most vulnerable, for without the Jerusalem Temple they are unable to bring a passover offering. The case of Passover therefore objectively proves that from the perspective of the Christian tradition, Judaism and the literal meaning of the Hebrew Bible are obsolete, being fulfilled and surpassed in Christianity and Jesus. Origen and Justin make this very point. Justin writes:

> "Let us examine this together," I replied, "and see whether anyone is able now to observe all of the Mosaic precepts."
> "No," he answered, "for we recognize, as you said, that it is impossible to sacrifice the paschal lamb anywhere else, or to offer the goats required for the fast, or to present all the other oblations."[38]

Not all Christians saw the Last Supper as a Passover meal and Jesus as a paschal sacrifice, but those who did were motivated by the importance and power of the metaphor of the passover offering. This is not surprising in the light of the biblical heritage. The exodus from Egypt had brought redemption and remained a sign of God's continued involvement with Israel. When Israelites offered the passover sacrifice they recalled this historic event and the assurances given them about their future. The sacrifice took on an increasingly essential role (Numbers 9 cannot conceive of the holiday without the sacrifice), and its significance grew when centralization of the cult changed the holiday from a family celebration to a national one, as evidenced in accounts of Josiah's and Hezekiah's passovers as well as in Philo's and Josephus' descriptions of the celebration. To be sure, the sources indicate that certain features were added to the celebration in Second Temple times. But the extra rejoicing, eating, drinking, and singing by the Levites entirely surrounded and accompanied the passover sacrifice. The problem, therefore, was aptly put by Melito, Justin, and the other early Christians: How could Jews observe this holiday without the passover offering? If early rabbinic authorities believed Judaism could continue without a temple, they had to offer an answer. They found the raw materials for their solution in Exodus's location of the ritual in the home, albeit around a sacrifice, in the Bible's juxtaposition of Passover and the Feast of Unleavened Bread, and in the mention of secondary elements that supplemented the passover sacrifice. Still they had to recast this answer to the loss of the Temple in a form such that Jews might continue to feel connected with their past heritage. How the Mishnah accomplished this is the subject of the next two chapters.

3

MISHNAH AND TOSEFTA
PESAHIM 10

THE EARLIEST FULL DESCRIPTION of the Passover evening celebration, later called the seder,[1] is found in Mishnah Pesahim 10, a translation of which is presented here. In the absence of a critical edition of the Mishnah, I have based the translation on the manuscripts and early editions of the Mishnah listed in the Abbreviations and Bibliography, section II-A. This text is free of later interpolations and changes generated by material in the Gemara (the postmishnaic collection of teachings edited in two recensions, one in Palestine, ca. 350–400, and the other in Babylonia, ca. 500) or by developments in the seder and the haggadah. A Hebrew text appears in appendix B.

A reading of the entire Mishnah reveals the distinctive narrative style of the text, which anonymously sets out the evening procedure in sequence and contains only several attributed statements and disputes. It is immediately obvious that this description differs from the premishnaic accounts of the rite.

Mishnah 10:1

A. On the eve of Passover, close to [the time of] *minhah* [the daily afternoon offering = about the ninth hour of the day], a person should not eat until it gets dark.[2]

B. Even a poor person in Israel should not eat until [he] reclines.[3]

C. [Those who serve] should not give him fewer than four cups of wine even if [the funds come] from the charity plate.[4]

Mishnah 10:2

A. [They] poured for him the first cup [of wine].

B. The House of Shammai say, [He] says the blessing over the day and afterward [he] says the blessing over the wine.

And the House of Hillel say, [He] says the blessing over the wine and afterward [he] says the blessing over the day.[5]

Mishnah 10:3

A. [They] served him[6]—[he] dips the lettuce (HZRT) [= the vegetable used for the bitter herbs] before he reaches the bread condiment.

B. [They] served him unleavened bread and lettuce and *haroset* [= a mixture, e.g., of nuts, fruit, and vinegar pounded together],[7] even though the *haroset* is not a *misvah* [= a commandment].

R. Leazar b. Sadoq says, [It is a] *misvah*.[8]

C. And in the Temple [they] serve him the carcass of the passover offering.[9]

Mishnah 10:4

A. [They] poured for him the second cup—

B.1. and here the child asks,

B.2. and if the child lacks intelligence, his father instructs him.[10]

C. How is this night different from all the [other] nights?

D.1. For on all the [other] nights we dip once, this night twice.

D.2. For on all the [other] nights we eat leavened and unleavened bread, this night we eat only unleavened.

D.3. For on all the [other] nights we eat meat roasted, steamed, or cooked [in a liquid = boiled], this night only [or "all of it"] roasted.[11]

E. According to the child's intelligence, his father instructs him.

F. [He] starts [reading] with the disgrace [section of the Bible] and ends with the glory;

G. and [he] expounds [the biblical section] from "A Wandering Aramean was my father" (Deut. 26:5), until he finishes the entire portion.[12]

Mishnah 10:5

A. Rabban Gamaliel said, Whoever did not say these three things on Passover did not fulfill his obligation:

B. *Pesah, massah,* and *merorim* [= passover offering, unleavened bread, and bitter herbs].

C.1. *Pesah*—because the Omnipresent skipped over the houses of our ancestors in Egypt.

C.2. *Merorim*—because the Egyptians embittered the lives of our ancestors in Egypt.

C.3. *Massah*—because they were redeemed.

D. Therefore we are obligated to give thanks, to praise, to glorify, to crown, to exalt, to elevate the One who did for us all these miracles and took us out of slavery to freedom,

and let us say before Him Hallelujah (Ps. 113:1ff.).[13]

Mishnah 10:6

A. Up to what point does he recite [the Hallel]?

B. The House of Shammai say, Until "[He sets the childless woman among her household] as a happy mother of children" [= end of Ps. 113].

And the House of Hillel say, Until "[Tremble . . . at the presence of the LORD . . . who turned] the flinty rock into a fountain" [= end of Ps. 114].

C. And [he] seals with [the term or prayer for] "redemption." [He ends with a blessing formula that has the motif of "redemption."]

D. R. Tarfon says, ". . . Who has redeemed us and redeemed our ancestors from Egypt and brought us to this night" [some texts add: "to eat thereon unleavened bread and bitter herbs"]—and [he] does not seal [with a concluding formula].[14]

E. R. Aqiva says, [One adds to the blessing:] "Thus O LORD, our God and God of our ancestors, bring us in peace to the approaching festivals which are coming to meet us, happy in the building of Your city [some texts add: "joyous in Your service"],[15] [so as] to eat from the passover and festive offerings whose blood will reach the wall of Your altar with favor,

and let us thank You for our redemption.

Praised art thou, O LORD, Who redeemed [or "redeems"] Israel."[16]

Mishnah 10:7

A. [They] poured for him the third cup [of wine]—[, he] says the blessing (MBRK) [alternatively: "and (he) said the blessing" (WBYRK)] over (ʿL) his food.[17]

B. [At] the fourth [cup]—[he] finishes the Hallel [i.e., through Ps. 118], and says over it the blessing over the song.[18]

C. Between the former cups, if [he] wants to drink [further] he may drink. Between the third and fourth, [he] should not drink.[19]

Mishnah 10:8

A. After [eating from] the passover offering, [they] do not end [with] *afiqimon* [= revelry].[20]

B. [If they] fell asleep:

[if it was] some of them—[they] may eat [again because the remaining individuals of the group, who stayed awake, maintained the group];

and [if it was] all of them—[they] may not eat [again].

C. R. Yose says, If [they] dozed—[they] may eat [again]. And if [they] slumbered—[they] may not eat [again].[21]

Mishnah 10:9

A. After midnight the passover offering imparts uncleanness to the hands; *piggul* [= the "offensive" sacrifice] and *notar* [= the "remnant"] impart uncleanness to the hands.[22]

B. [If one] said the blessing over the passover offering (BRKT HPSH), [he] is exempt from that over the festive offering (ŠLZBH),

that [blessing] over the festive offering, [he] is not exempt from that over the passover offering—the words of R. Ishmael.

C. R. Aqiva says, [Saying] the former does not exempt [one from saying] the latter, and [saying] the latter does not exempt [one from saying] the former.[23]

TOSEFTA PESAHIM (PISHA) 10

Tosefta Pisha 10 is keyed to Mishnah Pesahim 10 and glosses, complements, and supplements the teachings of the Mishnah. Since I frequently make use of the Tosefta to analyze the Mishnah, I present it in translation. The translation is based on Saul Lieberman's critical edition, *The Tosefta* (vol. 2, pp. 196–199 [New York, 1962]). Italicized portions are either quotations from the Mishnah or foreign words. Since Lieberman presents a complete critical apparatus, the notes to the text are limited to cross-references and variant readings important for the purposes of this study.[24]

Tosefta 10:1

A. *On the eve of Passover, close to [the time of] minhah, a person should not eat until it gets dark.*

B. *Even a poor person in Israel should not eat until [he] reclines.*

C. And [Erf MS without the W-, "and"] [*those who serve*] *should not give him fewer than four cups of wine,*

D. which contain the amount of a fourth [of log = 1½ eggs, in liquid measure],

E. whether it is raw or diluted,

whether it is fresh or old [from the previous year].

F. R. Yehudah says, And [Erf MS without the W-, "and"] as long as it has the taste and appearance of wine [= taste, even though possibly diluted; appearance, even though old].[25]

Tosefta 10:2, 3

A. *[They] poured for him the first cup [of wine]—*

B. *The House of Shammai say, [He] says the blessing over the day and afterwards [he] says the blessing over the wine,*

for the day causes the wine to come, and the day has already become sanctified and the wine has not yet come [= the day, which automatically comes at the appropriate time irrespective of the presence of wine, has already started].

C. *And the House of Hillel say, [He] says the blessing over the wine and afterward [he] says the blessing over the day,*

for the wine causes [provides the occasion for] the Sanctification of the day to be recited.

Another matter [= a second reason]: The blessing over the wine is constant and the blessing over the day is not constant [and that which is constant, not intermittent, takes precedence].

D. And the *halakhah* follows the words of the House of Hillel.[26]

Tosefta 10:4

A. A man is commanded to make his children and his wife happy on the holiday.

B. With what does he make them happy?

With wine, as it is written, "and wine gladdens the human heart" (Ps. 104:15).

R. Yehudah says, Women with what is appropriate for them, and children with what is appropriate for them.[27]

Tosefta 10:5

A. The waiter dips innards [in salt water] and serves them to the guests [even before darkness, since this hors-d'oeuvre whets the appetite and does not satiate the guests].

B. Even though there is no proof on this matter, there is a mention [= a hint] of it: "Plow a line and do not sow among the thorns" (Jer. 4:3). [= One starts with something to direct that which is to follow; the line will direct the seeding, and the hors-d'oeuvre will direct the food.]

Tosefta 10:6 [=A], 7 [=B, C], 8 [=D, E], 9a [=F, G]

A. [As to] one who leads in reciting the Hallel (HMQR' 'T HHLL)—they go to him and read [with him] and he does not go to them.

B. [As to] one who leads in reciting to his minor sons and daughters—he must respond with them in the places that they respond [i.e., he must read with them the portions with which they respond, for as minors they cannot perform the act on his behalf].

C. In what place does he respond?

[When] he reaches, "Praised [be He] who comes"—he responds with them, "in the name of the LORD."

[When] he reaches, "We bless you"—he responds with them, "from the house of the LORD."

D.1. Townspeople who lack someone to lead them in reciting the Hallel—[They] go to the house of assembly and read the first portion [chapters 113–114], and [they] go home and eat and drink,

D.2. and [they] return and finish the Hallel.

D.3. And if they are unable [to return to the house of assembly] they finish all of it [i.e., they finish all the Hallel before going home the first time].[28]

E. The Hallel is not abbreviated or expanded.

F. R. Leazar b. Parata used to keep the praises plain [literally, "flat," that is, he did not double them].

G. Rabbi used to repeat the praises.

Tosefta 10:9b

A. R. Leazar said, [They] grab unleavened bread [from each other] for [the sake of] the child [to astonish him] so that he will not fall asleep.

B. R. Yehudah says, Even if [the adult] has eaten only one hors-d'oeuvre, even if [he] has dipped only one [piece of] lettuce [and is still hungry], [he and the others] grab unleavened bread for [the sake of] the child, so that he will not fall asleep.[29]

Tosefta 10:9c

A. *Up to what point does he recite [the Hallel]?*

The House of Shammai say, Until "As a happy mother of children" [= end
of Ps. 113].

B. *And the House of Hillel say, Until "the flinty rock into a fountain"* [=
end of Ps. 114].

C. *And he seals with [the term or prayer for]"redemption."*

D. Said the House of Shammai to the House of Hillel.

And have [the Israelites] already gone forth that [they] mention the
exodus from Egypt? [The communal meal over the paschal lamb, as depicted in
Ex. 12, precedes the actual exodus from Egypt. Hence in recreating the events,
it is inappropriate at the evening meal to give thanks for the exodus.]

E. Said the House of Hillel to them,

Even if he waits until the cock crows [, early in the morning, to mention
the redemption, it is still inappropriate]. Lo, these [Israelites] did not go forth
until the sixth hour of the day [= later, after the hour at which the cock crows].
[Therefore, following your logic,] how can [one] mention "redemption" [later
or in the special selection of the Psalms in the morning service] while [the
Israelites] have not yet been redeemed [and yet people do mention "redemption" at that time]![30]

Tosefta 10:9d, 10

A. The *unleavened bread and* the *lettuce (HZRT) and* the *haroset, even
though the haroset is not a misvah* [= a commandment].

R. Leazar b. R. Sadoq says, [It is a] misvah.

B. *In the Temple [they] serve him the carcass of the passover offering.*

C. A Case (M'SH W-): R. Leazar b. R. Sadoq said to merchants of Lod,
"Come, take the prescribed (MSWH) spices."[31]

Tosefta 10:11, 12

A. *After [eating from] the passover offering they do not end [with]
afiqomon* [Erf = *afiqimon*],

such as nuts, dates, and parched grain.[32]

B. A person is obliged to engage himself in the [study of the] *halakhot* [=
laws] of Passover all night,

even with [only] his son,

even with [only] himself,

even with [only] his student.

C. Case concerning (M'SH B-): Rabban Gamaliel and the elders were
reclining in the house of Baitos the son of Zonin in Lod,

D. and [they] were engaged in the *halakhot* of Passover all night, until the cock's call.

[They] raised up [the table] from in front of them, and [they] stirred and went along to the house of study.[33]

Tosefta 10:13

A. What is the blessing over the passover offering (*BRKT HPSH*)?

"Praised [be Thou King of the Universe] who has sanctified us through His commandments and commanded us to eat the passover offering."

B. What is the blessing over the festive offering (*BRKT HZBH*)?

"Praised [be Thou King of the Universe] who has sanctified us through His commandments and commanded us to eat the festive offering."[34]

4

THE MISHNAH'S
RESPONSE: THE MEANING
OF PASSOVER CONTINUES
WITHOUT THE PASSOVER
SACRIFICE

INTRODUCTION

B
Y ANALYZING MISHNAH PESAHIM 10, this chapter shows how the Mishnah draws upon earlier biblical accounts of Passover eve and recasts them so as to provide the celebration with a new basis. As the prerabbinic descriptions make clear, everything in the evening rite had revolved around the passover sacrifice. And if, as early rabbinic authorities claimed, Judaism could continue without a temple, then what would be their solution concerning Passover?[1] The Mishnah solves this by outlining a viable evening protocol consisting of old and new elements. Through the choice, formulation, and sequence of contents within the chapter as well as the chapter's placement within the tractate, the Mishnah creates the impression that the new order constitutes a tried and valid evening ritual that will continue to remind people of past redemption and assure them of future redemption. Owing to the nature of its argument, the Mishnah intentionally presents an anomaly. That is, despite the disparity with the previous observance, the Mishnah writes as if nothing were new, and as if the new order were that which had always been followed.[2]

ANALYSIS OF MISHNAH PESAHIM 10

The Mishnah's effort to reinterpret and supplement the earlier heritage can be discerned in nine distinct ways. At several points, the Tosefta and other sources will throw light on the Mishnah.

1. The Passover meal is synchronized with the biblical sacrificial meal. Mishnah 10:1 proscribes starting the meal until nightfall: "On the eve of Passover, close to the [time of] *minhah*, a person should not eat until it gets dark." The Bible requires that the sacrifice and eating take place in the evening or during the night and uses different phrases to specify the exact time. Exodus 12:8 states, "They shall eat the flesh *that same night*," and Deuteronomy 16:6 says, "there alone shall you slaughter the passover sacrifice, *in the evening, at sundown*, the time of the day when you departed from Egypt." As shown in chapter 2, later works, including Ezekiel the Epic Poet, Jubilees, the Temple Scroll, and Josephus, choose one of these phrases or other expanded descriptions to define the proper moment to slaughter the animal and to eat it.[3]

The Tosefta extends the Mishnah's definition of the proper time for the meal. Tosefta Pesahim 10:1 cites Mishnah 10:1, and Tosefta 2:22 spells out the regulation:[4]

A. The lettuce [= bitter herbs] (HHZRT) and the unleavened bread and the passover offering:
the evening of the first day of the holiday—obligatory;
and the remaining days—voluntary.
B. R. Simeon says, For men [Lieberman:[5] the passover offering]—obligatory; for women—voluntary.
C. Hillel the Elder would fold together the three of them [= the items in A] and eat them.
D. From when do [they start to] eat them [the three items in A]?
From when it gets dark [immediately].[6]
[If they] did not eat them when it got dark—they eat them all night.
[If they] did not eat them all night—they should not eat them from then on.
E. The lettuce and the unleavened bread and the passover offering do not preempt each other.[7]

(T. Pes. 2:22, p. 150, ll. 65–69)

Tosefta Pesahim 2:22 emphasizes two points. First, clause D treats the time requirement and distinguishes between the preferred and tolerated times to eat the three items. Second, the passage makes all three items essential, which is an issue that will be discussed further.

Mishnah Pesahim 10:9 reminds us that the time of eating the sacrifice is important: "After midnight, the passover offering imparts uncleanness to the hands; *piggul* [= the 'offensive' sacrifice] and *notar* [= the 'remnant'] impart uncleanness to the hands."

In asserting that the Passover eve ritual starts at the same hour at which the sacrificial meal started during the time of the temple, the Mishnah strengthens the identification between the two. As a consequence, the evening ritual resembles or takes the place of the passover offering.

2. The unleavened bread and bitter herbs are equated with the passover sacrifice. While the unleavened bread is part of a specific biblical law, it is also mentioned along with bitter herbs in conjunction with the passover sacrifice. In this setting, however, the unleavened bread and bitter herbs are secondary to the passover offering. Mishnah 10:3, quoted in Tosefta 10:9–10, subtly presents the two as primary elements and assigns them equal status with the sacrifice:

> B. [They] served him unleavened bread and lettuce [= the vegetable used for the bitter herbs] and *haroset* [= a mixture, e.g., of nuts, fruit, and vinegar pounded together], even though the *haroset* is not a *misvah* [= a commandment].
> R. Leazar b. Sadoq says, [It is a] *misvah*.
> C. And in the Temple (WBMQDŠ) [they] serve him the carcass of the passover offering.[8]

In clause B, the masters differ as to the basis of *haroset*. The anonymous authority uses the phrase "even though" in mentioning that *haroset* is not a commandment, implying, as a consequence, that the other two items are commanded. Moreover, since only the *haroset* is disputed, one is left with the impression that all of the authorities agree that the other two items are divinely prescribed.

Clause C must be seen in this light. I have presented the text according to the manuscripts, which have the verb in the present tense, "they serve," MBY'YN. Printed texts include the auxiliary HYW, "used to," thus restricting the statement to the past and changing its import. In using the present tense, as Lieberman points out, the Mishnah employs language commonly used to contrast practices inside and outside the temple. The clause therefore refers not to two stages in the law but to two pre-Destruction customs. Through this projection of a precedent from temple days, the Mishnah legitimizes the rite as it is performed without the sacrifice and outside the temple precincts.[9]

The equalization of components and the presentation of a pre-70 precedent are more explicit in Tosefta Pesahim 2:22. Clauses A–C and E treat the requirement of bitter herbs, unleavened bread, and the passover offering. Clause A suggests that even when a sacrifice was available it shared the same law as governed the bitter herbs and unleavened bread. Therefore all three items are equally important, and as a consequence the bitter herbs and unleavened bread do not fall into desuetude because a more important third element is missing. Clause C presents a precedent for the combined use of all three items by the pre-70 master Hillel. And finally, clause E concisely states that none of the three preempts the others; therefore the loss of one item does not vitiate the use of the other two.[10]

The problem of the continued applicability of unleavened bread and bitter herbs after the temple's destruction is discussed even more directly in the Mekilta of Rabbi Simeon ben Yoḥai to Exodus 12:18 (p. 22):

> A. "[At evening, you shall eat unleavened bread] until the twenty-first of the month, at evening" (Ex. 12:18). Perhaps you are obligated as to unleavened bread all seven [days]?
> [Therefore] the teaching says, "[You shall not eat] with [or "upon"] it [anything leaven]" (Deut. 16:3). "With it" [= the passover sacrifice] you are obligated concerning unleavened bread; and you are not obligated concerning unleavened bread all seven [days].
> B. If so, why does it say, "Until the twenty-first of the month at evening"?
> For [otherwise] I might have [assumed] that it applies [only] when you have the passover offering. When you do not have the passover offering whence [do you learn it]?
> [Therefore] the teaching says, "Upon it you shall eat unleavened bread" (Deut. 16:3). The verse makes it an obligation.
> C. I only know [from this] concerning the time when the Temple exists.
> Concerning when the Temple does not exist, whence?
> [Therefore] the teaching says, "At evening you shall eat unleavened bread" (Ex. 12:18).
> D. I only know [from this] concerning within the Land of [Israel], outside the Land, whence?
> [Therefore] the teaching says, "In all your settlements you shall eat unleavened bread" (Ex. 12:20).

Several factors are operating in this text. The unleavened bread is associated with the passover offering (A), yet it also appears as the subject of a separate rule (B). An extra verse is needed to indicate that its requirement is not contingent upon the temple (C) or the land of Israel (D). The issue concerning unleavened bread could be even more forcefully applied to bitter herbs, which lack an independent prescription.

The Midrash thus finds biblical support for the continued use of unleavened bread. In contrast to the Mishnah, the Midrash is absolutely clear on the point that there are different practices and that they are all rooted in Scripture. The Mishnah makes a comparable claim, but does so quite subtly.[11]

3. The biblical pedagogic device of a parent responding to a child's inquiry can continue without the sacrifice. Exodus 12:25−27, 13:8, and 14−16 present

three instances in which a parent explains the themes of Passover to a child. Only the first instance appears in the context of the evening ritual:

And when your children ask you, "What do you mean by this rite ('BWDH)?" You shall say, "It is the passover sacrifice to the LORD, because He passed over the houses of the Israelites in Egypt when He smote the Egyptians, but saved our houses."

As seen in chapter 2, "this rite" refers to putting blood on the doorposts and making other preparations contingent upon the sacrifice.[12] When there is no sacrifice, what will prompt the child's inquiry? Mishnah Pesaḥim 10:4 responds:

A. [They] poured for him the second cup—
B.1. And here the child asks,
B.2. and if the child lacks intelligence, his father instructs him.
C. How is this night different from all the [other] nights?
D.1. For on all the [other] nights we dip once, this night twice.
D.2. For on all the [other] nights we eat leavened and unleavened bread, this night we eat only unleavened.
D.3. For on all the [other] nights we eat meat roasted, steamed, or cooked [in a liquid = boiled], this night only [or "all of it"] roasted.
E. According to the child's intelligence, his father instructs him.[13]

The Mishnah suggests alternative questions concerning dipping the bitter herbs twice and eating only unleavened bread and roasted meat. In this way, one is assured that the biblical pedagogic device will remain in use.[14]

4. The various regulations concerning the use of wine, first mentioned in Jubilees (and therefore nonbiblical though possibly a traditional element of the rite), indicates that wine may continue to play a role in the celebration. Mishnah Pesaḥim 10:1, 2, 4, and 7 specify the number of cups, when they are drunk, and when the blessings are said. At the same time wine takes on a distinct meaning within the rabbinic celebration, as will be seen later.

5. Gamaliel's requirement to verbalize the "three things" (M. Pes. 10:5) results in an added synchronization with the passover sacrifice. This requirement also makes the unleavened bread and bitter herbs as prominent as the sacrifice.

A. Rabban Gamaliel said, Whoever did not say these three things on Passover did not fulfill his obligation:
B. *Pesaḥ, maṣṣah*, and *merorim* [= passover offering, unleavened bread, and bitter herbs].

C.1. *Pesah*—because the Omnipresent skipped over the houses of our ancestors in Egypt.

C.2. *Merorim*—because the Egyptians embittered the lives of our ancestors in Egypt.

C.3. *Massah*—because they were redeemed.

D. Therefore we are obligated to give thanks, to praise, to glorify, to crown, to exalt, to elevate the One who did for us all these miracles and took us out of slavery to freedom,

and let us say before Him Hallelujah (Ps. 113:1ff.).[15]

(M. Pes. 10:5)

Gamaliel's requirement to say the words is intended to make people focus or concentrate on the items. This brings to mind the requirement to "concentrate," which rabbinic authorities believed the Bible applied only to the passover sacrifice and one other offering. These authorities held that an individual had to have special intention while slaughtering the passover lamb and the *hatat*, or sin offering. The coincidence of the Mishnah's rule and the required concentration was noticed by Samuel Eliezer ben Judah Ha-Levi Edels (1555–1631) and Meir Friedmann and provides another instance of early rabbinic attempts to link the celebration to the sacrificial meal.[16]

By requiring that all three items be verbalized, Gamaliel in effect equates them. This contributes to the larger effort of making the unleavened bread and bitter herbs as important as the sacrifice, which was shown in Mishnah 10:3, Tosefta Pesahim 2:22, and Mishnah 10:4.

Support for this analysis of the purpose of the Mishnah can be found in Alon's suggestion that the references, in clause B, to the *pesah*, or "passover [offering]," and, in Mishnah 10:4D, to the "roasted [meat]" are to a nonsacrificial animal roasted to resemble the passover sacrifice. People performed this practice so as to continue whatever part they could of the earlier rite.[17] As will be seen in chapter 7 and the appendix, other sources may likewise reveal this practice.

The following clauses in this Mishnah, Mishnah 10:5C–D (apparently later than A–B), enlarge on the assertion that the loss of the sacrifice does not end the celebration. Clause B makes its point indirectly, as is often the case with the Mishnah, while clause C adds a symbolic interpretation to the three items in clause B, therefore preparing the way for the much broader statement in clause D. In giving significance to what the three foods represent, rather than to the literal act of eating, clause C reflects a greater, though not yet total, acceptance of the changes in Judaism. Relating to an activity symbolically is a way of coping with its loss, for its physical presence is no longer as consequential. The old ways are continued, and at the same time it is less painful to acknowledge the change. This is a transitional stage of adjustment: one is still tied to the old structures and not yet relating to the current practices in their own terms.[18]

The author of clause C thus builds upon Gamaliel's tradition. In equating the three items, clause B decreases the sense of loss since two of the three items are still present in their original form and the third, if Alon is right, in imitation. The sense of loss is also decreased, to an even greater extent, by Gamaliel's specific requirement for an individual to "say," that is, to verbalize and concentrate on the three things. The author of clause C develops this approach, making it possible to overcome the loss in an even more profound manner now that the physical is no longer essential.

The symbolic approach to the sacrifice is further reflected in the custom of putting two cooked foods on the table to represent the passover and festival sacrifices. This custom would have developed when people no longer roasted a lamb to resemble the sacrifice. The two foods are mentioned in the Gemara, in a baraita, and have been anachronistically interpolated into the text of Mishnah Pesaḥim 10:3, which delineates the evening menu.[19]

6. The special psalms that previously accompanied the passover sacrifice could be sung without professional singers and without the offering. Mishnah Pesaḥim 10:5D and 10:6 require individual Jews to sing these praises of God, called *Hallel*.[20]

> Therefore we are obligated to give thanks, to praise, to glorify, to crown, to exalt, to elevate the One who did for us all these miracles and took us out of slavery to freedom,
> and let us say before Him Hallelujah (Ps. 113:1-).

(M. 10:5D)

A. Up to what point does he recite [the Hallel]?

B. The House of Shammai say, Until "as a happy mother of children" [the end of Ps. 113].

And the House of Hillel say, Until "the flinty rock into a fountain" [the end of Ps. 114].

C. And [he] seals with [the term or prayer for] "redemption."

D. R. Tarfon says, " . . . Who has redeemed us and redeemed our ancestors from Egypt and brought us to this night" [some texts add: "to eat thereon unleavened bread and bitter herbs"]—and [he] does not seal [with a concluding formula].

E. R. Aqiva says, [One adds to the blessing:] "Thus O LORD, our God and God of our ancestors, bring us in peace to the approaching festivals which are coming to meet us, happy in the building of Your city [some texts add: "joyous in Your service"], [so as] to eat from the passover and festive

offerings whose blood will reach the wall of Your altar with favor,
    and let us thank You for our redemption.
Praised art thou, O LORD, who redeemed [or "redeems"] Israel."

                                                              (M. 10:6)

Second Temple sources, seen in chapter 2, mention singing by experts in
conjunction with the sacrifice.[21] Tannaitic sources, including Mishnah Pesaḥim 5:5, 7, and 9:3, associate the songs with special singers. One can therefore
appreciate the Mishnah's point that lay people without experts to lead them may
still offer prayers and thanksgiving: even without the sacrifice, the purpose of
thanksgiving remains.[22] The Mishnah may be implying as well that singing
does not require musical instruments no longer used in the liturgy.[23]

One medieval rabbinic commentator, Menaḥem Meiri, aptly sensed the
transformation:

And it was their custom to read the Hallel in the synagogue while it was still
daylight in memory of the Hallel that they used to say in the precincts at the
time of the slaughter of the paschal lamb.[24]

Meir Friedmann further observes:

The primary place of the Hallel is in the evening of Passover over eating of
the paschal lamb. . . . And when the Temple was destroyed, they established that one should say the Hallel even without the eating of the paschal
lamb.[25]

We may now comment further on the formulation and structure of Mishnah
10:5, cited earlier in subsection 5. The passage consists of Gamaliel's statement
(A−B), the symbolic interpretation of the "three things" (C), and the requirement to give thanks by saying Hallel (D). In the manuscripts, *maṣṣah* "unleavened bread" precedes *merorim* "bitter herbs" in clause B, while in clause
C the sequence is reversed. The order in clause B accords with the usual
sequence in lists: words with fewer syllables precede those with more syllables.
In clause C the order has been deliberately reversed to fit the context. The
explanation given to *maṣṣah*, "because they were redeemed" constitutes the
basis for clause D and must immediately precede it. According to this arrange-
ment, the presence or absence of the sacrifice does not affect the recitation of
the psalms. What counts is the memory of their history of redemption, which in
post-70 days is still an event full of meaning.[26]

The dispute, in Mishnah 10:6 (quoted above), between the Houses of Hillel
and Shammai over the selection of the biblical psalms implies the appropriateness of saying the psalms as an effective means to recall the promise of
redemption. Although it is unknown whether this dispute concerned a private

custom or a standardized practice, in the present context the masters of the Mishnah deal with the latter possibility. The Houses of Hillel and Shammai existed before 70 C.E. and presumably by then, Hallel had a place in the Passover rite, something likewise seen in the prescriptions to say blessings after the recitation. In Mishnah 10:6C−E, the Yavnean masters R. Aqiva and R. Tarfon consider the proper reference to redemption to be in the blessing that closes the first part of Hallel, and in Mishnah 10:7B the anonymous Mishnah requires a blessing after the final part.

> A. They poured for him the third cup [of wine]—[, he] says the blessing (MBRK) [alternatively: "and (he) said the blessing" (WBYRK)] over ('L) his food.
> B. [At] the fourth [cup]—[he] finishes the Hallel [i.e., through Ps. 118], and says over it *birkat hashir* [= "the blessing over the song"].[27]

These requirements form part of the gradual rabbinic standardization of the liturgy and, at the same time, legitimize the use of Hallel outside the context of the sacrifice.

The additional subtlety in the argument of the Mishnah can be appreciated in its use of the *birkat h-* pattern, one of the standard constructions used to specify a blessing. The same *birkat h-* pattern is used in Mishnah 10:9 for the blessings over the paschal and festival sacrifices, *birkhat hapesah* and *birkat hazevah*.

> A. After midnight, the passover offering imparts uncleanness to the hands; *piggul* [= the "offensive" sacrifice] and *notar* [= the "remnant"] impart uncleanness to the hands.
> B. [If he] said the blessing over the passover offering (BRKT HPSH), [he] is exempt from that over the festive offering (ŠLZBH), that [blessing] over the festive offering, [he] is not exempt from that over the passover offering—the words of R. Ishmael.
> C. R. Aqiva says, [Saying] the former does not exempt [one from saying] the latter, and [saying] the latter does not exempt [one from saying] the former.[28]

In associating a blessing with each of these items, the Mishnah sets up a comparison, so that by implication, the psalm's recitation has as solid a foundation as the sacrificial offerings.

7. Without the meat of the sacrifice, a person can still fulfill the biblically ordained requirement to be happy, an essential element of any holiday.[29] The connection between "meat" and "joy" first appears in Chronicles and Jubilees, which emphasize the festivity and the large number of sacrifices. Jubilees, the first source to mention wine, does so in the context of the meal. In the Mishnah and the Tosefta, wine becomes a distinctive element of the ritual.

Mishnah 10:1, 2, 4, and 7 prescribe the drinking of wine and Tosefta 10:4 deals with its significance. The need of the latter to provide biblical support concerning the prescription of wine may reflect an awareness of wine's new role in insuring festivity.

> A. A man is commanded to make his children and his wife happy on the holiday.
> B. With what does he make them happy?
> With wine, as it is written, "and wine gladdens the human heart" (Ps. 104:15).
> R. Yehudah says, Women with what is appropriate for them, and children with what is appropriate for them.[30]
>
> (T. Pes. 10:4, p. 196, lines 8–10)

The Gemara contains a version of this passage from the Tosefta, glossing it with another passage which makes explicit the new use of wine.

> A. It is taught (TNY),
> R. Yehudah ben Betira says, When the Temple exists, "joy" derives only from meat (BZMN ŠBYT HMQDŠ QYYM 'YN ŚMḤH 'L' BBŚR).
> as it is said, "You shall offer peace offerings and eat them, and be happy before the LORD your God" (Deut. 27:7).
> And now (when the Temple does not exist),[31] "joy" derives only from wine,
> as it is said, "And wine gladdens the human heart" (Ps. 104:15).
>
> (b. Pes. 109a)

One anthropologist has noticed how wine has taken on this special role within the seder:

> At the Seder, sweet wine suggests joy and life, continuing at this festival its associations throughout the year. Wine is present on all occasions where future happiness is anticipated, such as the Sabbath, weddings, and the circumcision, and the common, informal toast over wine is *"L'chayim"*— "to life." It may be that wine is compatible with life and joy because of its sweet taste and its ability to suggest warmth and light, but these physical sensations are contingent and not necessary to its use. Other objects could be made to carry the same meanings. Wine is made "happy" by circumscribing its use. It is through mandated participation in situations defined as joyous that wine is a positive item, and through proscription in situations defined as sad—funerals or the days of mourning for the Temple—that wine becomes incompatible with the expression of individual or social despair.[32]

8. The place of the chapter within tractate Pesaḥim may also be significant in the Mishnah's argument that the holiday's celebration can "continue" as in

pre-70 days. Chapters 1 to 4 treat aspects of Passover that remained applicable after the temple's destruction, such as definitions of leavened and unleavened bread, while chapters 5 to 9 deal with the Passover sacrifice. Medieval authorities questioned why chapter 10 occurs at the close of the tractate, and not after chapter 4. Some commentators have suggested that chapter 10 initially followed chapter 4 but was later placed at the end as a "fitting conclusion."[33] The evidence, however, does not support such an explanation. The present order of the Mishnah is the original sequence, including the close that reverts to the sacrifice, Mishnah 10:8–9.

The first argument in favor of the original order of the chapters is the relationship of Tosefta chapter 10 to Mishnah chapter 10, which attests to the present structure of the Mishnah. Even Tosefta 10:13, which defines the *birkat hapesaḥ* and *birkat hazevaḥ* (the blessings over the paschal and festive offerings, mentioned in M. 10:9), attests to the resumption of sacrificial matters.[34]

The second argument is that the role of chapter 10 as the concluding chapter accords with the Mishnah's practice of placing the application of a principle at the end of a tractate. For example, Mishnah Miqvaot 1–8:4 deals with water used and not used in purification and the conditions under which the water is effective, while 8:5–10:8 treat the use of pools. The latter reference "stands by itself" with "no redactional interest in linking it—e.g., thematically—to the first eight chapters."[35] Likewise, in tractate Negaʿim, chapters 1 to 13 present the themes and laws of plagues, while chapter 14 applies these materials in terms of the rite of purification. The last chapter is unrelated to the earlier ones in its mode of thought and the manner of presentation; but coincidentally, its style is quite similar to that of Mishnah Pesaḥim 10 in that it uses predominantly declarative sentences.[36]

The third argument is that Mishnah Pesaḥim 10 constitutes an integral unit that should not be separated into "sacrificial" and "nonsacrificial" elements. Not only does the Tosefta attest to it, but internally it makes sense. Mishnah 10:1–7 describes the evening ritual, and Mishnah 10:8 provides a transition to Mishnah 10:9–10, which reverts to the offering.

A. After [eating from] the passover offering, [they] do not end [with] *afiqimon* [= revelry].[37]

B. [If they] fell asleep:

[if it was] some of them—[they] may eat [again]; and [if it was] all of them—[they] may not eat [again].

C. R. Yose says, if [they] dozed—[they] may eat [again]. And if [they] slumbered—[they] may not eat [again].

(M. Pes. 10:8)

The references in clause A to eating the paschal sacrifice and to revelry focus attention on the meal and its festive dimension. The festive aspect would appeal especially to people without the sacrifice. By contrast, clauses B—C deal with a rule that has unmistakable cultic associations. Commentators generally explain that the rule is intended to prevent eating the passover offering either after its fixed time or without the required concentration.[38]

Moreover, the transitional element of Mishnah 10:8 and the mention in Mishnah 10:9 of the blessings over the paschal and festive offerings correspond to earlier elements in the chapter. The concern for the time of eating has an analogue in Mishnah Pesaḥim 10:1, while the mention of blessings echoes the reference to the blessing over the song, *birkat hashir*, in Mishnah 10:7.[39]

Finally, the sequence suggests that the evening ritual, now without the passover offering, is a continuation of the earlier situation in which the offering was made. The components of the rite are inherently connected with what precedes (M. Pes. 5—9), and with what follows (10:8—9).

9. The loss of the passover sacrifice is no greater than the loss of the other sacrifices. This is the implication of the last Mishnah in chapter 10. In Mishnah 10:9, cited before in subsection 6, Ishmael and Aqiva differ as to whether or not an individual must recite a separate blessing before each of the sacrifices. Ishmael holds that the blessing over the passover offering serves also for the festive offering, but not the reverse. This accords with the obvious reasoning found in the Bible that the paschal lamb is primary and the additional festive offering secondary. But Aqiva equalizes the blessings: neither exempts the other. In denying that the passover lamb has greater significance than the festive offering, Aqiva implies that the loss of the paschal rite, after the temple's destruction, should not produce any extraordinary concern, for its loss forms part of the general loss of the sacrificial cult. To conclude the chapter and the tractate with this opinion drives home the point that the end of the paschal sacrifice is not a unique catastrophe.[40]

CONCLUSION

The evidence repeatedly shows that the choice of subjects, wording, and sequence of Mishnah Pesaḥim 10 as well as its location within the tractate can be effectively explained by a single proposition: the editor of the Mishnah desires to emphasize that the Passover celebration can and should continue even without the paschal lamb. Although the argument in the Mishnah is indirect, this proposition has been demonstrated by tracing the biblical antecedents and the history of the Passover celebration as well as by examining the peculiarities of the text of the Mishnah. Since the proposition stated above appropriately explains numerous and diverse details of the chapter, it is highly unlikely that something is being read into the text that is not there or that we are dealing with a series of coincidences. Moreover, as is discussed extensively in chapter 7, an author who wants to promote acceptance of change while at the same time trying to convince people that nothing has changed is forced to resort to a subtle argument. Other sources, including portions of the Gemara and the Midrash that reflect the ability to acknowledge the change openly, make the argument explicitly.

The Mishnah's assertion that the celebration can continue produces a new problem. Pre-70 sources indicate that the passover lamb was not only essential but also the distinctive feature of the evening celebration. Unless a new distinguishing characteristic was found, the evening celebration might be mistaken for a symposium, the Greco-Roman banquet that often provided an occasion for intellectual discussions. What the Mishnah did to prevent this misunderstanding is the subject of the next chapter.

5

A JEWISH SYMPOSIUM?
THE PASSOVER RITE AND
EARLIER PROTOTYPES OF
MEAL CELEBRATIONS

INTRODUCTION

T HE ARGUMENT OF THE Mishnah might well convince people that the Passover eve ritual without the passover lamb is a continuation of the earlier rite. What, however, might prevent them from confusing this festive meal with a symposium or some other merry occasion? The striking affinities between the two events have in fact caused some scholars to suggest that the Passover celebration is in effect a Jewish symposium. After all, the intellectual discussions, which in the seder were structured around the mythic history of Israel, had a well-established place at Hellenistic and Roman symposia and drinking parties. Moreover, Jews, including rabbis, obviously belonged to the wider Hellenistic and Roman late-antique society and frequently shared common cultural habits and literary forms. The question that follows is thus whether the Hellenistic elements of the Passover evening rite determined its character. In the present chapter, I argue that they did not. The editor of the Mishnah and his sources were aware of the similarities but strove to differentiate between the Jewish rite and other types of banquets so as to maintain the distinctive character of the Passover celebration.

The *Oxford Classical Dictionary* provides the following definition of a symposium:

SYMPOSIUM. A symposium was a Greek drinking-party that followed the evening meal. After libations had been poured and a hymn sung there was drinking according to an agreed procedure; the wine was diluted with water in various proportions. The participants were garlanded and many used perfume. Some did not drink; others displayed riotous intemperance. In addition to conversation the guests told riddles and fables, and sang capped drinking-songs, and pieces of verse from traditional classics or recent drama. Games were played, particularly *kóttabos*. There was usually a woman pipe-player, and displays of dancing, acrobatics, and miming were often given by hired performers.[1]

Ancient accounts of symposia formed a loosely defined literary genre for which scholars have traced several stages. Initially, as illustrated in Plato's *Symposium*, they comprised sets of speeches on a single philosophical subject integrated with dialogues. Xenophon's Socratic symposium treats more than one topic and includes extensive descriptions of entertainment. Later the dialogues become a framework for philosophical and other learned discussions or series of questions and answers. Plutarch (first- to early second-century C.E.) develops the genre to describe diverse and numerous discourses on philosophy, historical events, ethics, courage, table manners, and the like. In the *Learned Banquet* by Athenaeus (ca. 200 C.E.), the genre totally becomes a literary device for the exposition or collection of excerpts; here the discussions are not even portrayed as actual speeches.[2]

The following description by Plutarch highlights certain features of the symposium:

Some of the preparations which are made for dinners and drinking-parties rank as *necessities*, my dear Sossius Senecio; such are the *wine, the food, the cuisine, and of course the couches and tables*. Others are diversions introduced for pleasure's sake, and no essential function attaches to them; such are the *music*, spectacles, and any buffooning Philip-at-Callia's. With these latter, if they are present, the guests are pleased, but if they are absent, the guests do not very much desire them or criticize the party as being deficient. So it is with the *conversation*; some topics are accepted by the average run of men as the proper entertainment because they possess an attractive theme more suitable to the moment than pipe and lyre. Examples of these were mixed together in my first book. To the first category belong the *conversation on philosophical talk at drinking-parties*, that on the subject of whether the host himself assigns places or allows the guests to take their own, and such matters; as to the second category belong the conversation with poetical dispositions of lovers and the one concerned with the phyle Aiantis. The first group indeed I also call specifically drinking-party topics, but both together generally suitable table talk.[3]

Scholars who have analyzed this and other accounts of symposia point to numerous parallels between them and accounts of the Passover evening celebration. In addition to linguistic analogues, seven procedural similarities are found in the Mishnah, as are two additional ones in the Tosefta.[4] These include:

1. The use of waiters to bring in the food (M. Pes. 10:1, 2, 3, 4, 5, 7; T. Pes. 10:1, 2, 5, 9b, 12).
2. Reclining at the meal (M. 10:1, T. 10:1).
3. Dipping the food (M. 10:3).
4. Hors-d'oeuvres (M. 10:3; T. 10:5, 9b, 9d–10).
5. The use of wine before, during, and after eating (M. 10:1, 2, 4, 7; T. 10:1, 2, 4).
6. Being festive (T. 10:4).
7. The pedagogic use of questions and intellectual discussion (M. 10:4; T. 10:11–12).
8. Singing and praises to God (M. 10:5, 6, 7, and T. 10:6–9a).
9. Games to keep children awake (T. 10:9b).

Siegfried Stein presents the most comprehensive argument for the seder as a "Jewish symposium." While admitting that the seder follows a distinct Jewish purpose to commemorate the redemption from Egypt and that its components are made to fit this overriding theme, he argues that the Greco-Roman influence lies in "more than words and habits." According to Stein, this influence is also clearly seen in the literary form of the seder liturgy, which includes aspects of both the religious service and the required discussions.[5]

> A detailed comparison between Symposia literature and Seder liturgy must distinguish between a general similarity of dining habits—such as foods and drinks, the attendants who serve them, tables and couches and the reclining at dinner—and specific affinities of literary form—such as religious services and the statutory talk woven around the meal. An occasional overlapping will be unavoidable, and here and there an analysis of the tannaitic sources of the Haggadah will be necessary for the elucidation of the main purpose of our enquiry.[6]

Devoting the second half of his study to the affinities in the religious and literary forms, Stein concludes:

> The compilers of the Haggadah have made their own contribution to sympotic writings.[7]

Many of the parallels, especially those drawn to the postmishnaic stages of the celebration, are appropriate. But Stein argues that the symposium literature "gave the *impetus* to the extension from the unspecified Biblical ordinances to the elaborate ritual of the Haggadah as it now stands before us.''[8] Such a thesis must take into account the Mishnah, which represents the first formulated version of the expanded rite, and which sets the pattern for later developments. On such ground, Stein's argument fails. As seen in chapter 4, the impetus for recasting the celebration lay in the need for continuity with the past and for overcoming the loss of the paschal lamb. Only after acknowledging these facts can one appreciate the actual role of the symposiac elements and understand how they too have been integrated into a new context.

THE MEAL AND RELIGIOUS GATHERINGS

Several of the analogues between the symposia and the Passover rite are characteristic, in general, of dinners in antiquity. This is why parallels to both the symposia and Passover gatherings may be found elsewhere in Tannaitic literature, either as passing references or as part of the detailed descriptions of dining habits.[9] A special banquet would naturally include elements of a normal dinner. But why should a religious celebration be in the form of a meal?

The communal and ritual meal is not an invention of the Hellenistic period. The Bible mentions meals at which people gather or eat meat from sacrifices,[10] and it describes Passover as a rite that occurs at a meal. Since much of the Bible perceived and interpreted religious matters through the perspective of a cult, it is only natural that the meal, being part of a cultic ritual, became infused with cultic meaning and the participants seen as cultic officials. The description of the Passover celebration in Exodus 12 contains several elements that may be seen as cultic: lay people bring a sacrifice; they are to consume the paschal offering before the night's end; and they are not to break the animal's bone. In that way they act as priests, following the rules that priests follow in regard to other sacrifices.[11] Exodus 12 thus provides a model for a home celebration around a meal, in which the central element is eating part of the paschal lamb.

Before 70 C.E., did such meals take place *without* the paschal lamb? No firm evidence exists that confirms this, but it is worth considering ''circumstantial evidence.'' Passover always involved more than offering a sacrifice and eating the lamb. Likewise, the meaning of the sacrificial rite transcended the details of the animal's preparation and slaughter. The holiday had a wider historical and national meaning as a memorial to God's saving act in Egypt and the demonstration of His superiority over the Egyptian gods (Ex. 12:12 and 27; Deut. 16:1). Some might have found the seven-day Feast of Unleavened Bread a satisfying means to celebrate the redemption, for it does not appear to depend on the paschal lamb. Indeed, although the Bible assumes the Festivals of

Passover and Unleavened Bread are combined, it does not fully integrate the two, and their original distinctive dimensions can be discerned. In Numbers 9:9−14, for example, Israelites who are unable to observe the rite of Passover are given a second opportunity to bring the paschal offering—and the text's concern is for the sacrifice rite alone.[12] Nevertheless, it is possible that some people may have believed it important to mark the evening of Passover in some way, a sentiment expressed in Exodus 12:44:

> That was for the LORD a night of vigil to bring them out of the land of Egypt; that same night is the LORD's, one of vigil for all the children of Israel throughout the generations.

It is not unreasonable to assume that Israelites who did not have access to a cultic center and could not eat of the paschal lamb may have wanted to celebrate the festival and may have gathered at a meal on the night of Passover. If local altars existed in Palestine until the religious reforms of the sixth century B.C.E., most Palestinians could join in bringing and eating from the passover offering. But after the centralization of the cult, followed by the exile in 586 B.C.E. and the Diaspora, there must have been people who could not come to Jerusalem. These people may have adopted the holiday's existing structure of a meal. Indeed, the meal would have been most appropriate since, as sociologists and anthropologists have pointed out, it provides a natural context to celebrate important historical and religious experiences and to bind a group together.[13] Communal meals are described, not in connection with the Passover celebration but as part of the ongoing communal life of the Diaspora. Josephus, for example, cites a first-century B.C.E. Roman decree confirming the privileges of Jewish associations.[14]

Despite the probability that some Jews who lacked access to a paschal sacrifice felt the need to do something on Passover eve, none of the prerabbinic accounts of the celebration mentions a meal without a sacrifice, much less comes close to matching the multifaceted description of the gathering in the Mishnah.

Although communal meals did take on greater importance among various Jewish groups in Hellenistic and Roman times,[15] it does not necessarily follow that these gatherings simply took over a Hellenistic institution. Rather, upon examining these gatherings, one notices obvious differences. In fact, early rabbinic Judaism's structuring of the Passover rite around a communal meal constitutes but a single adaptation of the Hellenistic meal; moreover, it develops aspects of Passover to which the Bible has already referred, both directly and indirectly. Therefore, given the presence of these diverse factors and the lack of actual references to a communal Passover meal in prerabbinic times, its existence in that period remains only a speculation.

Since my claim that the symposia did not provide the impetus for the development of the Passover seder is partly supported by the existence and nature of other Jewish communal meals, a review of the main aspects of these meals is now in order. As I will demonstrate, the theory that the elaboration of the Passover rite took place for ideological purposes applies to these communal gatherings as well.

1. The meals of the Pharisees. Much of the rabbinic tradition concerning the Pharisees deals with purity rules and tithing, especially as they affect procedures at a meal and the preparation of food. The teachings attributed to the Pharisees also treat religious observances and liturgy at a meal, such as the recitation of the Sanctification and Havdalah blessings to usher in or escort out a Sabbath or holiday. The fact that the rabbinic tradition accords with the gospel depiction of the Pharisees has led Jacob Neusner to suggest that the Pharisees made up a "table fellowship." Since the Pharisees believed that lay people eating their profane food at home could act as priests act in eating consecrated food in the temple, and that the divine presence could therefore be experienced in daily life outside the temple, the meal provided an appropriate occasion to express theology.[16] This gathering was apparently not a special communal ritual meal, but the ordinary meal of everyday life.

2. The meals at Qumran. Qumran texts refer to meals at which the members gather together, eat and drink, "search out" or study the Bible, and praise God. For example, the Rule Scroll 6:2−8 reads:

In these [precepts] all of them shall walk in all their dwellings, each man with his companion: The man of lesser rank shall obey the greater in matters of work and money. They shall eat in common and bless [= pray] in common and deliberate in common. Wherever there are ten men of the Council of the Community there shall not lack a Priest among them. And they shall all sit before him according to their rank and shall be asked their counsel in all things in that order. And when the table has been prepared for eating, and the new wine for drinking, the priest shall be the first to stretch out his hand to bless the first-[portion] of the bread and new wine. And where the ten are, there shall never lack a man among them who shall study (DWRŠ) the Torah continually, day and night, one man exchanging for his fellow [= by turns]. And the Congregation shall watch in community for a third of every night of the year, to read the Book and to study (WLDRWŠ) [its?] judgements and to bless [= pray] together.[17]

Many scholars consider these gatherings community meals, while some argue that they do not constitute ritual meals per se. The latter believe that the Scrolls refer either to procedures that apply when members gather at a normal meal or to a form of messianic banquet anticipating the redemption, apparently explicit in Rule Annex 2:17−22. At the minimum, the meal appears as a setting at which advising, learning, and liturgical activities and significant religious experiences might occur.[18]

3. Philo's description of the meals of the Therapeutae. Philo devotes a treatise to the contemplative group called Therapeutae and describes their communal "spiritual" meals and meetings. The members recline, praise God with hymns, and, led by a president, discuss the Scriptures. The gatherings are infused with cultic meaning.[19] Philo is explicit that the Therapeutae act like priests:

> In this banquet . . . no wine is brought. . . . Abstinence from wine is enjoyed by right reason *as for the priest when sacrificing.* . . .[20] When everyone had finished his hymn the young men bring in the tables mentioned a little above on which is set the truly purified meal of leavened bread seasoned with salt mixed with hyssop, out of reverence for the holy table enshrined in the *sacred vestibule of the temple* on which lie loaves and salt without condiments, the loaves unleavened and the salt unmixed. For it was meet that the simplest and purest food should be assigned to the highest caste, namely the priests, as a reward for their ministry, and that the others while aspiring to similar privileges should abstain from seeking the same as they and allow their superiors to retain their precedence.[21]

Philo moreover discusses extensively the differences between these gatherings and the Hellenistic and Greco-Roman symposia:

> I wish also to speak of their common assemblages and the cheerfulness of their convivial meals as compared with those of other people. Some people when they have filled themselves with strong drink behave as though they had drunk not wine but some witch's potion charged with frenzy and madness and anything more fatal that can be imagined to overthrow their reason. . . .[22]
>
> Some perhaps may approve the method of banqueting now prevalent everywhere through hankering for the Italian expensiveness and luxury emulated both by Greeks and non-Greeks who make their arrangements for ostentation rather than festivity. . . .[23]
>
> Among the banquets held in Greece there are two celebrated and highly notable examples, namely those in which Socrates took part, one held in the house of Callias . . ., the other in the house of Agathon. Yet even these if compared with those of our people who embrace the contemplative life will appear as matters for derision. Pleasure is an element in both, but Xeno-

phon's banquet is more concerned with ordinary humanity. There are flute girls, dancers, jugglers, fun-makers, proud of their gift of jesting and facetiousness, and other accompaniments of more unrestrained merry-making. . . .[24]

But since the story of these well-known banquets is full of such follies and they stand self-convicted in the eyes of any who do not regard conventional opinions and the widely circulated report which declares them to have been all that they should be, I will describe in contrast the festal meetings of those who have dedicated their own life and themselves to knowledge and the contemplation of the verities of nature, following the truly sacred instructions of the prophet Moses.[25]

While scholars today tend to agree that the Therapeutae did exist and were not the product of Philo's imagination, one cannot know the degree to which Philo's own interests affected his perception and description. As was seen in chapters 1 and 2, Philo emphasizes elsewhere the point that lay Israelites act as priests. Likewise, his overall philosophy is devoted to uncovering the higher spiritual dimensions of things. Nevertheless, Philo's account provides us with a well-developed instance of the application of cultic imagery and themes to a nontemple context.[26]

All of these groups exhibit several similarities in terms of the dinner etiquette and the various activities delineated. At the meals of Qumran, Philo's Therapeutae, and the rabbinic Passover rite, people gather communally, eat together, study and expound Scripture, and pray or sing songs in praise of God. However, they interpret the meals in different ways. The rabbis cast the gathering as a cultic replacement for the lost paschal sacrifice meal, whereas the Pharisees see the meal as a way to express their ideas concerning God's presence and the temple. Philo, by contrast, explicitly transfers cultic notions to the Therapeutae meal. The Qumranites also see their meals through an external perspective, though it may be in eschatological rather than cultic terms. But if cultic transference does not apply to the Qumranites' meals, it does apply to their concept of the community, which is seen as the location of the divine presence, that is, the temple.

Some scholars have used the term "transference" to explain the type of religious development we are examining here. Like an individual, a group perceives reality through its own existing system of beliefs and adjusts to new situations on the basis of this world view. When groups that share a heritage and values in common experience an analogous crisis, they very well may respond in analogous ways. If they lose the institution that has provided meaning and direction to their piety but still want to maintain their values, they have to work out a substitute for the central institution. It seems likely that this replacement would come out of their new context and would have transferred to it notions associated with the old institution. Each group would do this according to its practical situation.[27]

In the present case, the groups fill the void left by the loss or inaccessibility of the Jerusalem Temple through transference. Philo alludes to this phenomenon in his description of Passover:

> After the New Moon comes the fourth feast, called the Crossing-feast which the Hebrews in their native tongue call Pascha. In this festival, many myriads of victims from noon till eventide are offered by the whole people, old and young alike, *raised for that particular day to the dignity of the priesthood*. For at other times the priests according to the ordinance of the law carry out both the public sacrifices and those offered by private individuals. *But on this occasion the whole nation performs the sacred rites and acts as priest with pure hands and complete immunity. . . .*
>
> *On this day every dwelling-house is invested with the outward semblance and dignity of a temple*. The victim is then slaughtered and dressed for the festal meal which befits the occasion. *The guests assembled for the banquet* have been cleansed by purificatory lustrations, and are there not as in other festive gatherings, to indulge the belly with wine and viands, but to fulfill with prayers and hymns the custom handed down by the fathers.[28]

As in his description of the Therapeutae, Philo explicitly differentiates this gathering from a communal banquet. The seder is "pure" and the participants offer praises and hymns to God. In gathering together and in making the sacrifice in a dignified home, the participants act like priests in the temple. Philo adheres to his philosophical persuasion and assumes a metaphysical orientation toward one's material service to God. As such, the pure, spiritual service is superior to the physical. Incorporating this hermeneutic into his interpretation, he claims that the whole community has transferred cultic language, rites, and significance to its own activities.[29]

Qumran and the Therapeutae share a common situation with the later rabbinic circles. Each is without the actual temple—the Qumranites and the Therapeutae due to choice or distance and the later rabbinic circles due to events and chronology. The absence of the temple likewise applies to the community to which Philo addressed his explanation of the Torah. Even if the Alexandrians occasionally go on pilgrimage to Jerusalem, in their daily lives they are outside of Jerusalem; while they may revere the Jerusalem Temple, they normally live without it.[30]

The concept of transference helps explain why these examples of a meal have parallels with the rabbinic development of Passover, even though they do not involve Passover and derive instead from "sectarian" groups, a point which surprised Stein.[31] All of these groups find the meal an appropriate context for the transfer of cultic notions. The transference indicates that the impetus to develop and use the meal comes not from the symposia literature but from the religious situation to which each group responded in common—the need to find a substitute for something unavailable.

Transference also helps explain other similarities among the groups. Shemaryahu Talmon has applied this perception to Qumranite and rabbinic substitution of prayer and blessings for sacrifices and the public cult.

> Now the sectaries' voluntary renunciation of sacrifice, which is to be explained as arising from socio-historical circumstances, and not as a result of ideological opposition to sacrifice as such, placed the sect, even before the destruction of the Temple, in a sociological and religious situation parallel to that in which normative Judaism was to find itself after the destruction. The sectaries were thus obliged to anticipate the development that later occurred on a national scale and to institute prayers to take the place of the sacrifice in the divine service.[32]

Neusner suggests that the same dynamic explains postbiblical developments in the idea of purity. Philo and the later rabbis offer allegorical interpretations of purity and use it as a subject of ethical homiletics.

> Allegory . . . occurs primarily among those for whom the Temple is not a physical presence, because of distance either of space, as with Philo, or of time, as with the later rabbis. We may generalize that nearness to the cult will yield concrete and socially significant interpretations of purity, while distance from the Temple will result in the interpretation of purity-rules in terms other than of cultic symbols.[33]

On the basis of these analogues, Neusner observes:

> What makes the *yahad*, the *havurah*, and the Christian community, Philo, and especially the rabbinic movement interesting is their shared capacity to construct a surrogate for that foundation-stone of Judaic life [the Temple]. . . .
> But they all addressed themselves to what we know to have been the absolutely inescapable dilemma of their day: what to do when the Temple, the place on which, for them, the lines of cosmic and social structure converged and were clearly defined, either was no longer acceptable or would no longer exist? And these nonpriestly groups all proposed the same solution: the Temple as it then was perceived no longer serves, but may be replaced by something—anything—else.[34]

Transference affects the self-image of these groups, for they apply the cultic notion of temple to the community of believers. Elisabeth Fiorenza has compared the early Church's adaptation of this notion to that of Qumran. In several

Qumran writings, the community replaces the temple but not the priesthood. The community is the locus of cultic purity and holiness and atones for the sins and transgressions of Israel.

> While the notion of temple is transferred to the community so that the community as the holy house could replace the temple in Jerusalem during the interim period, the members of the community did not replace the priests of the Jerusalem cult, but acknowledged the leadership of an institutional priesthood. Cultic language is used in the literature of Qumran because the community is now, in the endtime when the cultic institutions of Israel are desecrated, the place where atonement, ritual purity and holy worship of God are possible. This theological interest leads to the transference of the notion of Temple and to the ethicizing of the concept of sacrifice, but not to the understanding that all members of the community are priests.[35]

Transference of cultic language in the New Testament takes a different form than in Qumranite writings, as is expectable since the early Christians viewed the loss of the temple from a very different position:

> Whereas the transference and reinterpretation of cultic language in Qumran underlined the basic validity of the Jerusalem cult and expressed the hope for its renewal, the transference and usage of cultic language in the NT presupposes the conviction that the eschatological salvation in Jesus Christ meant the end of the temple of Jerusalem and of all cultic institutions.[36]

Fiorenza argues that transference in the New Testament is generally made for missionary purposes:

> Cultic terms such as temple, priest, sacrifice are employed by the NT writings solely to describe the Christ-event or to characterize the Christian community and its mission.
> The NT writers never make the connection between the community as temple and the atonement of sins and trespasses. . . .[37]
> Sins are forgiven and cultic access to God is achieved in the death of Jesus Christ. No further atoning sacrifice and cult is necessary. Christian worship, therefore, is no longer dependent upon cultic institutions and persons, but is actualized in everyday life. In the Christian community, true worship is possible, because the community is *the* eschatological temple and priesthood and not merely a temporary replacement for a concrete cultic institution.[38]

The various groups in question therefore employ modes of religious expression appropriate to their particular context and interests. Drawing upon the heritage these groups share in common, they transfer meaning to new institutions and practices accordingly. This phenomenon explains the common treatment of a meal among the Therapeutae, pre-70 Pharisaism, and possibly Qumran, and the perception of the community as a temple among the Therapeutae, pre-70 Pharisaism, Qumran, early Christianity, and nascent rabbinism.[39]

What of the biblical precedents for the new institutions and practices? Certainly the biblical repertoire of extratemple notions and means of piety that already existed had to take on a new role within the system. In the Second Temple period, the extratemple developments took on a secondary role to the temple cult. Psalms and prayers supplemented the official sacrificial system and constituted a means of private devotion. The Deuteronomic approach which perceived reality from the eyes of the community as a whole still gave the cult a prominent position. The very fact that these groups needed to transfer cultic notions to their institutions and practices indicates the degree to which the cult had monopolized the religious imagination. Nonetheless, extratemple practices had gained at least some currency and legitimacy.[40]

The post-Destruction experience of 586 B.C.E. was also part of the common heritage. Jews undoubtedly evolved religious structures appropriate to their situation, although direct evidence of these developments is meager.[41] What distinguishes the efforts of this earlier period, however, is the belief that the temple cult would be reestablished. The Samaritans, in fact, believed that the cultic life had never been lost. In contrast, early rabbinic authorities soon realized that their system had to replace the temple cult and would be, therefore, a direct continuation of it, rather than a mere supplement, whether temporary or permanent.

Because the biblical Passover was a home ritual and a prototype of a communal meal, Passover provided a natural setting in which the new or alternative piety could be expressed. All the people, not just the priests, could actively participate. For this reason, aspects of the rabbinic Passover ritual may be analogous to communal practices adopted by Jews who lived before 70 C.E. and whose lives were not structured around Jerusalem or its temple. In addition to the changes in the meal itself, several groups began to use vocal music instead of instruments, to emphasize the study of Scriptures, and to require the saying of a blessing or prayer.[42]

To summarize my argument, the meal appears prominent among several Jewish groups as the context to celebrate key religious moments, both for Passover and for other occasions. The groups in question are not identical in their conception of the meal though they draw upon analogous notions. All of the groups assume the importance of the temple, and draw upon temple concepts and earlier examples of extratemple practices, which they perceive in terms of the temple. The Hellenistic culture these groups shared in common contributed to their increased receptivity to alternatives to a central temple and may have influenced their choice of the features to be developed from the ancient heritage. It is therefore not surprising that rabbinic circles may have drawn upon banquet practices to enrich what they were doing. It is unlikely, however, that they were prompted to expand the biblical rite by their observation of Hellenistic symposia or on account of their knowledge of the symposia literature.[43]

THE DISTINCTIVE NATURE OF THE CELEBRATION

If Philo felt the need to differentiate between the symposia and the original paschal lamb—oriented version of the Passover gathering, would not there have been an even greater need to differentiate between the two when the passover sacrifice was no longer present?[44] Clearly this was the case. The Mishnah responds to this need by changing common features and by dissociating itself from elements in the symposia and earlier Jewish models for the rite.

1. The Passover gathering, in contrast to earlier dinners, follows a pre-scribed structure imposed on everyone. The Mishnah's description of the rite standardizes it and provides guidelines for all Jews. This delineation is one example of the overall practice of early rabbinic Judaism of mandating and systematizing extratemple practices that previously had been left to the choice of the pious individual.[45]

2. The framers of Mishnah Pesaḥim explicitly require everyone to partici-pate in the evening ritual, thus setting the evening rite apart from other meal gatherings, in particular the symposia, which pertain to a more limited social context.[46] Mishnah Pesaḥim 10:1 states that all Jews, not just the leisurely wealthy, are to share in the meal:

> A. On the eve of Passover, close to [the time of] *minḥah*, a person should not eat until it gets dark.
> B. Even a poor person in Israel should not eat until he reclines.
> C. [Those who serve] should not give him fewer than four cups of wine even if [the funds come] from the charity plate.[47]

Clause B applies this principle to reclining on couches and clause C to drinking of wine. The lower classes who generally ate humble meals in an unleisurely manner are to follow the practice of the more well-to-do and intellectual circles.[48]

3. The Passover drinking of wine differs from that of the symposium. The requirement of Mishnah 10:1 to have at least four cups of wine indicates that

the wine is more than just a good drink, and is not part of a drinking bout or revelry. While wine drinking may have originated in customs of dining and celebrating, here in the Passover ceremony it is attached to key parts of the ritual.[49] The first cup provides the occasion for a benediction marking the special character of the evening (M. 10:2); the second precedes the child's questions and accompanies the discussion (M. 10:4); the third cup is taken prior to saying grace (M. 10:7A); and with the fourth, the participants finish the Hallel (M. 10:7B).[50]

The reference in Mishnah 10:7 to drinking additional cups of wine indicates that the four required ones are to be considered separately from the voluntary or additional cups. Moreover, three of the four cups are known from other occasions, so their presence in the Passover meal cannot be directly attributed to the symposia literature. In their usual dinners, people drank wine with appetizers, with the main meal, and after the meal. Two of these cups of wine became associated with specific religious rituals and form the basis for the first and third cups in the Passover celebration. The first cup is for the opening Qiddush, or Sanctification, recited to usher in the Sabbath and holiday, while the third cup accompanies the saying of grace after meals.[51]

The fourth cup, not regularly found at dinners, was apparently added to the Passover ritual to accompany the Hallel. While Stein aptly points to symposiac parallels for the drinking of wine to accompany after-dinner praises and singing, I suggest another possible explanation for this cup of wine. In Temple days, Levites sang psalms to accompany the slaughter of the sacrifice; whereas in the rabbinic rite, individual Jews did the singing. Since the individual Jews also needed a context for the psalms, the wine may have filled the void created by the loss of the sacrificial meal.[52]

The details concerning the wine further clarify the point that the drinking is something special. The Mishnah requires the wine to be "poured" or "mixed" (MZG), which means appropriately diluted. Otherwise it would be too strong and might make one drunk too quickly or even induce a Bacchic frenzy.[53]

Similarly, Tosefta 10:1 cites and glosses Mishnah 10:1 and specifies the nature, amount, and potency of the drink:

C. And [*those who serve*] *should not give him fewer than four cups of wine*,

D. which contain the amount of a fourth [of log = 1½ eggs, in liquid measure],

E. whether it is raw or diluted,

whether it is fresh or old [from the previous year].

F. R. Yehudah says, And as long as it has the taste and appearance of wine.

Of particular interest is Yehudah's opinion, in clause F, which would exclude not only overly diluted wine but also the fancy wine drinks commonly served at symposia, such as those flavored with honey, cinnamon, or saffron.[54]

Tosefta 10:4 gives the wine drinking a specific purpose: to enable people to fulfill the requirement to be happy on the holiday.[55] Postmishnaic authorities, characteristically uncovering significance in every detail of a rite, see a symbolic dimension to each of the four cups. While their interpretations typologically differ from those of earlier masters, both Amoraim and Tannaim agree that wine should not be considered solely a good drink.[56]

4. The eating and dipping of food, specifically bitter herbs, prior to the meal takes on new meaning and cannot be considered the standard partaking and dipping of hors-d'oeuvres.

> A. [They] served him—[he] dips the lettuce (ḤZRT) before he reaches the bread condiment.
> B. [They] served him unleavened bread and lettuce and *haroset*, even though the *haroset* is not a *misvah*.
> R. Leazar b. Ṣadoq says, [It is a] *misvah*.
> C. And in the Temple [they] serve him the carcass of the Passover offering.[57]

(M. 10:3)

The dispute in clause B, as demonstrated above, gives the impression that the procedures not under dispute are assumed to be prescribed.[58] Accordingly, clause A must be speaking of a required special dipping that precedes the bread condiment. The distinct nature of this dipping is reflected in one of the three questions presented in Mishnah Pesaḥim 10:4:

> A. [They] poured for him the second cup—
> B.1. and here the child asks,
> B.2. and if the child lacks intelligence, his father instructs him.
> C. How is this night different from all the [other] nights?
> D.1. For on all the [other] nights we dip once, this night twice.[59]

Clause D.1 refers to two dippings, one familiar from "all the [other] nights," the other special to this night. The meal thus has procedures not common at regular banquets.

5. In contrast to symposia, the Passover gathering should not let its singing degenerate into frivolous songs. Mishnah Pesaḥim 10:7 explicitly addresses this issue and provides a preventive measure:

A. [They] poured for him the third cup [of wine]—[, he] says the blessing [alt., "and (he) said the blessing"] over his food.

B. [At] the fourth [cup]—he finishes the Hallel, and says over it the blessing over the song (*birkat hashir*).

C. Between the former cups, if [he] wants to drink [further] he may drink. Between the third and fourth, [he] should not drink.[60]

Between the third and fourth cups of wine, one recites the second half of the psalms and praises to God. The ban on additional cups of wine prevents one from getting drunk at that point and singing hymns in a light manner, as is common at drinking parties or symposia.[61]

6. The dissociation from a symposium is reflected as well in the rule of Mishnah Pesaḥim 10:8 proscribing after-dinner revelry. The relevant portion of this text reads: "After [eating from] the passover offering, they do not end [with] *afiqimon*." Numerous studies have analyzed the meaning of the word *afiqimon* (or *afiqomon*). Most agree that it refers to some type of banquet custom, an interpretation found in the Palestinian Talmud. Specifically, the term denotes after-dinner revelry commonly found at banquets or symposia. After the symposium meal, the participants would go to other homes for further festivity.[62] It is this practice that the Mishnah prohibits.

The Mishnah's attempt to avoid degeneration in the Passover meal, apparent in the rules of Mishnah 10:7 and 8, constitutes one aspect of its effort to distinguish the Passover rite from other ancient banquets and symposia. The same effort may be perceived in other ancient writings. Philo distinguishes between Hellenistic symposia and the true spiritual meals of the Jews.[63] Josephus, in a passage describing Passover, sets the Passover rite apart from regular banquets with the phrase "feasting alone not being permitted."[64] Plutarch decries the degenerate music often played at banquets.[65] Clement of Alexandria provides a vivid example of this revelry in the *Paidagogos*, where he informs Christians how to act at banquets.

In feasts of reason that we have, let the wild celebrations of the holiday season have no part, or the senseless night-long parties that delight in wine drinking. The wild celebration ends up as a drunken stupor, with everyone freely confiding the troubles of his love affairs. And as for all-night drinking parties, they go hand-in-hand with the holiday celebration, and, in their wine-drinking, promote drunkenness and promiscuity. They are brazen celebrations that work deeds of shame. The exciting rhythm of flutes and harps, choruses and dances, Egyptian castanets and other entertainments get out of control and become indecent and burlesque, especially when they are reenforced by cymbals and drums and accompanied by the noise of all these instruments of deception. It seems to me that a banquet easily turns into a mere exhibition of drunkenness. The Apostle warned: "Laying aside the works of darkness, put on the armor of light. Let us walk becomingly as in the day, not occupying ourselves in revelry and drunkenness, not in debauchery and wantonness" (Rom. 13:12–13).

. . . In general, we must completely eliminate every such base sight or sound—in a word, everything immodest that strikes the senses (for this is an abuse of the sense)—if we would avoid pleasures that merely fascinate the eye or ear, and emasculate. Truly, *the devious spells of syncopated tunes and of the plaintive rhythm of Carian music corrupt morals by their sensual and affected style, and insidiously inflame the passions.* . . .

It is fitting to bless the Maker of all things before we partake of food; so too, at a feast, when we enjoy His created gifts, it is only right that we sing psalms to Him. In fact, a psalm sung in unison is a blessing, and it is an act of self-restraint. . . . *Even among the ancient Greeks, there was a song called the skolion which they used to sing after the manner of the Hebrew psalm at drinking parties and over their after-dinner cups.* All sang together with one voice, and sometimes they passed these toasts of song along in turn; those more musical than the rest sang to the accompaniment of the lyre.

Yet, let no passionate love songs be permitted there; let our songs be hymns to God. . . . We may indeed retain chaste harmonies, but not so those tearful songs which are too florid in the overdelicate modulation of the voice they require. These last must be proscribed and repudiated by those who would retain virility of mind, for their sentimentality and ribaldry degenerate the soul. *There is nothing in common between restrained, chaste tunes and the licentiousness of intemperance. Therefore, overcolorful melodies are to be left to shameless carousals*, and to the honeyed and garish music of the courtesan.[66]

Thus the effort of the Mishnah to distinguish between banquets and the Passover celebration follows a pattern shared by religious writers. Those with philosophical interests, such as Philo, make the distinction in philosophical terms.[67] The Mishnah does so indirectly, by changing elements of the banquet, providing them with new and distinct meaning, and dissociating the Passover rite from inappropriate symposiac practices. This task became critically important as the Mishnah, reflecting the ideology of early rabbinic Judaism, presented the Passover ritual without the paschal lamb but, nevertheless, as a continuation of the earlier protocol.[68]

6

THE PERSPECTIVE OF EARLY RABBINIC JUDAISM

A LTHOUGH THE MISHNAH TRIES to de-emphasize the discontinuity with the past, its account of the Passover rite is influenced by the later concerns and world view of early rabbinic Judaism. This influence can be seen in two ways. First, the Mishnah changes various pre-70 aspects of the celebration, dissociating elements from the temple cult and providing extra-temple practices with a new significance. Second, it enriches the rite with items not attested in earlier sources, or revises old elements to the point where they take on a distinct, vital role. In earlier chapters I have analyzed the recasting of pre-70 elements of the ritual. I have also noted that the fixed etiquette for passover found in Mishnah and Tosefta Pesahim 10 reflects the tendency of early rabbinic Judaism to standardize and mandate practices that previously had been left up to the individual. In the present chapter I point to the additions and totally transformed features of the celebration that are shaped by the rabbinic world view.

BROADENED IMPORTANCE OF INTELLECTUAL EXCHANGE

During the period of early rabbinic Judaism, intellectual discussion became a central activity incumbent upon everyone. The Bible, for example, explains the meaning of Passover and its rituals through the literary device of parental instructions to a child. As seen in Exodus 12:26, the parent responds to a child's questions concerning the details of the evening rite and, in Exodus 13:14, also the dedication or redemption of the firstborn humans and animals. Exodus 13:8 shows the parent, on his own initiative, explaining the requirement to eat unleavened bread for seven days. These verses may provide not only the rationale for the elements of the holiday but also a prescriptive model that a child and parent should follow—the child should ask a question and the parent should supply an answer. The Mishnah assumes this understanding, but re-phrases the biblical prescription so as to extend the paradigm beyond a parent-child discussion.[1] Mishnah 10:4 thus reads:

A. [They] poured for him the second cup—

B.1. and here the child asks,

B.2. and if the child lacks intelligence, his father instructs him.

C. How is this night different from all the [other] nights?

D.1. For on all the [other] nights we dip once, this night twice.

D.2. For on all the [other] nights we eat leavened and unleavened bread, this night we eat only unleavened.

D.3. For on all the [other] nights we eat meat roasted, steamed, or cooked [in a liquid = boiled], this night only [or "all of it"] roasted.

E. According to the child's intelligence, his father instructs him.

F. [He] starts [reading] with the disgrace [section of the Bible] and ends with the glory;

G. and [he] expounds [the biblical section] from, "A Wandering Aramean was my father," until he finishes the entire portion.[2]

According to clause B.2, the parent may open the discussion without the child's prompting. The Mishnah thus does not strictly follow the paradigm of Exodus 12:26. Nor is the rendition in the Mishnah based on Exodus 13:8, for that verse does not deal with the evening rite. To be sure, rabbinic circles elsewhere rely on both of these verses along with Exodus 13:14 to formulate several questions that typify different types of children and to supply appropriate answers by a parent. But the formulation of the dialogue does not necessarily indicate that its perspective is fixed by the Bible, for one of the questions and answers employs Deuteronomy 6:20 which does not even deal with Passover![3]

In contrast, Mishnah 10:4 is obviously not unrelated to the biblical prescription. As was seen in chapter 4, the Mishnah suggests appropriate questions applicable now to the evening ritual without the paschal sacrifice, and it thereby indicates that the old pedagogic device is still viable. The Mishnah therefore shapes the biblical material to fit its own interests. This tendency is further confirmed by the choice of the three questions in clause D, concerning bitter herbs, unleavened bread, and roasted meat: these are also the three items on which Gamaliel focuses attention and through which he de-emphasizes the unique role of the passover sacrifice.

The language of Mishnah 10:4 enables us to see how rabbinic issues became prominent. The words "lacks intelligence" or "has intelligence" are regularly used as the criterion to exclude or include an individual, especially a child, from a provision of a law, whether a privilege, responsibility, or liability. If a person is physically and mentally able to do something, he or she can be held responsible to do it. Similarly, if a person can understand the import of an action, he or she can be required to have the proper intent.

Mishnah Baba Meṣʿiaʾ 7.6 shows a typical usage of "intelligence":

A. A man extracts terms [in return for an agreement not to exercise the right to eat fruit from the field in which he is working] for himself, for his adult son and daughter, for his adult bondman and bondwoman, for his wife—because theŷ have intelligence (MPNY ŠYŠ BHN DʿT).

B. But a man does not extract terms for his minor son and daughter, nor for his minor bondman and bondwoman, and not for his animal—because they lack intelligence (MPMY ŠʾYN BHN DʿT).[4]

At times the term "intelligence" applies to a specific procedure, as in Mishnah Sukkah 3:15 concerning the laws of Sukkot:

And every minor who knows how to shake [the *lulav*] (ŠYŠ BW DʿT LNʿNYʿ) is liable as to *lulav*.

Tosefta Ḥagigah 1:2 presents eleven definitions tailored to different laws:

[A minor who] knows how to shake, is liable as to *lulav*; [who] knows how to wrap [around a garment] is liable as to fringes; [who] knows how to speak, his father instructs him [in] (ʾBYW MLMDW) Shemaʿ, and Torah, and the holy tongue [= Hebrew] . . . ; . . . [who] knows how to slaughter, his slaughter is valid; [who] is able to eat. . . an olive's amount of roasted meat, they slaughter the passover sacrifice for him.[5]

The format of Mishnah Pesaḥim 10:4 of a parent instructing a child is also found elsewhere in connection with teaching a child about the Torah and Judaism. The passage cited earlier from Tosefta Ḥagigah 1:2 provides one example of this usage.[6] In all of these references, the texts refer to a person who either knows and understands or does not know and understand the matter under discussion.

The Mishnah therefore reflects the rabbinic concern that parents teach their children what they should know.[7] The biblical model for the pedagogic dialogue is thus adapted to the standard rabbinic formulation that is designed to determine a child's involvement. Considering the Mishnah's choice of this standard twofold typology, it is not surprising that the Mishnah does not use the well-known typology of four kinds of children each with a different character or level of intelligence.[8]

In demonstrating that the device of a question remains a viable educational tool and religious ritual, the Mishnah determines when during the rite the child "asks the question" and therefore adapts the pedagogic device to its own purposes.[9]

In Tosefta 10:11–12, one can actually see the biblical model juxtaposed to and subsumed under a different model. One also finds the emphasis on the study of the *halakhah*, another central rabbinic concern.

> A. After [eating from] the passover offering they do not end [with] *afiqomon* [alt., *afiqimon*]. . . .
> B. A person is obligated to engage himself in the [study of the] *halakhot* of Passover all night,
>> even with [only] his son,
>> even with [only] himself,
>> even with [only] his student.
> C. Case concerning (M'SH B-): Rabban Gamaliel and the elders were reclining in the house of Baitos the son of Zonin in Lod,
> D. and [they] were engaged in the *halakhot* of Passover all night, until the cock's call.
>> [They] raised up [the table] from in front of them,
>> and [they] stirred and went along to the house of study.[10]

Clause B refers to the situation mentioned in the Bible, of a parent and child, and to a rabbinic setting, that of a master and student. Though clauses C–D illustrate the latter academic-rabbinic perspective, they do not deal with its specific case. Since they thus cannot have been generated merely to serve as an example, one should assume that they originally circulated as a separate teaching.[11] The compiler, however, uses the Gamaliel story because it fits his purpose to exemplify the issue with a case of studying *halakhot*, or the "laws." This contrasts with the more famous variant story incorporated into the Passover haggadah, in which the sages spend the whole night "talking about the exodus from Egypt," a subject with wider interest than "laws."[12] Since the haggadah is a liturgical text aimed at popular audiences this famous story fits its context.[13] In contrast, the formulation in the Tosefta accords with tannaitic usage. The Mishnah and the Tosefta regularly speak of the laws that govern a holiday. For example, according to Tosefta Megillah 3:5, prior to Passover, "They ask concerning the laws of Passover" (ŠW'LYN HLKWT HPSH. . . ŠW'LYN BHLKWT [London MS = HLKWT] HPSH).[14]

A text in Mekilta *Pisha*, number 18, provides an insightful view of the Passover gathering from the perspective of the rabbinic social world. Based on Deuteronomy 6:20—"What mean these exhortations, laws, and norms"—the passage appears in the context of the child's question in Exodus 13:14:

A. "What mean these exhortations, laws, and norms," etc.

B. R. Eliezer says, From where can you say that if there was a group (HBWRH) of sages or of students, they are required to engage themselves in the [study of the] *halakhot* of Pesaḥ until midnight?

C. It is for this that it says, "What means these exhortations, laws," etc.[15]

Here we find not a parent-child discussion, as illustrated in the biblical text, but a "fraternity" of sages and students studying the laws of Passover.

Finally, the reference to "the house of study," BYT HMDRŠ, in clause D of the Tosefta, likewise fits the rabbinic background. The Tosefta projects not only the situation of an individual's home, with a parent and child, but also of a rabbinic gathering.[16]

The biblical device of a child's inquiry is thus expanded in Mishnah 10:4 into a ritual for all Jews, assuming that even an adult may be the one to open the discussion. The Mishnah supplies three questions on the three things Gamaliel considered essential and employs its standard terminology to lay out the requirement, especially in regard to a parent's responsibility toward his child. The Tosefta goes further in freeing the question from its biblical parameters, and even reflects a specific rabbinic concern for *halakhah* and the rabbinic social group.

How does the Tosefta's extension relate to the charge in Mishnah 10:1 that all Jews should be involved? It is not necessarily inconsistent, because if everyone should be included then the ritual is not just for lay people. Moreover, the sages believe that they provided a model for all Jews to emulate: all should act as students of the Torah and, in this instance, should be engaged in the study of Passover. The Tosefta also reflects a tendency in early rabbinic Judaism to focus attention on the social forms of the rabbinic group. It is therefore important to note that the Mishnah lacks these overt references to contemporary social institutions. Mentioning them might work against the impression of timelessness the Mishnah seeks to create, which in turn serves its purpose of showing that the present Passover rite continues the pre-70 structures.

EXPOUNDING THE BIBLE

As prescribed in Mishnah 10:4F−G and cited earlier, the reading and exposition of the Bible is in accord with the rabbinic emphasis on these activities. Specifically, one starts reading from a section reflecting the "disgrace" or "shame" of Israel and ends with a section reflecting its "praise"; then one expounds (DRŠ) the biblical section that begins, "A wandering Aramean was my father'' (Deut. 26:5). As several scholars have noted, the reading and exposition constitute two requirements.[17] It would not be surprising if people had recited and discussed the biblical narrative in pre-70 days. Indeed, the prescriptions in Exodus 12:26, 13:8, and 13:14 as well as in Deuteronomy 6:20 call for such a retelling of the exodus, and the Bible also presents several historical reviews that trace the Israelites' origins and God's redemptive intervention. These include Deuteronomy 4:37−38, 6:21−24, 26:5−10; Joshua 24:2−14; and Nehemiah 9:6−37,[18] which adds an account of the Sinaitic revelation. In addition, as was seen in chapter 2, numerous biblical and postbiblical books recount this period of history, and several treat the exodus experience in particular. Deuteronomy 26:5ff. was an apt choice for special focus since this text was formulaic in nature and was commonly known. Its popularity stemmed from its original use as part of the ''first-fruits'' ceremony, when people annually brought their first fruits of the harvest to the sanctuary.[19]

The exposition of a scriptural passage, though, is something relatively new and differs from a simple retelling or embellishing of a biblical account. In Qumranite writings, in Philo's description of the Therapeutae, and in his allegorical interpretations of Scripture, one finds the first extant examples of expositions that are distinct from the biblical text. In rabbinic Judaism these expositions, and the study and interpretation they required, took on central importance. Philo and rabbinic and Qumran expounders all had a similar need to replace an inaccessible cult, in particular to find a substitute for the cult's role in providing a religious experience and divine instruction. Unable to use the traditionally defined institutions of the biblical world, they turned to the study of Scripture as one way to provide a new basis for their systems. All of them, however, perceived the act of study and exegesis differently. Philo endeavored to find the deeper spiritual dimension of the Bible. Qumran writers believed that their group had access to a key which enabled them to uncover the plain sense of the Bible. The rabbis, in contrast to both of these, had a notion of ''oral Torah,'' and searched the Scriptures to discover parts of a second revelation. Study became the highest form of piety and a ritual in its own right.[20] The Mishnah's requirement to expound the formulaic account of Jewish history, set out in Deuteronomy 26:5ff., reflects this new dimension of study and distinct type of encounter with the biblical text.[21]

EXTENDING THE MEANING OF REDEMPTION

The redemption motif of the Passover celebration is made applicable to the Jews of the post-70 era by the liturgical text attributed to Aqiva in Mishnah

10:6E. Aqiva is in dispute with Tarfon concerning the blessing that follows the first portion of Hallel.

> D. R. Tarfon says, " . . . Who has redeemed us and redeemed our ancestors from Egypt and brought us to this night" [some texts add: "to eat thereon unleavened bread and bitter herbs"]— and [he] does not seal [with the concluding formula].
>
> E.1 R. Aqiva says, [One adds to the blessing:] "Thus O LORD, our God and God of our ancestors, bring us in peace to the approaching festivals which are coming to meet us, happy in the building of Your city [some texts add: "joyous in Your service"], [so as] to eat from the passover and festive offerings whose blood will reach the wall of Your altar with favor,
>
> E.2. and let us thank You for our redemption.
>
> E.3. Praised art Thou, O LORD, who redeemed [K and P MSS: redeems] Israel."[22]

Tarfon speaks of the past redemption and, according to some readings, mentions the unleavened bread and bitter herbs. Aqiva, in contrast, refers to an ever-recurring redemption that applies not only to the ancient Israelites but also to the current generation, explicit in clause E.2, and possibly in clause E.3, if the Kaufmann and Parma manuscripts preserve the original reading. He also mentions in E.1 the cult and the passover sacrifice, and, in passing, the "building of Your city," that is, rebuilding Jerusalem.

Aqiva draws on the message in the Bible where, as S. S. Loewenstamm has demonstrated, the exodus event inherently carries the promise of future redemption.[23] This promise is interpreted in diverse ways. Jubilees, for example, asserts that whoever participates in the passover sacrifice will experience a year free from the plague.[24] Aqiva revises the message to Jews to conform with the loss of their temple. By mentioning the notion of an ongoing redemption at the point when people finish singing God's praises in acknowledgement of past redemption, Aqiva provides Jews with a firm foundation of hope for future redemption and strengthens their plea for divine assistance.[25] But his message is still based on the old religious structures. Not only does it speak of the future only in terms of a continual present (God redeemed and is redeeming) but it also refers only by implication to the changed situation in expressing hope for the reestablishment of "your city" so that Jews will be able to eat from the passover and festive offerings. This posture sharply contrasts with the amoraic extensive treatment of the theme of redemption. The postmishnaic masters, openly dealing with the disparity between the rite with its message of redemption and the current social and political situation under Roman and Iranian rule, either reinterpret redemption or else speak of experiencing it in the future.

Overall, then, although the Mishnah is informed by current realities, it does not make redemption a central theme. Indeed, considering the situation under Roman and Iranian rule, focus on the present lack of redemption would be counterproductive to the Mishnah's design to portray current practices in a timeless manner, as if they had existed in pre-70 days.[26]

<h3 style="text-align:center">ESTABLISHMENT OF FIXED BLESSINGS</h3>

The Mishnah requires seven different blessings to accompany key parts of the celebration; the Tosefta mentions five of these and provides actual blessing formulas for the last two:

1−2. Mishnah 10:2 and Tosefta 10:2, blessing over the day; blessing over the wine.

3. Mishnah 10:6 and Tosefta 10:9, blessing of "redemption," following the first part of Hallel.

4. Mishnah 10:7A, blessing over food.

5. Mishnah 10:7B, blessing over the song, *birkat hashir*, at the conclusion of Hallel.

6−7. Mishnah 10:9 and Tosefta 10:13, blessing over the passover offering, *birkat hapesah*; blessing over the festive offering, *birkat hazevah*.

Recitation of a blessing in association with a religious act serves either to prepare one for a religious experience or to interpret that emotional encounter in a specific way. In particular, for those without the temple, the saying of a blessing became an important way to ensure that religious acts would involve an experience of the divine. In rabbinic Judaism, these blessings became an institution required of every Jew, designed to sensitize people to the presence of God in the world. It was only natural that the Passover eve celebration would include a series of blessings: people would have welcomed reassurance that the rite still provided an effective way of relating to God and fulfilling the requirement to participate in the Passover event.[27]

<h3 style="text-align:center">SUMMARY</h3>

Four characteristic aspects of early rabbinic Judaism can be identified in the Mishnah, none of which would have been central in the pre-70 sacrificial meal. The first is the intellectual discussion of the celebration which is geared to all Jewry and therefore is freed from its biblical structure. This intellectual discussion is designed to make the adults participate in the event and understand its significance and is no longer solely a means of educating children. This accords

with the presence of additional educational features aimed at all the participants, including (a) Gamaliel's requirement to mention the passover lamb,
unleavened bread, and bitter herbs and therefore to concentrate on them as the
three central components of the rite, and (b) the anonymous symbolic interpretation of each of the three items.

Second, the form of the discussion includes not only retelling the events but
also expounding a classic text that reviews the mythic history in which God
redeems and provides for Israel. This requirement to expound accords with the
rising importance of midrash, the "searching out" of Scripture. The present
and the past illuminate each other, enabling the participants to relate more fully
to the exodus experience and to see it as paradigmatic of their own situation.

Third, the explicit mention of redemption reminds people both of the present
reality without the temple cult and of the hope for a change. This theme,
however, is not extensively developed, and the aspirations for the future are
channeled into a liturgical composition, a process characteristic of rabbinic
Judaism in general.

Fourth, the prescribed recitation of seven blessings ensures that people see
the celebration as a religious rite and become sensitive to its divine dimension.
The very need to emphasize this matter is characteristic of rabbinic Judaism,
which has tried to impart a new meaning to the world of mundane experience
through the system of blessings.

7

FROM FORM TO MEANING: THE SIGNIFICANCE OF THE PASSOVER RITE AND ITS PLACE IN EARLY RABBINIC JUDAISM

INTRODUCTION

W HAT LIGHT DOES THIS study throw on the nature of early Rabbinic Judaism? This question can be answered by placing the results in a larger context. Specifically, first, how does the Mishnah's restructuring of the ritual affect the meaning of the rite and the projected experience of the participants? Second, what is the significance of the way in which the Mishnah conveys its message, describing the current ceremony as if it had also been in effect in pre-70 days? As I will demonstrate, both the message and the style were essential to meet the needs of Jews troubled by the destruction of the temple and the paganization of Jerusalem. The Mishnah afforded Jews a sense of continuity with the past while it set them on a new path for the future.

THE SIGNIFICANCE OF THE PASSOVER RITE

Some scholars have argued that we should not attach much significance to the Passover rite as described in the Mishnah, since several of the novel elements predate 70 C.E. This argument is invalid. First, all the references to pre-70 elements derive from descriptions of the ceremony that centered on the passover offering and not on a nonsacrificial gathering. While it is reasonable to assume that even without the sacrificial meal some Jews may have employed certain features of the rite, there is no direct evidence to that effect.

Second, even if we could demonstrate that some features predate 70 C.E., that fact is not substantiating because those features took on a new role in the rabbinic rite. The Mishnah does not just add items but restructures the rite in several distinct ways, which may be summarized as follows: (1) It elevates the unleavened bread and bitter herbs to equal status with the passover offering and makes all features of the celebration independent of the offering. (2) The child's question does not depend on the procedures surrounding the sacrifice and its blood. (3) Individual Jews, not just Levites accompanying the sacrifice, may offer psalms of praise and thanksgiving to God. (4) Even without the meat of the sacrifices, participants can still be happy and express their joy with wine. (5) Even without the sacrifice, the gathering maintains its religious and ritual dimension and does not become a mere banquet.

The narration of the mythic history of Israel also imparts a distinctive meaning to the elements of the rite. The participants hear how God's intervention and redemption brought Israel out of its humble origins to its present honorable status, from darkness to light. Specifically, Jews are to focus on the classic formulaic text that recounts the mythic history of Israel, Deuteronomy 26:5−8(9). This passage imposes its perspective on whoever recites it. As Gerhard von Rad observes:

> The speaker divests himself of all his personal concerns and aligns himself fully with the community. Indeed, he identifies himself with the community: at this moment, as he pronounces its confession of faith, he is its mouthpiece.[1]

As has been seen, the narration of the Exodus experience is not novel. But now it becomes a central part of the ceremony. The sacrifice and its rituals no longer elicit an explanation of past history; but rather their actions and symbols are designed to exemplify and lead into the narrative. Moreover, the participants do not passively listen or go through empty motions. Just as the child is to ask a question or an adult is to instruct the child or another adult, so the participants are to expound (DRŠ) the account in Deutenonomy 26 of the history of Israel and thereby become engaged with those events. This is an example of midrash, the exegetical activity that became so important in rabbinic Judaism, described by Judah Goldin as follows:

> Midrash. . . is not mere reference to the past: it is the enlightment of the past in the service of the present. Even more specifically, it is a reinsertion into the present of the original divine Word, "memory making past present."[2]

But the myth in Deuteronomy 26 had to be readjusted by those who wished to see in their contemporary situation the fulfillment of the past. As David

Hoffmann has observed, it was incongruous for Jews after the destruction of the temple and the later paganization of Jerusalem to recite Deuteronomy 26:9:

> He brought us to this place [= the central sanctuary or temple] and gave us this land, a land flowing with milk and honey.[3]

Not surprisingly, rabbinic sources declared that the recitation of Deuteronomy 26 should end with verse 8:

> The LORD freed us from Egypt by a mighty hand, by an outstretched arm and awesome power, and by signs and portents.

Although Jews could not deny the aspect of their history that included the temple and their dwelling in the land of Israel, they could overcome the dissonance of their present situation by seeing it as one stage in the traditional paradigm. Aqiva's addition to one of the prayers in Mishnah 10:6 exemplifies how the loss of the temple could find a positive reference within the rite. There had been several instances of the transition from darkness to light. The present reality made up one such cycle, and Jews could believe that they lived somewhere between the existing darkness and the future light.

The mythic history is therefore enlarged to include their contemporary situation. Theodore M. Ludwig analyzes a comparable problem in the prophetic response to the destruction of the First Temple, in 586 B.C.E., and uses the term "remything" to desribe this phenomenon:

> Yet the paradigm [of the old bases of salvation] itself provides the vision for an extension or remything of the old traditum [= tradition] that can incorporate present experience. In a sense, present history is thus mythologized, but under the pattern of the religious paradigm. The theologoumenon of the traditum gives rise to mythologoumena relating directly to present experience. The remythed paradigmatic traditum carries a new authority, as authenticated in the personal experience of the transformers of the tradition; as such, it serves as the basis for new communal esoteric experience.[4]

While the prophetic response may differ substantively from the rabbinic, the dynamics of the process are similar. The Mishnah reflects a "remything" of the paradigm. As we know from explicit tannaitic sources, rabbis asserted that just as Israel was redeemed in the past, so Israel would be redeemed in the future.[5] Mishnah Pesaḥim conveys this obliquely, making use of the Deuteronomic formulaic text that emphasizes the mighty role of God in redeeming Israel.

The Mishnah's selection of a text from Deuteronomy (which generally downplays Moses' role in the events) is also significant. This choice may be related to the fact that the Mishnah and later versions of the haggadah do not cite any passage from Exodus mentioning Moses. A tannaitic comment that the haggadah adapts and applies to Deuteronomy 26:8 seems to point out the reason for these choices.

> And the LORD freed us from Egypt, not by means of an angel, and not by means of a seraph, and not by means of a messenger. On the contrary, the Holy One, blessed be He, by His glorious self, as it is said (Ex. 12:12), "For that night I will go through the land of Egypt and strike down every first-born in the land of Egypt, both man and beast; and I will mete out punishments to all the gods of Egypt, I, the LORD."[6]

Considering this perspective, the lack of reference to Moses is only natural. While Moses had a role in the Egyptian liberation, he does not figure in any of the later instances of redemption. It is God who repeatedly intervened for Israel, and it is His historical record that assures the people of hope.[7]

The narration of the mythic history and the exposition of a specified text direct the discussion and provide evidence supporting the overall message of the rite. *In its "remythed" form, the message was undoubtedly distinct from any pre-70 version that might have existed, whether from a temple or an extratemple context.*[8] Specific procedures in the Mishnah that serve to impart the meaning of the actions and symbols reflect this revised message. The teaching lesson in Mishnah 10:3 aimed at an adult and child and consisting of three questions related to the passover offering, unleavened bread, and bitter herbs; Gamaliel's statement in Mishnah 10:5A-B that equates these three elements and makes their verbalization the crucial action; and the anonymous authority's insistence on their symbolic signficance in Mishnah 10:5C are all obvious responses to and solutions for the problem of the loss of the temple and reflect the new perspective.

Mishnah 10:5C, in particular, contains the potential to transcend the sacrifice:

> C.1. *Pesaḥ* [= the paschal lamb]—because the Omnipresent skipped over the houses of our ancestors in Egypt.
> C.2. *Merorim* [= bitter herbs]—because the Egyptians embittered the lives of our ancestors in Egypt.
> C.3. *Maṣṣah* [= unleavened bread]—because they were redeemed.

By asserting that there is a cognitive meaning behind the rituals, their physical performance appears secondary, for when one becomes aware of their purposes, do not the rituals ipso facto achieve their desired result?[9] The specific symbolic explanations further attest to the new message. The unleavened bread, rather than sacrifice, symbolizes redemption, and the sacrifice only recalls the detail that God skipped over the houses of the Israelites. Finally, the juxtaposition of this passage with the prescription in Mishnah 10:5D to praise

God for the act of redemption makes the unleavened bread, an object still available in post-70 days, the basis for the praises:

> D. Therefore we are obligated to give thanks, to praise, to glorify, to crown, to exalt, to elevate the One who did for us all these miracles and took *us* out of slavery to freedom,
> and let us say before Him Hallelujah.

The participants assert that they too have been redeemed. This experience of identification and thanksgiving is central to the mythic dimension of the rite.[10]

THE EXPERIENCE OF THE CELEBRATION

The rite takes place at a meal which gives the participants a special opportunity to strengthen their bonds of friendship. In Victor Turner's terminology, the setting permits *communitas*, an atmosphere that liberates individuals from social structures that normally separate them. They become more open to personal "interrelatedness" and to a common experience of the divine.[11] The Mishnah relaxes social structures in very specific ways. The rite is not exclusive: not just for the intellectuals, the wealthy or the priests; not contingent on the presence of expert singers; not limited to the adults in a household. The concern for the participation of children is such that the Tosefta suggests that adults even play games with the unleavened bread to keep the interest of the children aroused (T. 10:9b).

In the practices related to children and the poor, one can also see a form of Turner's "status elevation," which often occurs in transitional or liminal phases of rituals when an individual or group passes from a structured situation to an experience of *communitas*:

> There [in the Nbembu society] liminality occurs in the middle phase of the rites of passage which mark changes in a group's or an individual's social status. The intervening liminal period or phase is thus betwixt and between the categories of ordinary social life. I then tried to extend the concept of liminality to refer to any condition outside, or on the peripheries of, everyday life, arguing that there was an affinity between the middle in sacred time and the outside in sacred space. For liminality among the Nbembu is a sacred condition. Among them, too, it is one in which communitas is most evident.[12]

One of the characteristics of this threshold or changing reality is the elevation of those with low social status:

> In the liminal phases of ritual, one finds a *simplification, even elimination of social structure* in the British sense and an amplification of structure in Levi-Strauss's sense. *We find social relationships simplified, while myth and*

ritual are elaborated. That this is so is really quite simple to understand: if liminality is regarded as a time and place of withdrawal from normal modes of social action, it can be seen as potentially *a period of scrutinization of the central values and axioms of the culture in which it occurs.* [13]

However different the Passover meal may be from the rituals Turner describes, it certainly simplifies social relationships, emphasizes mythic history, and sets up an atmosphere of *communitas* in which the culture's central values may be examined. The Mishnah therefore provides an exact protocol for the rite as well as boundaries in which one can let oneself go. One anthropologist who has analyzed the developed form of the seder offers observations that fit the description in the Mishnah and which are similar to Turner's:

> The structure of the Seder permits, indeed requires, each person to join the ritual whatever his or her degree of learning, belief, social status, or ritual participation at other times. "Society" is defined in its widest sense, as opposed to many other ritual procedures in Jewish culture that exclude people because of their age or sex. All communication that takes place at the Seder must be available to everyone.
>
> Formal public ritual is like a game that everyone agrees to play. The participants consent to abide by the rules of the evening and to let the decisions concerning their own actions be taken out of their hands and placed in Haggadah's program. For the success of the game, they allow themselves to be freed for the evening from the mentally divisive process of decision making, which focuses the mind on ideas in opposition, and also tacitly agree to ignore the personal matters and status considerations that separate individuals in nonritual time. In relaxing the barriers that divide people mentally and socially, *the focus of the evening may now be socially shared ideological considerations and not private concerns.* [14]

It may be illuminating at this point to compare the rabbinic Passover rite with certain aspects of the pre-70 rite. Before 70 the ritual was tied to a pilgrimage. This had been the ideal from the centralization of the cult in the seventh century B.C.E., and the actual practice, at least for many Jews, during the Second Temple period. Both the similarities and the differences between the old practices and the rabbinic ritual are significant.

The meal around a sacrifice, like that of the rabbinic seder, would have provided a special sense of interrelatedness, strengthened the bonds of friendship, and provided a release from normal social structures. Moreover, as Turner has demonstrated, the pilgrimage would have provided a dramatic break from regular patterns of life and contributed to a liminal experience. [15] Peter Brown summarizes Turner's insight:

> As Victor Turner has pointed out, the abandonment of known structures for a situation where such structures are absent, and the consequent release

of spontaneous fellow feeling, are part of the enduring appeal of the experience of pilgrimage in settled societies. The accustomed social world looks very different from even a short walk outside the town.[16]

Turner reviews numerous elements of the pilgrimage, including the preparations, the relationships with those who help the pilgrims along the way, and the pilgrims' social organization and behavior. Many of these elements are portrayed in biblical and postbiblical sources,[17] such as the following description from Philo:

> Countless multitudes from countless cities come, some over land, others over sea, from east and west and north and south at every feast. They take the temple for their port as *a general haven and safe refuge from the bustle and great turmoil of life, and there they seek to find calm weather, and, released from the cares whose yoke has been heavy upon them from their earliest years, to enjoy a brief breathing-space in scenes of genial cheerfulness.* Thus filled with comfortable hopes they devote the leisure, as is their bounden duty, to holiness and the honouring of God. Friendships are formed between those who hitherto knew not each other, and the sacrifices and libations are the *occasion of reciprocity of feeling and constitute the surest pledge that all are of one mind.*[18]

While the respite from normal life is common to both the pilgrimage and the rabbinic seder, the Passover gathering outside of one's usual environs involves an added experience of a national character. Peter Brown describes this aspect of a pilgrimage in relation to processions to a local shrine. He first quotes William Christian:

> As images of social wholeness, the processions have an added significance. The villagers for once in the year see the village as a social unit, abstracted from the buildings and location that make it a geographical unit.[19]

Brown then describes Romans going to the countryside to visit the shrine of Saint Hippolytus:

> Here was the *true* Rome: Rome shorn for a blessed day of its blatant social and topographical distinctions. [Quoting Prudentius, a fourth-century Christian Latin poet]: "The love of their religion masses Latins and strangers together in one body. . . . The majestic city disgorges her Romans in a stream; with equal ardor patricians and the plebian host are jumbled together, shoulder to shoulder, for the faith banishes distinctions of birth."[20]

A shrine serving both city and country, or serving a number of villages, united people from several locations. This would be even more dramatically true of a national pilgrimage center such as Jerusalem. One should not be surprised, therefore, by Philo's and Josephus's descriptions of the huge number of

pilgrims that came to Jerusalem during the festivals or by their explanations of
the significance of Passover as a national holiday of thanksgiving for the exodus
from Egypt. Note how Josephus emphasizes the national function of the
holidays in the summary of the laws that he attributes to Moses:

> Let them assemble in that city in which they shall establish the temple, three
> times in the year, from the ends of the land which the Hebrews shall conquer,
> in order to render thanks to God for benefits received, to intercede for future
> mercies, and to *to promote by thus meeting and feasting together feelings of
> mutual affection*. For it is good that they should not be ignorant of one
> another, being members of the same race and partners in the same institu-
> tions; and this end will be attained by such intercourse, *when through sight
> and speech they recall those ties to mind, whereas if they remain without
> ever coming into contact they will be regarded by each other as absolute
> strangers.* [21]

At a time when Jews had a national center and a semblance of national
freedom, they would naturally see Passover primarily as a national celebration
of thanksgiving for the historic event of the Exodus. [22] This contrasts with the
first Passover ceremony described in Exodus, in which the participants sought
to protect the community in general and their firstborn in particular from death.
The first Passover participants thus dealt with what an anthropologist would call
a structural problem or danger in their social order. At most one could personal-
ize the redemptive message, as in Jubilees, and think of it in terms of plague
prevention or (judging from pilgrimages in other cultures) for the purpose of
obtaining some change of condition "from sin to grace, or sickness to
health."[23]

All of these elements of Passover contrast with the post-70 experience, when
the gathering is not part of a national celebration and redemption is not the
contemporary reality. Now individual families or social units gather together
locally with fewer distractions than in Jerusalem, and thus with greater inti-
macy. There is still a national dimension: participants know they share a
common lot with other Jews and that Jews elsewhere celebrate a similar rite.
While this provides them with some sense of unity with their brethren, it can
hardly compare with the experience of pilgrims amid the crowds in Jerusalem. [24] Further, there is a new attitude toward history. The exodus, more than a
unique event in the past, takes on a mythic quality to a far greater degree. The
ritual emphasizes this quality and adjusts its account of the past redemption to
show that the present is a stage between darkness and light. It helps people
continue to believe that a new social and national order can and will come
about.

On a practical level, this means that the Passover celebration provided Jews, after the destruction of the temple and the subsequent paganization of Jerusalem, with a channel in which to direct their hopes and anxieties concerning redemption. This is not to deny that in terms of the normal, everyday structured existence the rite afforded Jews with an opportunity for a release and revitalization. Nevertheless, in terms of the national situation, it provided them with a means to cope with this unsettling problem. Whenever Jews followed the Mishnah's protocol, they could reexperience the liminal, unstructured and, in their case, disoriented condition of Jews after the Destruction. But the Mishnah then provided an outlet and a new structure for these feelings in the Passover rite. People did not have to admit to any discontinuity with the past; despite the loss of the temple and the end of the sacrificial service, they could still observe the celebration. They could even experience the divine in a more intimate fashion through examining and expounding the Scriptures. Accordingly, from this perspective the Mishnah and the etiquette it sets out made some degree of personal and social renewal possible. [25]

Anthropologists emphasize that an act or symbol cannot be fully understood in isolation but must be examined in terms of its role in a series of other actions and symbols and within its entire fabric of associations. This proposition holds true for the particular elements in the Mishnah's description of the Passover evening celebration. One must analyze individual teachings in the Mishnah as parts of units and larger blocks of tradition. [26] It is therefore justifiable to treat the Mishnah as a historical datum in its own terms, even if some of the threads it weaves were spun in an earlier period. The components are infused with meaning by the world view and the mythic reality that the whole document projects.

THE FUNCTION OF THE DESCRIPTIVE-NARRATIVE:
THE CULT CONTINUES

The style of Mishnah Pesaḥim 10 differs from the Mishnah's regular style. The Mishnah usually consists of individual teachings in the form of statements of law or disputes, attributed or unattributed, and with a protasis and apodosis. The various units of a chapter generally make up a whole by the logical connection of the legal principles and the use of a similar syntax. The units of Mishnah Pesaḥim 10, however, are interrelated by the very structure of the chapter. In describing the order of Passover eve and in setting out the rules of etiquette in chronological sequence, the Mishnah creates a single narrative in which even the attributed comments and the occasional disputes are integrated. It formulates much of the narrative with a participle construction used for the present tense and therefore suggests a timeless procedure that ostensibly remains unaffected by history. But, as I have demonstrated, the etiquette does not strictly accord with the way the rite was performed in the premishnaic period. This timeless quality and the resulting historical anomaly serve the purposes of the Mishnah's editor. I have not, however, explained exactly how this style fits the needs of the Mishnah. Why did the editor of the Mishnah choose this style to formulate its teachings?

The timeless quality of the style of the Mishnah is suited to the specific mythic nature of the Passover rite. Various writers have pointed to the mythic character of Passover. Biblical scholars have found it in the Scriptures. Von Rad, as noted before, sees it in the recitation of Deuteronomy 26:5−8, which plays a central role in the seder. Brevard Childs comments on it in his analysis of Exodus 12−13:16:

> But once again, the narrative momentarily pauses, and turns briefly from the historical setting into a parenetic style. Because this rite is to become a permanent institution within Israel, later generations must need to know its significance. How does Israel transmit its faith to the next generation? The writer poses the questions in terms of a child's query [= Ex. 12:26−27]. When your sons ask in time, what is the meaning of this ritual, then you will say: 'It is the passover offering to YHWH through which we are redeemed.' This response is not simply a report, but above all a confession to the *ongoing participation of Israel in the decisive act of redemption from Egypt.*[27]

The concern of the Bible that the event be experienced has wider implications:

> Finally, the redactor's use of the dialectic between redemption as hope and redemption as memory has important theological implications. Those commentators who are disturbed over the detailed instructions for future celebration before the initial event has transpired have failed to see that far more is at stake in the text than chronological consistency. The interplay in vv. 1−20 and 21−28 between the now and the then, between what is to come and what has already happened, is not dissolved after the event, but once again picked up and maintained in a new dialectic between the past and the future. *Israel remains a people who has been redeemed, but who still awaits its redemption.*[28]

Scholars have discussed the significance of this paradigmatic quality of Passover. While they draw upon the haggadah, many of their references go back to the Mishnah or develop mishnaic themes. Jacob Neusner, for example, writes:

> Through the natural eye, one sees ordinary folk, not much different from their neighbors in dress, language, or aspirations. The words they speak do not describe reality and are not meant to. When Jewish people say of

themselves, "We were the slaves of Pharaoh in Egypt," they know they never felt the lash; but through the eye of faith that is just what they have done. It is *their* liberation, not merely that of long-dead forebears, they now celebrate.

To be a Jew means to be a slave who has been liberated by God. To be Israel means to give eternal thanks for God's deliverance. And that deliverance is not at a single moment in historical time. It comes in every generation and is always celebrated. Here again, events of natural, ordinary life are transformed through myth into paradigmatic, eternal, and ever-recurrent sacred moments. Jews think of themselves as having gone forth from Egypt, and Scripture so instructs them. God did not redeem the dead generation of the Exodus alone, but the living too—especially the living.[29]

Neusner clarifies what he means by this mythic interpretation of history:

The redemptive promise that stood by the forefathers and "stands by us" is not a mundane historical event, but a mythic interpretation of historical, natural events. Oppression, homelessness, extermination—like salvation, homecoming, renaissance—are this-worldy and profane, supplying headlines for newspapers. The myth that a Jew must think of himself or herself as having gone forth from Egypt . . . and being redeemed by God renders ordinary experience into a moment of celebration.[30]

Ruth Fredman recently has offered an anthropological interpretation of the timeless quality of the seder. Citing numerous elements of the developed ritual, she suggests that the rite places the participants in an "inbetween state," moving from darkness to light. She speaks further of the "mythic quality" of the event:

The Seder works with time on many levels, presenting the Exodus from Egypt as a historical event as well as a paradigmatic sequence explaining the experience of the Jews for all times. The Exodus is both history, a sequence of events, and myth, a timeless explanatory model for the society's existence, and this "mythical history" is made objective and palpable through the objects and actions of the ritual.[31]

Amoraic comments make the point clear. One master refers to the lowly origins of Israel, which Mishnah 10:4 requires the participants to mention, by saying "*we* were slaves."[32] Another tradition requires the participants to say, " 'And us He freed from there' (Deut. 6:23)."[33] The same thought is expanded in a gloss to Mishnah Pesahim 10:5, which has found its way into the haggadah:

In every generation a person is required to regard himself as if he went out from Egypt, as it is said, "And you shall tell your child on that day saying, '[It is] because of that which the LORD did for me when I came out of Egypt' " (Ex. 13:8).[34]

The present study indicates that the Mishnah creatively plays with this mythic quality. In addition to the explicit reference in Mishnah 10:5 to "the One who . . . took *us* out of slavery to freedom,"[35] it is reflected in numerous words and actions. For example, the special exposition of Deuteronomy 26 is meant to draw the participants into a relationship with the specifics of slavery and liberation.

The "timeless" style also appears in other sections of the Mishnah concerned with cultic matters—for example, Mishnah Tamid, Middot, and Parah 3.[36] Neusner, analyzing the use of this technique in the divisions of Qodashim and Tohorot, finds that it serves to lay out the "cosmology" or construction of the temple in its usual and daily practices.[37] With this style, the Mishnah restates and reaffirms the world of the sanctuary and the sacrifice:

> We have a system before us: the system of the cult of the Jerusalem Temple, seen as an ordinary and everyday affair, a continuing and routine operation.[38]

In contrast with a work such as the Letter to Hebrews, which explains away the physical cult as being inherently inferior and therefore to be transcended, the restatement in the Mishnah asserts that the cult exists and is important. It pretends that nothing has changed:

> Mishnah's refusal to reinterpret in any detail and in any aspect a single rule of Scripture, its dogmatic insistence upon the literal meaning of such Scriptures as it does resort to, and, more important, its extensive access to all those facts and conceptions of Scripture which generate Mishnah's own rules—these facts in context cannot be taken as routine and unexceptional. The pretense that nothing has changed in five hundred years . . . and that the ancient system goes forward unaffected by change and by time is the most eloquent apologetic.[39]

But the construction of the Mishnah is not escapist: while the rabbis insure that the cult will remain in people's consciousness, they do not suggest (in fact they deny the possibility) that the sacrifice can be moved outside the Jerusalem Temple.[40] As Neusner observes, by setting forth rules and protocols previously in the special domain of priests, the Mishnah is making priestly concerns available to all Jews. Anyone can study this document, and thereby be in touch with the cult, at any time and in any place:

> If Mishnah plans to have its materials studied, its intention therefore is to turn whoever studies the document into someone who knows what priests know and, excluding only the matter of proper pedigree, *can* do pretty much what priests can do. . . .[41]

In truth, the profound shift in Israelite symbols, effected by our document (at least) for those who make and memorize it, is a movement towards a society where, as I said, all know what priests know. But in this society all know it in the form and language given by sages, accessible only among their circles. To put matters simply: In the world of disaster and cataclysmic change, Mishnah stands as a statement of how the old is to be retained. It defines and effects the permanence amid change.[42]

A narrative description offers one way in which to portray the cultic world as a viable reality. Mishnah Pesahim 10 therefore uses techniques similar to other portions of the Mishnah to portray an appearance of an ongoing procedure. This does not denigrate the passover sacrificial rite or suggest that the cultic elements be forgotten or be performed outside of the temple. Indeed, Mishnah 10:3, which describes details of a protocol viable anywhere and ends with the clause "and in the temple they serve him the carcass of the passover offering," implies that only in the temple do people partake of the sacrifice.[43]

Again, like other "timeless" narratives in the Mishnah, Mishnah Pesahim 10 calls for the reader's active engagement with the world it describes. This is especially appropriate in relation to the Passover rite. It is not novel that all Israelites are to learn the rules for the rite: they were always involved in the Passover rite and sacrifice as they were not in the daily maintenance of the cult. The innovation of the Mishnah lies in its description of laypeople performing certain features of the celebration, for example the singing, which previously had been the monopoly of professionals, the Levites. Here it offers new roles to individual Jews, who may now act as cultic officials. I have demonstrated how Philo made this observation in his descriptions of several meal gatherings.

This last variation points to the main difference between the Passover narrative and those associated with the usual, everyday cult. The Mishnah portrays a reality which, as far as evidence indicates, did not exist in pre-70 times and which revises numerous details of the pre-70 rite. While unknown and now nonextant precedents for extratemple private Passover rites may have existed, those procedures would not have been considered the official celebration and could hardly have served as an adequate source for the picture of reality constructed by the Mishnah. According to the Mishnah, one is to believe, the only difference between a temple and an extratemple observance is that in the temple people ate from the passover sacrifice. Everything else was supposed to be thought of as identical!

It is fair to conclude, therefore, that the present-tense description and narrative style contribute to the purpose of the Mishnah. *The Mishnah wants the reader to believe that the text provides another description of a pre-70 cultic reality*. This type of cultic description, as Neusner suggests with regard to Qodashim, constitutes a statement that the cult is viable and not obsolete. Some scholars have assumed that the narrative-descriptive style is used in Pesaḥim, Qodashim, and elsewhere for "archaeological" descriptions—as if what is purported actually occurred in that way.[44] The error or gullibility of these scholars indicates the power of the Mishnah's argument.

The Mishnah wants us to believe that its directions on how to follow the mythic history of Passover point to a well-tried and established road. It does indeed provide Jews with an appropriate path in a time of turmoil and disorientation.

THE NEED FOR A SENSE OF CONTINUITY

Though we now understand how the literary construction and argument of the Mishnah operate, one may still pose the question: Why would the Mishnah not just openly assert that the rite continues without the temple and sacrifice?

The destruction of the temple in 70 C.E. and the paganization of the city in the second century undoubtedly led to a sense of despair over the possible rebuilding of the temple. Separately and together these posed a grave religious and psychological crisis. In chapter 1, I briefly noted the nature of this crisis. Early Christians saw the situation as proof that Judaism had become obsolete, for they believed that a temple-based religion constituted the only legitimate type of Judaism. They were led to this view by the nature of the prevailing religious institutions and by a simple reading of the Bible.[45] In chapter 2, I showed how Justin, Origen, and other Christian thinkers took up the charge: without the sacrifice, how could Jews observe the festival? And if Jews could not observe the festival, how could they observe other commandments associated with the holiday, for example, circumcision? Christian thinkers concluded that God's covenant of the flesh with Israel could not be eternal. While rabbis may have tried to answer this charge and while the Mishnah provided one kind of answer with regard to Passover,[46] the Christian polemics underscore the fact that the loss of the temple created a potentially destructive vacuum.

Rabbinic and nonrabbinic sources indicate that some Jews may have tried to fill the void by preparing a passover sacrifice outside of Jerusalem. Thus Tosefta Ahilot 3:9:

A. A case concerning (M‘SH B-): In Bet Daggan in Judah, a person died on the eve of Passover and they [= the local people] went to bury him.
B. And the women entered and tied the rope to the rolling stone [at the end of the grave]. The men pulled from the outside and the women entered

and buried him. And the men went and prepared their passover offerings in the evening.[47]

Since moving the stone with the rope does not convey uncleanness, the men were able to prepare their passover sacrifices in a state of ritual purity. And this occurred outside of Jerusalem!

Passages such as this, as well as nonrabbinic post-70 discussions of Passover that employ the present tense in describing the sacrificial rite, have been used by some writers to claim that the sacrifice was still being offered. In appendix A, I review this evidence more extensively. Here I will repeat that these sources at most report only some people's beliefs. Even if they accurately portray the events, scholars agree that such practices would have ceased by the middle of the second century. The Mishnah certainly does not entertain the possibility that a person might still bring a passover sacrifice. Even if the Mishnah's rejection of this possibility is a second-century development, my argument would not be affected. Because I analyze the Mishnah as a complete work and seek to understand its overall world view, it would not be problematic if the bulk of the Mishnah derived from the second century.

Several sources mention "local" practices according to which some people prepare a roasted lamb in the manner in which the sacrifice was previously prepared. For example, Mishnah Pesaḥim 4:4 reads:

> A place where they [= people] are accustomed to eat roasted meat (SLY) on the nights of Passover—they eat [it].
> A place where they are accustomed not to eat [it]—they do not eat [it].

This and similar references underscore the degree to which people felt the need to continue the cultic dimensions of the festival, to whatever degree possible.[48] Since we lack comparable stories suggesting that people brought other sacrifices or imitated the preparation of other temple offerings, evidently the passover sacrifice was perceived to be different and more vital.

An individual or group that suffers a traumatic loss must eventually confront and adjust to the new circumstances. But as long as the pain of loss is acute, one cannot openly alter one's relationship to the lost object or transcend it. To face the future, one needs to feel and demonstrate a continuity with the past. Mortimer Ostow, as I have shown in chapter 1, provides insight into the psychological plight of post-70 Jews:

> To those who are committed to a religious life, the existence of a crisis makes observance even more necessary. It is vital to retain the forms of observance and worship that have signified continuity with the past and that protect against discontinuity. Maintaining one's way of life under hostile

attack serves also to sustain one's self esteem, which is always at risk under pressure.[49]

But, to repeat, the Mishnah reflects a stage of coming to grips with the crisis and the beginnings of working through the events. Ostow further observes:

> We use the term "working through" to designate a relatively long process by means of which the individual, and possibly the group psyche—if we may use such a term—accommodates to the traumatic disruption of its ordinary activities and finds a new basis for functioning. Working through includes such activities as recollecting the traumatic events in detail so as to overcome the denial which was the initial response to overwhelming trauma; examining the implications of these events for the present and the future; recollecting similar events from the past and taking courage from the fact that they are overcome; *reconstructing personal and group myths which provide a sense of origin, continuity, identity, and destiny*; making practical plans for the future that will compensate for the losses of the trauma and that will promise a reasonable prospect of protection against similar trauma in the future. In a sense one constructs a new image of the universe to replace the one that has been lost. When the working through process has been completed the individual experiences a sense of invigoration, remoralization and renewal, which in the unconscious is represented as a feeling of being reborn.[50]

Some elements of this paradigm fit the treatment of the Passover rite in the Mishnah. Other elements, representing an ability to accept openly the implications of the Destruction and to advocate a new basis for life, are not found in the Mishnah and are not fully expressed until the postmishnaic period.

The rabbinic movement was made up of Jews who chose neither to give up Judaism nor to deny the events and their implications. They did not follow the old ways in a literal fashion, as the Samaritan community did.[51] Rather, early rabbinic authorities evolved a new way to stay on the old path. They found numerous precedents for extratemple practices, and they recast and supplemented the biblical heritage. In this fashion, the well-tried cultic ways could continue. Further, they adapted the group myth—the mythic history of Israel, represented in the Passover motto of "from slavery to freedom"—so that it would be applicable to comparable situations in the future.

It is not possible to trace all the steps of this development, for example, to know when temporary procedures were perceived as permanent. Undoubtedly the failure of the Bar Kokhba revolt (132–35) and the paganization of Jerusalem contributed to the belief that the old ways would not quickly return and that the new emergency measures would persist for a long while. By looking at the Mishnah as a whole, one can see these trends in their maturity.

Theological considerations also compelled the rabbis to demonstrate a continuity with the past. Rabbinic masters believed that the Torah was a divine revelation, eternally relevant, with infinite layers of meaning geared to all circumstances. They therefore held that the interpretive structures they evolved belonged to the divine plan. Scholars argue that these notions are central to the rabbinic world view. Judah Goldin demonstrates their role in midrash and in the study of the Oral and Written Torah, noting how they produce a mentality that anachronistically projects the present reality backward in time:

> Midrash which gave old statements ''new'' meaning and ''new'' direction—in other words, applicability in terms of the requirements or emphases of the later periods—could accomplish this because of what we may call anachronism, the assumption by a later generation that ideas uppermost in its mind are necessarily the ideas uppermost in the mind of the earlier generation. Anachronism, naturally, is always at work in every society. But what makes it so congenial to and operative in Classical Judaism is the combination . . . [of]: on the one hand, great painstaking at conserving what has been handed down by the past, but on the other, firm conviction that the once-upon-a-time revealed Word and the subsequent words which are its outgrowth continue with unceasing life and liveliness to release successive truths which are not novel, but only newly recognizable permanent elements of the original content.[52]

Anachronism enables people to believe that they stand in a continuity with the past:

> *If there is only change and adaptation, discontinuity remains a permanent possibility*—for the change may be so revolutionary that nothing less than a new beginning is required if there is to be either survival or revival.[53]
>
> It is therefore not with change and adaption as such that the rabbis are preoccupied; this is not their fundamental orientation. *It is with the preservation of that intimate relationship between the inexhaustible Word and human society that they are concerned.*[54]

Mishnah Pesaḥim 10 is an example of the anachronistic process which aims at continuity and cannot acknowledge the existence of change, but which at the same time is motivated by a desire to express a new meaning. The need to demonstrate conformity with the past indicates that the framers of the Mishnah are still affected by the traumatic loss of the cult. But in structuring the rite on a new basis and in adding new features, they are coming to grips with the crisis. Moreover, the very construction of this altered reality to some degree enables the framers of the Mishnah, and those who follow the Mishnah, to experience a sense of closure.

The dynamics of Mishnah Pesaḥim represent a phenomenon seen in the history of all teachings. As Neusner points out, it is the nature of traditions to be constantly contemporized:

> Tradition, as a process of handing on and passing forward, thus is dynamic and not static. Its interest is not in what was originally said alone but in how what was said in the past endows with meaning, imposes sense upon, the issues of the new age.[55]

> [The] tradition does make room, through the process of retelling and reinterpreting, for the most current concerns.[56]

By tracing the history of the Passover rite, one both finds how the past is made relevant to a new reality and also obtains a glimpse of that new reality.

In addition to the historical-psychological and theological influences at work, one should appreciate the difficult task rabbis faced as teachers of new ideas. Even if they were fully conscious of the novelty of their ideas, they could not just propound a theory and expect that it would capture people's minds and imaginations. Peter Brown brings out some of the psychological factors at play in the development of Christian ideas about the afterlife:

> The late-antique cult of the martyrs represents . . . a consistent imaginative determination to block out the lurking presence, in the cemeteries of the Mediterranean world, of "black death."
> *We should not underestimate the psychological momentum behind this effort.* In itself belief in the afterlife does little to explain it. What we shall have to follow . . . is the working of an imaginative dialectic which led late-antique men *to render their beliefs in the afterlife palpable and directly operative* among the living by concentrating these on the privileged figure of the dead saint.[57]

The posture of the Mishnah concerning the Passover rite is a sign of the vitality of the Mishnah framers and of the society that produced them. As Goldin comments on anachronistic "imaginativeness":

> Anachronism is one of the firmest signs of the vitality of a tradition. . . . [T]he equation of past with present is not failure of intellect. It may be innocent of historical discipline, but it is a pious act of imaginativeness.[58]

Neusner remarks on the creativity of the Mishnah in his discussion of the Order of Qodashim, which deals with the everyday cultic affairs:

> Brandon's judgement of the world framed by Mishnah to begin with hardly exhibits understanding (or even knowledge) of those ways in which the destruction of the Temple turned out to inaugurate not a time of decay and dissolution, but a remarkable age of reconstruction and creativity in the history of Judaism.[59]

Accordingly, the response of early rabbinic Judaism to the crisis of the day is not a sign of denial or of the feebleness of the community. If any religious tradition is to remain vibrant, it must adapt to changing realities in such a way that the present is not seen as a departure from the past. This ability to maintain a sense of continuity is what creates a living religion. Joseph Blau puts it this way:

> Each living religion *must* change thus, if it is to continue to have relevance to the lives of those who accept it. But, although it is constantly changing, each religion must seem to be as unchanging as possible, for though we want our religions to be always relevant, we also want them to serve as our link to the past, the root of our sense of continuity.[60]

The study of the Passover rite thus broadly illuminates the history of Judaism and the community's response to the destruction of the temple cult. It also provides an opportunity to trace the formation of rabbinic Judaism. Rabbis faced an identical task in dealing with the entire earlier heritage. But in the case of Passover, a considerable amount is known concerning the prehistory of the rabbinic ritual, including its state as a family-home gathering prior to the centralization of the cult in the seventh century B.C.E., and its later biblical and postbiblical form as a celebration at a central cultic place. One can therefore determine what existed before the rabbis recast the rite, and how they drew upon earlier extratemple items, adapted, restructured, and supplemented the antecedent materials, and developed a ritual and mode of piety not contingent upon the temple and sacrificial cult.

In claiming that first- and second-century historical events provided the impetus to expand the biblical rite, one denies that other forces played a central role. I rule out, for example, the possibility that the symposia literature had a major impact. This literature at most may have enriched various features of the celebration, especially in its postmishnaic versions. The present study of rabbinic and nonrabbinic sources has enabled us to trace the actual recasting of the cultic elements in the celebration. Further, as seen in chapter 5, banquet habits and the use of meals for a gathering are not unique to Passover. Different groups adapted the communal meal for many different purposes and, most importantly, one can observe a pattern in their adaptation. The descriptions of the meals, whether of Passover or not, in Qumran, Philo, and Philo's account of the Therapeutae, apply cultic language and other notions to these gatherings in the manner in which the Mishnah extends cultic significance to the Passover rite. One must conclude that the need to show continuity with a cultic background is the operative principle.

THE SYSTEM OF THE MISHNAH AND BEYOND:
FROM CONTINUITY TO DISCONTINUITY

I have demonstrated the reason for the anomaly inherent in the Mishnah. To respond to the loss of the temple and the passover offering, the Mishnah has to claim, anachronistically, that the present rite is not discontinuous with the past. This effort is geared to those still troubled by the loss of the temple and its cult. Gradually, however, as people felt more sure of themselves and less vulnerable concerning the temple's loss, they could relate to the restructured rite in its own terms. Jews could then admit that a discontinuity existed. The Mishnah only hints at such a stage. I have suggested that the symbolic interpretation added to Gamaliel's statement of the three essential elements to the rite, in Mishnah 10:5, is the beginning of this practice. Several glosses and changes to the text of the Mishnah show further developments of this conception. Mishnah 10:3 provides two striking examples:

A. [They] served him—[he] dips the lettuce [= the vegetable used for bitter herbs] before he reaches the bread condiment.
B. [They] served him unleavened bread and lettuce and *ḥaroset* [= a mixture, e.g., of nuts, fruit, and vinegar pounded together], even though the *ḥaroset* is not a *miṣvah* [= a commandment].
R. Leazar b. Ṣadoq says [It is a] *miṣvah*.
C. And in the Temple [they] serve him the carcass of the passover offering.[61]

The loss of the sacrifice is implicit in a gloss to clause B. On the basis of a later comment or version, the mention of "two cooked foods," representing the lost passover and festival sacrifices, is interpolated into the passage:

B.' [They] served him unleavened bread and lettuce and *ḥaroset* and two cooked foods even though the *ḥaroset* is not a *miṣvah*.

Even more explicit is the transformation of clause C. That clause indicates that the Mishnah speaks of two contemporary practices: a general and ostensibly standard protocol for outside the temple, and an added special feature for inside the Temple. But printed editions change the verb to a past tense and turn the clause into an acknowledgment of change:

C.' And in the Temple [they] used to serve him the carcass of the passover offering.

Modifications in the list of typical questions concerning the evening's procedures found in Mishnah 10:4 likewise reflect changing attitudes.[62] In the course of this study, I have cited additional examples from the Tosefta, the

Gemara, and the Midrashim. These deal with the awareness that the rabbinic seder is temporally correlated with the sacrificial gathering; that the focus on three central items of the seder requires special intent just like that required for the preparation of the passover sacrifice; that one uses wine instead of meat from the sacrifice to express one's joy; that the unleavened bread and bitter herbs were originally secondary but have been elevated in status equal to that of the passover sacrifice; and that Israelites, instead of the Levitical professional singers, sing psalms to God. In addition, the special emphasis on the mythic dimension of Passover and on the required identification with the Exodus experience may also reflect this tendency.[63]

As I mentioned at the outset, my task has not been to examine the later stages of the tradition. However, it is worth noting the existence of these developments, for they provide a contrast to the Mishnah and highlight its distinctive perspective. An implication of the present study is that we have to refine overly general explanations for developments in the history of Judaism. Judaism evolved several types of responses to the end of the passover cult. Only by paying attention to the exact relationships of these responses can one fully understand their significance and function. Moreover, this effort will enable us to correlate and map out the religious and historical situation reflected in the different teachings. For a vivid illustration of this point I will now examine two additional texts which, in contrast to the Mishnah, present the viewpoint that the passover offering lacks any inherent importance. The first, Mekilta, an early (i.e., third-century) Midrash,[64] suggests that God added details to the preparation of the passover rite to provide Israel with merit to be redeemed. The second, from Exodus Rabbah, a Midrash edited in the posttalmudic period,[65] extends this notion to the sacrifice as a whole. God prescribed the offering only as a ruse so that Jews would circumcise themselves. First, Mekilta *Pisḥa*, chapter 5:

A. "And you shall keep it until the fourteenth day of the same month" (Ex. 12:6). Why did Scripture require the purchase of the paschal lamb to take place four days before its slaughter?
B.1. R. Matia the son of Heresh used to say, Behold it says, "[You were still naked and bare] when I passed by you and saw that your time for love had arrived" (Ezek. 16:[7−]8). This means, the time has arrived for the fulfillment of the oath which the Holy One, Praised be He, had sworn unto Abraham, to deliver his children. But as yet they had no religious duties to perform by which to merit redemption, as it says, "your breasts became firm and your hair sprouted. You were still naked and bare" (Ezek. 16:7), which means bare of any religious deeds.
B.2 Therefore the Holy One Praised be He, assigned them two duties, the

blood [Lauterbach = "duty"] of the paschal sacrifice and the blood [Lauterbach = "duty"] of circumcision, which they should perform so as to be worthy of redemption. For thus it is said, "When I passed by you and saw you wallowing in your blood, I said to you, 'In thy blood live [, and I said to you, 'in thy blood live']" (Ezek. 16:6). And it says, "As for you also, because of the blood of your covenant I released the prisoners from dry pit" (Zech. 9:11).

C. For this reason Scripture required that the purchase of the paschal lamb take place four days before its slaughter. For one cannot obtain rewards except for deeds.[66]

The passover sacrifice thus has a purpose—if only to give the Israelites merit. The implication might be that the blood of the sacrifice, like the blood of circumcision, would continue to give Israel merit. While Jews may no longer be able to have the blood from that sacrifice, they can still perform circumcision.[67]

Two comments from Exodus Rabbah, clauses B−D and E−M, indicate that the passover sacrifice serves an ulterior purpose. The second comment in particular expands the tradition found in Mekilta and "improves" on it to fit later realities:

A. "This is the ordinance (HWQT) of the passover offering" (Ex. 12:43).

B. R. Simeon b. Halafta said, When Israel departed [or "were about to depart"] from Egypt, the Holy One Praised be He said to Moses, "Exhort the Israelites concerning the command of the passover offering. 'No foreigner shall eat of it. But any slave a man has bought may eat of it once he has been circumcised' (Ex. 12:43b−44)."

C. When the Israelites saw that the uncircumcised were disqualified from eating the passover sacrifice, they arose with the least possible delay and circumcised all their servants and sons and all those who [subsequently] went out with them, as it says, "And the Israelites went and did so" (Ex. 12:28). [This verse reports the Israelites' response to Moses' instructions to prepare the passover offering. Cp. Ex. 12:50.]

D. It can be compared to a king who arranged a banquet for his friends and who said, "Unless the invited guests show my seal, none can enter."

Similarly, God ordained a feast for them, "[flesh . . .] roasted with fire, with unleavened bread and bitter herbs" (Ex. 12:8), because he delivered them from trouble; [but] He commanded, "Unless the seal of Abraham is [inscribed] on your flesh, you cannot taste thereof."

E. Thereupon all those who had been born in Egypt were immediately circumcised, and concerning these it is said, "Gather My devotees unto Me, those who made a covenant with Me for ('LY) a sacrifice" (Ps. 50:5).

F. And rabbis said, Israel did not wish to be circumcised in Egypt, and all save the tribe of Levi had abolished circumcision in Egypt, as it says, "And

of Levi he said, Let Your Theummin and Urim be with Your faithful"
(Deut. 33:8). Why was this? "Your precepts alone they observed, and kept
Your covenant" (Deut. 33:9)—in Egypt.

G. And when the Holy One Praised be He was about to redeem them, He
could find no merit in them. So what did He do? He called Moses and said,
"Go and circumcise them."

(H. Some say Joshua was there and it was he who circumcised them, as it
says, "And circumcise again the Israelites a second time" [Josh. 5:2].)

I. But many of them would not agree to be circumcised.

The Holy One Praised be He commanded that the passover offering
should be prepared, and when Moses prepared the passover offering, God
decreed that the four winds of the world [should blow] and they blew in the
Garden of Eden.

J. And from the winds that blew in the Garden of Eden [a scent] went and
joined in that passover offering, for it says, "Awake, O north wind, Come,
O south wind! Blow upon my garden, that its fragrance may spread" (S.S.
4:16). And this scent spread over a distance of a forty days' journey.

K. All the Israelites [then] came flocking to Moses and said, "Do,
please, give us some of your passover offering to eat," for they were
famished on account of the odor that was in it.

L. The Holy One Praised be He said, "Unless you circumcise yourselves
you cannot eat [thereof]," as it says, "And the LORD said to Moses and
Aaron: This is the ordinance of the passover offering," etc. [= "No
foreigner shall eat of it. But any . . . may eat of it once he has been
circumcised"] (Ex. 12:43).

M. Thereupon they immediately offered themselves for circumcision,
and the blood of the passover offering mingled with that of circumcision.

N. And the Holy One Praised be He took each one, kissed him and
blessed him, as it says, "And when I passed by you and saw you wallowing
in your blood," etc. [= "and I said to you, 'In thy blood live,' and I said to
you, 'In thy blood live' "] (Ezek. 16:6). "[In thy blood] live"—refers to
the blood of the passover offering; "[In thy blood] live"—refers to the
blood of circumcision.[68]

The fact that Exodus Rabbah is a late Midrash is reflected in both interpretations, clauses B−E and F−N. They address an audience that can take the lack
of a passover offering for granted, and they assume that the sacrifice lacks any
specific inherent meaning.[69] The comments appropriately appear as interpretations of Exodus 12:43, which uses the word *huqqah*, "ordinance" or law, a
term often understood as a divine command on ritual matters, especially for
laws that appear to lack reasons.[70] Both clauses B−E and F−N present this
perception of the passover sacrifice. According to the first interpretation, God
prescribed the passover offering to induce the Israelites to circumcise themselves. The sacrificial meal was a banquet to commemorate the deliverance,

clause D, as if the liberation is a past fact. The second interpretation, clauses
F−N (with H, an interpolated gloss to G), is even more explicit in playing down
the sacrifice. Clauses G and M−N employ language found in the Mekilta
tradition, though here the circumcision is the sole focus of interest. Indeed, the
background of the Mekilta helps explain the mention of the blood of the
passover offering, in clauses M−N, which might otherwise seem strange in this
context.

In Exodus Rabbah, circumcision is thus assumed to be more important than
the sacrifice.[71] Surely, such an announcement of the meaninglessness of the
passover sacrifice would have seemed cruel and abrasive to people who had
been grieved by its loss, whether they had personally lived through the Destruction or had merely maintained faith in the central role of the sacrifice. By the
same token, once the rabbinic celebration became accepted as a ritual in its own
right, it did not have to be justified on the basis of old cultic notions. People
soon forgot that the sacrifice had provided the structure for everything else. It
was sufficiently remembered through a symbol. This attitude indicates that the
Mishnah had indeed triumphed.

The seder constitutes one of the most effective products of early rabbinic
Judaism. It provides examples of the central rabbinic institutions of prayer,
blessings, study, acts of loving kindness, and fellowship. Each activity was an
act of piety and available to all Jews, not just the wealthy, or adults, or
intellectuals. It moreover epitomizes the rabbinic mythic world view.[72] In word
and deed it provided Jews with a way to look at and to live in the world. They
had been redeemed but they had also been slaves. Those who felt themselves in
a state of redemption needed to know that they had been slaves and to be
thankful to God who redeemed them. Those who saw themselves as enslaved
should remember that they had once been redeemed from slavery in Egypt. As
they had experienced a redemption once, so they would experience it again. In
innumerable situations, Jews could "remyth" or adapt the paradigm to include
their own situation.

Students of religion have noted that a single event within the calendar can
have an impact that remains through the rest of the year. Joachim Wach, for
example, observes:

> The integrating force of worship is revealed in the creation of transient or
> permanent organizational forms. . . . Festivals and pilgrimages are out-
> standing examples. . . . It can easily be imagined to what extent organiza-
> tions such as those mentioned are able to influence the religious moods and

attitudes of the worshipers gathered together for a special purpose and so *exert a strong influence on the religion as a whole.*[73]

It is not surprising that the Passover evening celebration has had this kind of impact upon Jews and has proved to be one of the most popular Jewish observances.[74] It contains a message that Jews have found meaningful, powerful, and appropriate to their needs. The words, actions, and protocol involve each individual in the experience and provide all participants with a respite from the normal structures of society and history. They thereby become receptive to mythic history and can find their place in the mythic paradigm. While many customs and liturgical texts have enriched the rite, the basic framework goes back to Mishnah Pesaḥim 10.

Appendix A

ROASTED MEAT OR SACRIFICES AFTER 70 C.E.?

THE PROBLEM

SEVERAL SCHOLARS HAVE ARGUED that Jews did not lose their attachment to the passover offering even after the destruction of the temple in 70 C.E. Jews either continued to offer the sacrifice or else roasted a whole lamb in accordance with biblical requirements (Ex. 12:8−9).[1] This argument shares my view concerning the central role of the temple (see chapter 1) and the essential need for the passover sacrifice (see chapter 2). It might seem to contradict, however, the thesis that Jews experienced a traumatic loss at the temple's destruction and that this situation accounts for the expansion of the Passover evening celebration in the Mishnah. In chapter 7 I briefly discussed the issue and suggested that evidence for this view actually attests to the seriousness of the religious problem to which the Mishnah responds. In this appendix I will review more extensively the relevant sources.

RABBINIC MATERIALS

Scholars frequently cite one or more of the following six rabbinic sources:

1. Mishnah Pesaḥim 4:4:

A place where they [= people] are accustomed to eat roasted meat (ṢLY) on the nights of Passover—they eat [it].
A place where they are accustomed not to eat [it]—they do not eat [it].

In chapter 7 I cited and discussed this passage; and as I pointed out, and as Gedalyahu Alon has already suggested,[2] the pericope assumes that some people might want to continue to eat roasted meat even without the sacrificial rite. This underscores the degree to which people felt the need to preserve whatever they could from the cultic celebration.

2. Mishnah Pesaḥim 7:2:

A. They do not roast the passover lamb (HPSḤ) on a [metal] spit or on a grill.

B. R. Ṣadoq says, A case concerning (M'ŚH B-): R. Gamaliel said to Tebi his servant, "Go and roast the passover lamb (HPSḤ) for us on the grill."

This passage treats the "roasting" prescribed in Exodus 12:8 and elsewhere. Clause A requires that the animal come into direct contact with the fire. Gamaliel's position in clause B can be interpreted in one of two ways. The narrative may represent an opinion opposing clause A, to the effect that a spit is permitted. In this case Gamaliel refers to an actual sacrifice or to an animal to be prepared exactly as the sacrifice is prepared. Alternatively, the story illustrates the principle in clause A. After the temple's destruction, Gamaliel wants to have an animal prepared in a manner similar to but not identical with the passover offering and as a consequence he requests that it be put on a grill. Only if the first rendering is correct and the reference is to Gamaliel the second and to an actual sacrifice would the text purport to describe a post-70 passover offering. Alon suggests that in light of the other traditions attributed to Gamaliel (including number 3 immediately following), one should assume that the passage does not refer to an actual sacrifice.[3]

3. Mishnah Beṣah 2:7 = Mishnah 'Eduyyot 3:11:

Moreover ('P) he said three things to be lenient [= Rabban Gamaliel, as stated in M. Beṣ. 2:6, took the lenient position in three matters],

They sweep behind the couches and they put spices on the fire on a festival and they prepare a kid roasted whole (GDY MQWLS) on the nights of Passover [in the manner prescribed for the passover offering, in Ex. 12:9].

And sages forbid [it].

The term (GDY) MQWLS provides one definition of the particular type of roasting required by Exodus 12:9, "Do not eat any of it raw . . . but roasted— head, legs, and entrails—over the fire." While rabbinic sources and modern scholars differ on the exact meaning of this word,[4] the passage is universally understood to refer to the preparation of a nonsacrificial lamb in the manner of the actual passover offering. Otherwise there would be no reason for the dispute with the sages. No one need assert that the passover sacrifice is roasted whole, for that is what the Bible states.

Gamaliel's present tradition accords with our understanding of Mishnah Pesaḥim 10:5, where Gamaliel requires an individual to verbalize and thus concentrate on the passover offering, the unleavened bread, and the bitter herbs. He thereby equates all three as essential elements of the rite.[5] Here, though, Gamaliel appears to express his interest in continuity by prescribing cooking procedures associated with the sacrifice. The editor of the Mishnah who cites the opposing position attributed to the sages—or who adds that attribution, implying that the teaching is the majority opinion—apparently believes that such an imitative act is inappropriate. The view attributed to Gamaliel, by contrast, accords with Mishnah Pesaḥim 10:3—which projects a viable procedure without the sacrifice and outside of the temple—and, in fact, accords with the impression made by Mishnah Pesaḥim 10 as a whole. If the tradition does originate with Gamaliel, it might reflect one way in which Jews sought to continue old practices soon after the destruction of the temple.

4. Tosefta Yom Ṭov 2:15, pp. 290−91, lines 56−62, which comments upon and adds to Mishnah Beṣah 2:7:

A. What is a "kid roasted whole" (GDY MQWLS)?
B. Completedly roasted, [with] its head, legs, and entrails.
C. [If] he boiled any part of it, steamed any part of it—this is not a kid roasted whole.
D. They prepare a kid roasted whole on [even the nights of][6] the first day of the Festival and on [even the nights of] the last day of Passover; [they prepare] a calf roasted whole ('GL MQWLS) on [even the nights of] the first day of Passover but not a kid roasted whole. [Since a calf never served as a passover offering, it—even roasted whole—could not be mistaken for that sacrifice.][7]
E. Said R. Yosah, Todos of Rome directed the Romans to take lambs (ṬL'YM) on the nights of Passover and they prepared them roasted whole.
They [= anonymous sages] said to him,
And he borders on feeding them holy things [of the Temple area] outside [the holy precincts], because they [= the Roman Jews] called them [= the lambs] "passover offerings" (PSHYN).

Clauses A−C provide one definition of the phrase "kid roasted whole" (GDY MQWLS).[8] Clauses B−C emphasize the point that the animal be completely roasted and not at all boiled or steamed.[9] Clause D treats the time when one is prohibited from preparing the kid in this manner. This clause contains several textual variants, which Saul Lieberman discusses. According to all readings, clause D apparently accords with the view of the sages in Mishnah Beṣah 2:7. The proscription prohibits only the roasting of a whole kid and only on Passover eve.[10]

The implication of clause E is clear, though it can be interpreted in one of two ways. Yosah's citation may explain the position of the sages in the Mishnah who dispute Gamaliel, or it may throw light on Gamaliel's view. Only non-Palestinians, here Roman Jews, would consider the roasted nonsacrificial lamb as a passover offering, and as a consequence only they would be prohibited from preparing an animal in that fashion. According to either rendering, clause E indicates that rabbinic circles believed, first, that the sacrifice was important and was considered so even by non-Palestinians, but that it could not be offered; and, second, that some Jews might interpret their present practices in cultic terms.[11]

5. Tosefta Ahilot 3:9, p. 600, lines 16−18:

A. A case concerning (M'ŚH B-): In Bet Daggan in Judah a person died on the eve of Passover and they [= the local people] went to bury him.
B. And the women entered and tied the rope to the rolling stone [at the end of the grave]. The men pulled from the outside and the women entered and buried him. And the men went and prepared their passover offerings (PSḤYHN) in the evening.

This passage was discussed in chapter 7. The men took special precautions to maintain their state of cleanness in order to prepare their passover lambs in the evening.[12] The simple meaning of the text is that some people outside of Jerusalem were believed to offer a passover sacrifice. Alon, however, suggests that this passage be interpreted in light of the other accounts and be seen as a reference to preparing a nonsacrificial passover lamb in the manner in which the sacrifice had been prepared.[13] Whether or not Alon is correct, the passage points to the presumed importance of the sacrifice.

6. Tosefta Ahilot 18:18, p. 617, lines 21−23:

A. A case concerning (M'ŚH B-): Rabbi and R. Ishmael the son of R. Yose and R. Eliezer Haqappar spent the Sabbath in the stall of Pazzi in Lud, and R. Pinḥas b. Ya'ir was sitting before them.
B. They said to him, Ashkelon—what do you rule concerning it?
C. He said to them, They sell wheat in their basilicas and they immerse themselves and eat their passover offerings (PSḤYHN) in the evening.

The passage forms part of a section on the ritual uncleanness of Gentile lands, dwellings, and at times colonnades. The dialogue in clauses B−C concerns the status of the city of Ashkelon. Some people conduct their business in the city's basilicas, then immediately bathe and eat their passover offerings. These individuals do not assume that they are unclean for seven days, as they would have if they considered Ashkelon a Gentile land.[14] This passage may be interpreted similarly to the previous one. Ostensibly it indicates that Ash-kelonites were believed to prepare passover offerings in a state of ritual cleanness, though it could be construed to refer to nonsacrificial animals prepared and eaten so as to resemble an actual sacrifice.

We can divide these six sources into three groups. Numbers 3−4 unequivocally indicate that certain rabbis believed that some Jews wished to prepare an animal to resemble the passover sacrifice. Numbers 1−2 can reasonably be interpreted in the same fashion. That does not, however, seem to be the sense of numbers 5−6, although they could conceivably be construed in the same way as the other sources. All six indicate, first, that rabbinic circles deemed the passover offering important, and, second, that they believed Jews at large shared in this sentiment and tried to preserve as many aspects of the sacrifice as possible. Considering the history of the sacrifice in Second Temple times, people would believe that the passover lamb would have to be offered in Jerusalem. Even K. W. Clark, who recently revived the view that a sacrificial cult continued after 70 C.E., agrees that it would have ceased by 135 when the city of Jerusalem and the temple mount became paganized. From the viewpoint of the Mishnah, which was edited toward the end of the second century, all Jews who venerated Jerusalem would have experienced the loss of the passover sacrificial rite. Mishnah Pesaḥim 10 reflects the same need found in the above six sources, though as Mishnah 10:3 indicates, it found a different solution to the crisis. The sacrificial rite was seen as one of two valid procedures from temple days. Without the temple one can continue the extratemple practice which lacked the sacrifice but included all the other essential ingredients.

NONRABBINIC SOURCES

Several first- and early second-century nonrabbinic works, especially Josephus, seem to describe a sacrificial rite still in effect, particularly the one for Passover. For example, in *Antiquities* 2:312, Josephus recounts the exodus and comments:

> He accordingly had the Hebrews ready betimes for departure and ranging them in fraternities kept them assembled together; then when the fourteenth day was come the whole body, in readiness to start, sacrificed, purified the houses with the blood, using the bunches of hyssop to sprinkle it, and after the repast burnt the remnants of the meal as persons on the eve of departure. *Hence comes it that to this day* we keep this sacrifice in the same customary manner, called the feast *Pascha*, which signifies "passing over," because on that day God passed over our people when he smote the Egyptians with plague.[15]

Do the words "to this day" mean that the practice was carried on after 70 C.E., even into the early 90s when Josephus wrote *Antiquities*? Use of the present tense in the accounts of Josephus and Christian writers may refer to contemporary practices, which would attest to the perceived importance of the temple cult, particularly the passover offering. Scholars who hold this view agree, however, that after the Bar Kokhba revolt the sacrificial rite would have ceased.[16]

It is equally plausible, however, that the above citation of Josephus and the other references did not refer to contemporary practices. Numerous sources reflect the end of the cult, and the use of the present tense can be easily explained. The revised edition of Emile Schürer, for example, suggests that these references "are merely describing what was lawful, not what was actually practised."[17] Similarly, E. Mary Smallwood comments:

> References after that date [70 C.E.] which appear to imply the continued observance of the cult are to be explained as ideal accounts of a procedure which it was hoped would some day be restored, rather than as realistic accounts of actual contemporary practices.[18]

Smallwood observes that the analogous reference in *Antiquities* 3:224–57 merely follows the text of Leviticus and Numbers which it paraphrases.[19] David Altshuler puts Josephus's practice of using indicative verbs for cultic matters into a larger context. They are intended as apologetics, meant to de-emphasize the importance of cultic matters. These practices are presented as "customs the Jews happen to observe." By contrast, when Josephus uses the imperative form of the verb, as in *Antiquities* 4, he presents the materials as "commands of God through Moses."[20]

CONCLUSIONS

Both the nonrabbinic and the rabbinic evidence reflect the importance attached to the passover sacrifice. Even if everything purported actually took place and referred to an actual sacrifice, my thesis would not be disproved. While the nonrabbinic sources are inconclusive, and the rabbinic testimony varied and somewhat ambiguous, the evidence agrees in attesting to the importance of the passover sacrifice and the need to find some continuity with it. In the body of this study I have demonstrated the alternative path taken by Mishnah Pesaḥim 10, which provided a rich and meaningful rite without the sacrifice, fulfilling the needs of Jews in the second century while maintaining a sense of continuity with the past.

Appendix B

THE HEBREW TEXTS OF
MISHNAH AND TOSEFTA
PESAḤIM 10

OR THE HEBREW TEXT of the Mishnah, I reproduce the Kaufmann MS, generally considered the best MS of the Mishnah. It is not perfect, however, and the attached notes indicate wherever its readings are inferior to those of other MSS. More extensive notes are found on the English translation, in chapter 3. I express my thanks to the Hungarian Academy of Sciences for providing me with photographs of this text. For the Hebrew text of the Tosefta, I reproduce the critical edition of Saul Lieberman, *The Tosefta, According to Codex Vienna, with Variants from Codices Erfurt, London, Genizah MSS. and Editio Princeps (Venice 1521) together with References to Parallel Passages in Talmudic Literature and A Brief Commentary.* Vol. 2 (New York: The Jewish Theological Seminary of America, 1962), pp. 196–199. I gratefully acknowledge the permission of the late Professor Saul Lieberman and the Jewish Theological Seminary to reproduce this selection.

i. MISHNAH PESAHIM 10

פי ו

ערב פסחים סמוך   10:1
למנחה לא יאכל אדם עד שתחשך
אפי' עני שבישרא' לא יאכל עד
שיסב לא יפחתו לו מארבע' כוסות
שלהן אפי' מן התמחוי ב מזגו   10:2
לו כוס ראשון בית שמיי א' מברך
על היום ואחר כך מברך על היין וב
ובית הלל או' מברך על היין ואחריך
מברך על היום   ג הביאו לפניו   10:3
מטבל בחזרת עד שהוא מגיע
לפרפרת הפת הביאו לפניו מצה
וחזרת וחרוסת את על פי שאין
חרוסת מצוה ר' לעזר בר' צדוק או'
מצוה ובמקדש מביאין לפניו [לפני]
שלפסח ד מזגו לו כוס שני   10:4
וכן הבן שואל אם אין בבן דעת אב'

(M.10:4 cont.)

1

מלמדין מה נשתנה הלילה הזה
מכל הלילות שבכל הלילות אנו
מטובלים אפילו פעם אחת הלילה
הזה שתי פעמים שבכל הלילות
אנו אוכלים חמץ ומצן הלילה
הזה כולו מצה שבכל הלילות אנו
אוכלים בשר צלי שלוק ומבושל
הלילה הזה סרוי צלי יפי רעתו שלבן
אביו מלמדו מתחיל בגנות ומסיים
בשבח ודורשיה מארמי אבד אבי
עד שהוא גומר כל הפרשה ה:

10:5

רבן גמליאל או כל שלא אמ שלושה
דברים ביו בפסח לא יצא ידי חובתו
פסח מצה ומרורים פסח על שפסח
המקום על בתי אבותינו במ׳ צריים
מרורים על שמרדם המצרייה את
חיי אבותינו במעמ מצה על שם
כי נאלו לפיבך אנחנו חייבים להודות
להלו לשבח לפאר לרומם לגדל לעי
שעשה לנו ולאבותינו את כל הניסים
האלו והוציאנו מעבדות לחירות

 נ׳אמר לפניו הליויה: ו עד אוכן

10:6

הוא אוביית שמי אומרים עד אב
הבנים שמחה ובית הלל עד חלמיש
למעינו מים וחותם בנאלה: ז: ר
טרפון זו אשר או נאלנו וגאלאת
אבותינו ימיצ והיצענו הלילה הזה
ואינו חותם ר עקיבה אם מ צינו
ל כי אבותינו יגיענו לתלים ובאים

3 לקראתם לשלות שמשיכבביריין עולם
לאוכלימן הפסחיה וגמן הזבחים אשר
ביבע דמה על קיר מזבח לרעון ומוה
לך על גאולתינו בר אתה יי גאל ישר

(10:6 cont.)

4 ח מזני לו כוס שלישי מכך צל
מזונ רביעי גומר את ההלל ואומ
עליו ברכת השיר בין הכוסות האילו
אם רצה לשתות ישתה בין הכוס שלישי
לרביעי לא ישתה אין מפטירין אחר

10:7

הפסח אפיקומין ישנו מקצתם יאכל
וכולם יאכלו וחצה לא יאכלו אם נתנמנמו

10:8

יאכלו ואם נרדמו לא יאכלו ט
הפסח אחר חצות מטמא את הידים
הפיגול והנותר מטמאים את הידים

10:9

5 בירך ברכת הפסח פטר את הזבח
את שלובח לא פטר את שלפסח דעיי
רי ישמעו ר עקיבה או לא וז פטרת
וו ולא וז פטרתה

חסל פסח פר י

ii. TOSEFTA PESAḤIM (PISḤA) 10

1. ערב פסחים סמוך למנחה לא יאכל אדם עד שתחשך. אפי׳ עני
שבישראל לא יאכל עד שיסב, ולא יפחתו לו מארבע כוסות של יין שיש בהן
כדי רביעית. בין חי, בין מזוג, בין חדש, בין ישן. ר׳ יהודה או׳ ובלבד שיהא
בו טעם יין ומראה.   2. מזגו לו כוס ראשון, בית שמיי או׳ מברך על היום
ואחר כך מברך על היין, שהיום גורם ליין שיבא, וכבר קדש היום ועדיין יין
לא בא. ובית הלל אום׳ מברך על היין ואחר כך מברך על היום, שהיין
גורם לקדושת היום שתאמר.   3. דבר אחר, ברכת היין תדירא וברכת
היום אינה תדירה. והלכה כדבריי בית הלל.   4. מצוה על אדם לשמח
בניו ובני ביתו ברגל. במה משמחן, ביין, דכת׳ ויין ישמח לבב
אנוש. ר׳ יהודה או׳ נשים בראוי להם, וקטנים בראוי להם.   5. השמש
מכביש בבני מעים ונותן לפני האורחין, אע״פ שאין ראיה לדבר זכר לדבר,
נירו לכם ניר ואל תזרעו אל קוצים.   6. המקרא את ההלל,
הם הולכין אצלו וקורין, והוא אין הולך אצלם.   7. המקרא את בניו
ובנותיו קטנים, צריך להיות עונה עמהן במקום שעונין. באי זה מקום הוא
עונה, הגיע לברוך הבא אומ׳ עמהן בשם ה׳, הגיע לברכונכם
אומ׳ עמהן מבית ה׳.   8. בני העיר שאין להן מי שיקרא את ההלל,
הולכין לבית הכנסת וקורין פרק ראשון, והולכין ואוכלין ושותין, וחוזרין
ובאין וגומרין את כולו, ואם אי איפשר להן, גומרין את כולו. ההלל אין
פוחתין ממנו ואין מוסיפין עליו.   9. ר׳ לעזר בן פרטא היה פושט בו
דברים, ר׳ היה כופל בו דברים. ר׳ לעזר אמ׳ חוטפין מצה לתינוקות,
בשביל שלא ישנו. ר׳ יהודה או׳ אפי׳ או׳ לא אכל אלא פרפרת אחת, אפי׳ לא
טבל אלא חזרת אחת, חוטפין מצה לתינוקות, בשביל שלא ישנו. עד היכן
הוא אומ׳, בית שמיי או׳ עד אם הבנים שמחה. ובית הלל או׳ עד
חלמיש למעינו מים, וחותם בגאולה. אמרו בית שמיי לבית הלל
25 וכי כבר יצאו שמזכירין יציאת מצרים, אמרו להם בית הלל אפילו הוא
ממתין עד קרות הגבר הרי אילו לא יצאו עד שש שעות ביום, היאך אומר
את הגאולה ועדין לא נגאלו. המצה, והחזרת, והחרוסת, אף על פי שאין
חרוסת מצוה, ר׳ לעזר בי ר׳ צדוק אומ׳ מצוה. במקדש מביאין לפניו גופו
של פסח.   10. מעשה ואמ׳ להם ר׳ לעזר בר׳ [צדוק] לתגרי לוד, בואו
וטלו לכם תבלי מצוה.   11. אין מפטירין אחר הפסח אפיקומן, כגון אגוזין,
תמרים, וקליות. חייב אדם לעסוק בהלכות הפסח כל הלילה, אפלו בינו
לבין בנו, אפלו בינו לבין עצמו, אפלו בינו לבין תלמידו.   12. מעשה
ברבן גמליאל וזקנים שהיו מסובין בבית ביתוס בן זונין בלוד, והיו עסוקין
בהלכות הפסח כל הלילה עד קרות הגבר, הגביהו מלפניהן, ונועדו והלכו
35 להן לבית המדרש.   13. אי זו היא ברכת הפסח, ברוך אשר קדשנו
במצותיו וצונו לוכל הפסח. אי זו היא ברכת הזבח, ברוך אשר קדשנו
במצותיו וצונו לוכל הזבח.

NOTES

1. Defining the Problem

1. The haggadah as a literary work is posttalmudic. On the date of the developed liturgy and the haggadah see, e.g., Kasher, pp. 17–19, esp. 26–30, 40, 48; Goldschmidt, passim, esp. 3, 8–9, 12, 13, 17, 19, 28, 34, 38, 39, 46–47, 70–72; Heinemann (1960–1961), pp. 405–410, esp. 406; *EnJ*, "Passover," by Louis Jacobs; Freedman, who enables one graphically to see how the haggadah draws upon and integrates the earlier rabbinic sources; and cp. Epstein (1957), pp. 57, 331, 333–334.

2. See Green (1978), Halivni (1979), and Neusner (1981), as well as Halivni, Gereboff (1979), Kanter, Porton (1976–1982), and cp. Epstein (1957), pp. 205–226. For examples of this approach in biblical studies, see Weinfeld for Deuteronomy; Japhet for Chronicles; and Conzelmann (1960) for Luke.

3. See Neusner (1981) and esp. Bokser (1981).

4. Ostow, p. 11.

5. See Bokser (1981); Ostow, pp. 15–16; and n. 35 below.

6. See Goldschmidt, Segal, Kasher, and Tabory, as well as the earlier study by Friedmann.

7. See Stein and the literature he cites; Plutarch, *Moralia: Table Talk*, vols. 8–9; *InDB*, "Banquet," and "Meals," by J. F. Ross; Barrow; Fischel (1975), pp. 69–70; and chap. 5 below.

8. See, e.g., Daube; Bahr; esp. Lietzmann, pp. 220–286, 494–509, 596–652, for an evaluation of the appropriateness of the comparison; Tabory, p. 1, and chap. 2 below, nn. 26–30 and text thereto.

9. See Alon, pp. 164–166; Safrai; and the earlier attempts by David Hoffmann, in Hoffmann, Hoffmann (1924), and Hoffmann (1972). See also Goldschmidt, pp. 51–52; Urbach (1961), p. 148; Davies (1964), pp. 269–270; and Tabory, passim, esp. pp. 229–250. See also Fredman, who does not purport to trace the history of the seder but notes that the seder constitutes a post-70 rite to replace the lost temple and passover sacrifice, and offers an anthropological interpretation of the ceremony.

10. See, e.g., Beer, Baneth, and Albeck.

11. See, e.g., Weinfeld, *EnJ*, "Deuteronomy," by Moshe Weinfeld; *InDBS*, "Leviticus," by Jacob Milgrom, and "Prophecy," by M. J. Buss; and Sarna.

12. Philo, *Special Laws*, 1:66–68, vol. 7, pp. 136–141, on which see Daniel ed., pp. L–LI, and chap. 2, n. 19 below. On the glorification of Jerusalem and the temple, see also (a) Aristeas nos. 83–120, Hadas ed., pp. 12–15, 142–164, and esp. 48–50; and Pelletier ed., pp. 143–163 and nn., esp. 142–143, n. 3, 160–161, n. 3, and 163, n. 5; (b) Philo the Elder, to which see Gutman (1954); Gutman, 1:221–244, esp. 224,

238–239, 244; *EnJ*, "Philo (The Elder)," by B. Z. Wacholder; and Hengel, 2:71, n. 352; and (c) Philo, *Embassy to Gaius*, #277–292, esp. 281–284, vol. 10, pp. 140–147. See also Cohn.

Concerning the existence of temples outside of Jerusalem, see Hengel, 1:100, 272–275, esp. 275, and cp. 2:181–82; and esp. Smallwood, pp. 367–368.

13. See, e.g., Heinemann (1964), pp. 17–28; Sarna; *EnJ*, "Mishmarot and Ma'amadot," by Daniel Sperber, and "Synagogue," by L. I. Rabinowitz; and esp. Shanks, pp. 17–30, 176–177 (n.b. 16–20), and 177, n. 10; Kraabel, pp. 502–503; Strange, pp. 656–657, 664; and Schürer, 2:292–293.

14. See, e.g., Talmon (1978); Haran (1979), pp. 182–185; Sarna, pp. 290–295; Kraabel, p. 502; and Strange, pp. 656–657, 664.

15. Sarna, p. 295.

16. See Greenberg, and Tigay.

17. See Sarna; Talmon (1978); and Wach, pp. 41–42. Note, for example, how the Wisdom of Ben Sira describes the centrality of the Temple sacrificial cult and includes prayers of individuals. Because of the distinction made in the text, historians of other religions frequently differentiate between the official or public religion and private or personal religion. See, e.g., Rice and Stambaugh concerning Greek religion. On the sociological differences between private and communal prayer see Heilman, esp. pp. 65–69, 129–149.

18. Heinemann (1964).

19. Talmon (1978), p. 269. See also chap. 2, nn. 8–10 and text thereto.

20. See chap. 2 below, nn. 31–36; and cp. Wach, pp. 141–145, esp. 154.

21. See, e.g., Neusner (1981).

22. Smallwood, p. 124; see also pp. 124–127, 133, 136, 140, 143, 192–193, 558–560, and cp. 371–376, 416, 476; Liver (1963), pp. 173–198; Cohn; and Turner (1974), who throws light on pilgrimage as a unifying force for far-flung members of a group. Cp. Stone, pp. 75–82, esp. 76, 81, for a slightly different evaluation of the ostensibly conflicting evidence concerning the centrality of the temple. On the whole problem, see Townsend (1981) for a review of the literature.

23. See above, text to nn. 3–5; Neusner (1972); and Schürer, 1:501–528.

24. Philo, *Special Laws*, 2:145–146, 148, vol. 7, pp. 394–397. On Philo see chap. 2, nn. 16–17.

25. See chap. 2 below, nn. 4–6 and text thereto.

26. See chap. 2 below, nn. 1–4, 8, and text thereto where I point out that an Aramaic papyrus from Elephantine mentions unleavened bread alone.

27. See Loewenstamm, p. 21; Fishbane, pp. 121–140; cp. Hoffmann (1972), pp. 2–3; and chap. 6 below, nn. 22–24 and text thereto.

28. See, e.g., Plutarch, 3:645B, 660A–C, vol. 8, pp. 200–201, 292–293, 7:697, 708C–D, vol. 9, pp. 4–7, 62–65; Douglas; and *IESS*, "Food, II. Consumption Patterns," by Yehudi A. Cohen, pp. 509, 510.

29. Douglas, pp. 269, 272.

30. See, e.g., Philo, *Special Laws*, 1:70, vol. 7, pp. 139–141, and *Questions and Answers on Exodus*, 1:3, Sup. 2:8–9, on which cp. Wach, p. 42; esp. Plutarch, 5:678C–679E, vol. 8, pp. 406–413; Durkheim, p. 381; Delcor; Talmon (1978), p. 296; Wach, esp. pp. 27–34, 39–42, 58–79, 92–97, 109–112 (n.b. 110), 182,

196–205; Heilman, esp. pp. 50–52, 253–260; Fredman, pp. 10, 151; and Turner (1974), pp. 46–47.

31. See the references in n. 7 above and in chap. 5, nn. 1–3; and Tabory, pp. 252–256.

32. See Talmon (1978), esp. p. 283; Jer. 16:5 and Porten, pp. 179–186 concerning a *marzeaḥ*, a feast or banquet at a house of mourning and hence a different type of gathering around a meal; and chap. 2 below, texts to nn. 1–2. On Isa. 30:29, see Luzzatto, ad loc., p. 358.

33. See nn. 20–21 above and chap. 6 below, nn. 14–28 and text thereto.

34. M. Pes. 10:1. On the significance see *IESS*, ''Food, II. Consumption Patterns,'' p. 508; and chap. 5 below, nn. 46–48 and text thereto.

35. See Lieberman *TK*, 1:62; Bokser (1980), pp. 39–40, 144–145 (n. 130), 261, 279–80 (n. 18), and references there; and cp. Luzzatto, p. 358, to Isa. 30:29.

36. Fischel (1977), pp. xix–xx, whose approach follows M. Smith. On the didactic use of questions and answers and the device of a parent instructing a child, see Fishbane, pp. 79–83, 147–148.

37. See Bokser (1981). For an indication of some of these developments concerning Passover, see chap. 4, nn. 11, 16–19, 24–25, 31, chap. 5, n. 56, chap. 6, nn. 10–16, and chap. 7, nn. 61–70, and texts thereto; and chap. 4, n. 14.

2. *Prerabbinic Descriptions of Passover*

1. See Kaufmann, 1/1–3:104, 115–116, 125–126, 213, 535, 544, 545, 575–579, 2/4–5:487; Noth, pp. 87–102; Segal; Ringgren, pp. 186–188; *EnM*, ''MRWR'' and ''PSḤ,'' by Jacob Licht; *EnJ*, ''Passover,'' by Louis Jacobs and Ernst Kutsch; Loewenstamm; Weinfeld, pp. 216–217; Carmichael, pp. 89–94, 129; Childs, pp. 178–214, esp. 187, 191, 194, 197–198, 200, 204–206; Epstein (1957), pp. 323–331; *InDBS*, ''Exodus, Book of,'' by R. E. Clements; Haran, pp. 294, 317–348; Wambacq; Wambacq (1980); and note the observations of Bloch, pp. 137, 140. Segal; *EnM*, ''PSḤ''; and esp. Childs cite and evaluate the earlier literature.

2. See Segal, pp. 22–23, 231, 240, esp. 233, and cp. 163–165; Lauterbach, esp. pp. 239–241; esp. Le Déaut (1963), pp. 179–184; Loewenstamm, pp. 84–88, esp. 88; Weinfeld, pp. 216–217; and Childs, p. 207, n. to Ex. 12:46. Cp. Kaufmann 1/1–3:547, 573–574, 585; and Morgenstern. For a clear statement concerning the notion behind the apotropaic rule not to break the bone see Meyers, pp. 3, 12–14, 91–92.

3. Later sources refer to regular ceremonies for the first fruits of other harvests. See Baumgarten; and Yadin, 1:81–99.

4. See Segal, pp. 10–19, 225–230; Talmon, pp. 58–74; esp. Petersen, pp. 60–96; *EnJ*, ''Chronicles, Book of,'' by S. Japhet; Japhet, pp. 212–217, 253–254, 281–282, 354–355, 370–371; and Schürer, 2:254–256 and nn.

5. See Werner (1957), esp. pp. 28–32; Bayer; *EnM*, ''Neginah UZimrah,'' by Bathja Bayer; esp. Liver, pp. ix–x, 53–54, 64–72, esp. 66–67, 69–70, 71–72, 90–95; *EnJ*, ''Music,'' by Bathja Bayer and Hanoch Avenary, 12: 557, 559–566, 571; and Schürer, 2:254, n. 58, 288–290, 303–304 and nn., esp. n. 41. Cp. Büchler, pp. 94–118. See, in particular, The Wisdom of Solomon, 10:18–20, 18:8–9;

Winston, pp. 222, 316; text to n. 14 below; immediately below concerning Jubilees; and Philo, *Contemplative Life*, nos. 86−87, vol. 9, pp. 166−167, on which see Winston (1981), n. 45.

Concerning the use of Exodus 15 on the seventh day of Passover, see Muilenburg; Childs, pp. 245, 250; and n. 14 below and text thereto.

6. The cited translations are from Charles, pp. 1−82. See Segal, pp. 22−23, 231−240, esp. 233, and the other references in n. 2.

7. See Segal, pp. 23−25, 233, n. 4; Gutman, 2:51−54, 66−69; 151, esp. 54 (concerning the significance of the focus on sacrifices); *EnJ*, "Ezekiel the Poet," by M. S. Hurwitz; and Jacobson, pp. 121−136.

8. See Segal, pp. 8−10, 221−224; Porten, pp. 122−124, 128−133, 276−277, 279−282, 286, and 331−333 (for a new transcription with plates, of the papyrus). The ostraca are cited on pp. 131−132.

9. See Montgomery, pp. 37−40; Jeremias (1932); and Talmon (1977).

10. See esp. Talmon (1977).

11. See the index of verses in Fitzmyer, pp. 152−170.

12. See De Vaux (1973), pp. 12−16; and Schiffman (1979), pp. 46−49; and Baumgarten (1953).

13. See Yadin, 1:79−81, 2:54−55, esp. n. to l. 7; and, on the provenance of the scroll, cp. Schiffman (1979), p. 49, n. 21, and Baruch A. Levine, in Neusner (1980), pp. xvii−xx.

14. See Winston, pp. 20−25, and esp. 316, for a suggested emendation of the verse which would make it refer also to "joy"; and n. 5 above.

15. See Winston (1981), Introduction, for a critical statement and bibliographical references on Philo's method and relationship to the Bible and contemporary philosophy; and chap. 5 below, n. 29 and text thereto.

16. Philo, *Decalogue*, no. 159, vol. 7, pp. 84−87; *Special Laws*, 2:163−169, vol. 7, pp. 406−411; *Moses*, 2:224, vol. 6, pp. 560−561; and the passage quoted in chap. 1, to n. 24. Cp. Philo's description of the Therapeutae, who act as priests throughout their lives, *Contemplative Life*, nos. 10−39, esp. 74, vol. 9, pp. 118−137, esp. 158−159; and see chap. 5, nn. 19−21, 29, and text thereto.

17. *Special Laws*, 2:148, vol. 7, pp. 396−397. See also chap. 1, text to n. 24; and Philo, *Questions and Answers on Exodus*, 1:10, Sup. vol. 2, pp. 18−20.

18. See *Special Laws*, 2:146, vol. 7, pp. 396−397.

19. See ibid., 2:193−194, vol. 7, pp. 426−428 (concerning the Day of Atonement); *Cherubim*, nos. 91−97, vol. 2, pp. 62−69; *Moses*, 2:23−24, vol. 6, pp. 460−461; *Contemplative Life*, nos. 40−90, esp. 56, 58, 63−64, vol. 9, pp. 136−169, esp. 146−147, 150−151; and chap. 5 below, nn. 22−25, and esp. 29, and text thereto.

20. See *Questions and Answers on Exodus*, 1:1−23, Sup. vol. 2, pp. 2−34; *Special Laws*, 2:150−155, vol. 7, pp. 396−401; *Preliminary Studies*, nos. 161−162, vol. 4, pp. 541−543; *Sacrifices of Abel and Cain*, nos. 62−63, vol. 2, pp. 140−143; *Allegorical Interpretation*, 3:154, vol. 1, pp. 404−405.

21. *Moses*, 2:224−232, vol. 6, pp. 560−565; quotation from nos. 232, 233, vol. 6, pp. 564−565.

22. See, e.g., Scholem, pp. 34−35; and esp. Goldin (1965), pp. 282−284, in part quoted in chap. 7 below, n. 9.

23. See Josephus, *Wars*, 2:10, 224, 280 (vol. 2, pp. 326–327, 410–411, 432–433), 4:402 (vol. 3, pp. 116–117), 5:99–100 (vol. 3, pp. 229–231), 6:421–434 (vol. 3, pp. 496–501); *Antiquities*, 2:312–313 (vol. 4, pp. 300–303), 3:248–251 (vol. 4, pp. 436–439), 9:263–272 (vol. 6, pp. 138–145), 10:70–72 (vol. 6, pp. 194–197), 11:109–111 (vol. 6, pp. 366–369), 17:213–215 (vol. 8, pp. 470–473), 18:29–30, 90 (vol. 9, pp. 24–27, 64–65), 20:105–112 (vol. 9, pp. 446–469). See Thackeray, in his edition of Josephus, vol. 3, p. 118, n. a; and *Antiquities*, Shalit ed., vol. 2, note pp. 55 (n. 146), 71–72 (n. 177); Chenderlin, pp. 373–375, 386–390, 392–393; and Appendix below, for a discussion of Josephus' usage.

24. Vol. 3, pp. 498–499.

25. See *TDNT*, "Paska," by J. Jeremias; and esp. Childs, pp. 207–214, for a discussion of the different usages and bibliographical references. See also the works cited in nn. 26–31 below.

26. For the Last Supper see: Mark 14:1–52; Matt. 26:1–46, Luke 22:1–53; John 11:55, 12:1, 13:1–38. Some other references include: Luke 2:41–43; John 18:39, 19:14. See also Segal, p. 241; Le Déaut (1963), pp. 178, 200–208, 307–338, 374–375; and *RAnC*, "Eulogia," by A. Stuiber, esp. cols. 912–914. For references to the Primitive Church's celebration of a Christian Passover feast, see *TDNT*, "Paska," pp. 901–904.

27. See, in particular, Mark 14:12, 14, 16, 24; Matt. 26:17, 19, 26:28; Luke 22:1, 7, 8, 11, 13, 15. Jeremias, pp. 15–88, esp. 41–62, and Higgins lay out these and additional elements analogous to the Passover meal. See also *TDNT*, "Paska," esp. pp. 899–900; Daube, pp. 163–169, 186–195, 278–284, 330–335, 413–415, 434–436, esp. 192–195; and Petuchowski.

28. Conzelmann, p. 52.

29. Lietzmann, pp. 172–187, and Richardson, in Lietzmann, pp. 220–286, 494–509, have extensively argued for the secondary nature of the identification. See also Conzelmann, pp. 51–53, 76–77; Segal, pp. 33–37, 241–247; Davies (1964), pp. 59, 83–84; and, in general, *InDB*, "The Agape," "Eucharist," and "Lord's Supper," by M. H. Shepherd. For a discussion concerning the chronological problems and bibliographical references, see Fitzmyer, pp. 134–137, and Chenderlin, pp. 369–393.

Those who claim that the Passover interpretation of the Last Supper is secondary suggest alternative origins for the notion that Jesus' death was a saving event. See Le Déaut; Vermes (1973), pp. 219–227; and esp. Williams, pp. 1–56, esp. 203–254. See also below.

30. See, e.g., references to Lietzmann, Conzelmann, and Williams in n. 29. As Williams puts it: "Nevertheless the most that Jeremias can demonstrate is that the last supper *could* have been a Passover meal; the sources themselves, by their very nature, cannot yield positive proof that what could have been actually did occur"; p. 210. See also Raphael, pp. 82–85, for a brief but incisive analysis of the NT materials.

31. See also 1 Peter 1:13–21, esp. 19; John 1:29, 36; Davies, pp. 230–284, esp. 242–253; Neusner (1980), pp. 35–44; Melito, in Hall (1979), Introduction and notes, esp. pp. xxvi–xxvii, xliv; Perler, pp. 32–42; the references to Justin Martyr and Origen, nn. 36, 38 below. For additional patristic sources see Lietzmann; *TDNT*, "Paska," pp. 900–901; and Childs, pp. 209–211, 212–214; and esp. Lampe, s.v. *paska*, pp. 1046–1050, esp. entries C.1 and D. See also Lieberman (1946), pp. 332–

334; Zeitlin, pp. 444–449, 458–460; and Chadwick, pp. 84–85, 258–259.

32. Scholars point to actual parallels with the structure and language of M. 10:5. See Hall (1979), pp. xxvi–xxvii, 23 (n. 12), 35 (n. 32), 37 (n. 34), 45 (nn. 47–48), 51 (n. 53), and the references there, esp. Werner, to which add: Flusser, Pines, pp. 173–179. Pines, though, did not employ manuscripts of the Mishnah, and his comments should be compared to Cross, Hall, and Hall (1979). Cp. Childs, p. 210.

33. L. 1, Hall (1979), pp. 2–3.

34. L. 33, ibid., pp. 16–17. In general see Johnson, pp. 135–137.

35. Ll. 44, 46–47, Hall (1979), pp. 22–25.

36. Justin Martyr, *Dialogue with Trypho*, chap. 40, Falls, pp. 208–209. See Guéraud and Nautin, pp. 122–123.

37. See Hall (1979), p. 23, n. 11.

38. Justin Martyr, *Dialogue with Trypho*, chap. 46, Falls, p. 216. See Stylianopoulos, pp. 119–120. On Origen, see De Lange, pp. 94–95, 190, n. 30, which refers to *In Rom*. 2, 13 (*PG* XIV. 906–907) and fr. X (*JTS* 13 [1911–1912]:217–218). While Origen makes the polemical argument, he does not see the Passover account and the sacrifice as an allegorical prefiguration of the Passion. See Origen, *On Pascha*; Pagels; and Guéraud and Nautin, esp. pp. 112–113, 120–122, 137.

3. *Mishnah and Tosefta Pesaḥim 10*

1. On the date of the developed seder see chap. 1, n. 1.

2. See Rabbinovicz, p. 306, n. 1; Lieberman *TK*, 4:647, 510–511, 548; Lieberman, *The Tosefta*, 1:25, l. 1, Brief Commentary to T. Ber. 5:1. Usage elsewhere confirms that clause A closes with the word "dark" and B opens with "even a poor." See T. 10:1; M. Ket. 4:4, T. Pe'ah 2:3, p. 48, l. 26; T. Ket. 6:7, p. 77, ll. 27–28 (to which see Lieberman *TK*, 6:280); *Talmud Bavli. Masekhet Ketubot*, Hershler ed., 1:342–343, esp. nn. 21–22, 352–353; Halivni, 1:190, n. 3; and cp. Friedmann, pp. 15–16. Sarfatti (1976) astutely suggests that we follow K, P, and other manuscripts of the Mishnah that read "on the eve of passovers," meaning, on the eve when passover offerings are sacrificed, a phraseology fitting Second Temple realities when the fourteenth of Nisan was considered a distinct and special day. On the time element see chap. 4, nn. 3–7 below and text thereto.

3. See chap. 5, nn. 9, 46–48, and text thereto.

4. See chap. 4, nn. 29–32, and chap. 5, nn. 49–56, and texts thereto.

5. See Lieberman *TK*, 1:90, and 6:469, and, on the wine, n. 4 above.

6. The K, C, P, and Paris MSS and the Naples and Unk editions contain this reading, without the phrase "greens and lettuce," YRQWT WHZRT, which is a later gloss. See Rabbinovicz, p. 355, n. 5. One may find a clue to our usage in T. Ber. 4:8, which describes the customs of a meal and states, "They poured for them . . . they served them the bread condiment." M. Pes. 10:3 may employ or be patterned after this formulation and may interpolate what is appropriate to its context, viz. a first "dipping" prior to the regular appetizer. Clause A of the Mishnah serves to specify not what is brought but rather an action, "dipping," that occurs. Cp. Halivni (1981), p. 70; Nissim, s.v. HBY'W; Albeck, 2:455; Goldberg, p. 345; and esp. Safrai, pp. 305–306.

7. The K, P [text, in contrast to the margin which contains a gloss], and C MSS, the

Naples edition and the L MS to PT lack the phrase "and two cooked foods," found in later printed texts. This addition breaks the balance between two sets of clauses: First, in A, "they served . . . lettuce," and in B, "They served . . . *haroset*"; and, second, in A, "before . . . condiment," and in B, "even . . . *miṣvah*." Furthermore, it breaks the literary form used for a dispute, here between the anonymous authority and R. Eleazar b. Ṣadoq. See T. Pes. 10:9, p. 198, ll. 27–28; below, chap. 4, text to n. 19, and chap. 7, text to n. 61; Rabbinovicz, p. 355, n. 6; Lieberman *TK*, 4:654, and esp. Goldberg, p. 345, n. 9; and cp. Baneth, p. 241, n. 16.

8. See n. 7, and in general, chap. 4, nn. 8–9, below and text thereto.

9. The K, C, and P MSS, the UnK edition, and the L MS to PT lack the word "used to," HYW, found only in the Paris MS and the Naples and Ven BT editions. See T. Pes. 10:9, p. 198, ll. 28–29; Rabbinovicz, p. 355, n. 7; Friedmann, p. 36; and esp. Lieberman *TK*, 4:654; and below, chap. 4, n. 9 and text thereto; chap. 7, text to n. 61. While Safrai (1965) recognized this reading, at p. 209, n. 111, he disregards it, at p. 238, and in Safrai, p. 304. On the term for "the Temple" or "holy precincts," MQDŠ, see Milgrom, pp. 23–24, n. 72.

10. On the formulation of this clause and in general on the adoption of the biblical pedagogic device, see chap. 1, n. 36, chap. 4, nn. 12–14, and chap. 6, nn. 1–9, and texts thereto.

11. Numerous changes have been introduced into the Mishnah to adapt it to revisions and additions to the text and number of the questions. See Goldschmidt, pp. 10–13; and n. 10 above. The reference, in D.3, to roasting may be to the custom to roast a nonsacrificial animal in imitation of the roasted passover offering now no longer available. See chap. 4, n. 17, and Appendix A. On the three ways of preparing the meat, see T. Ned. 6:1, p. 107, l. 1, and on "steamed," see Lieberman *TK*, 1:446, n. 60, 4:577–578, esp. n. 15. See also Halivni (1981), pp. 70–74.

12. See chap. 6, nn. 17–21, and text thereto.

13. In A, the reading "said," with the word HYH, literally, "used to say," follows the printed editions, the P MS, the Naples and Unk editions, the L MS to PT, and the Columbia MS to BT. "Says" is found in the K, C, Paris, and Y MSS. See Goldschmidt, p. 125, variant to haggadah, and Kanter, pp. 236–237.

The order of C. 1, 2, 3 follows the K, C, P, Paris, and Y MSS and the text of the Naples edition and the L MS to PT. The end of C.3 provides the justification for D, as demonstrated below, chap. 4, nn. 18, 20–26, esp. 26, and texts thereto. Late texts of the Mishnah and the Gemara place C.2 after C.3, and after C.3 interpolate a clause that explicitly bids a person to empathize with the redemption and which relates to C.2 or C.3. In the L MS to PT, the interpolation appears as an actual marginal gloss. The version in the Naples edition is: "In every generation a person is required to regard himself as if he went out from Egypt, as it is said, 'And you shall tell your child on that day saying, "Because of that which the LORD did for me when I came out of Egypt." ' " This text may have been generated from the liturgy, as it is found in the haggadah (Goldschmidt, p. 125). Cp. the reading in the Unk edition, which has the correct order of C.1, 2, 3 but which includes the addition. See Solomon Haedani and Heller, in Vilna editions of the Mishnah, ad loc.; Friedmann, p. 58; Rabbinovicz, p. 362, n. 7; esp. Goldschmidt, pp. 53–54; and chap. 7, nn. 32–34 below and text thereto.

MSS and early editions vary in the text of clause D.

First, some include additional terms of praise and other contrasting conditions besides "slavery to freedom." Those familiar with the Homily of Melito of Sardis have pointed to apparent parallels between these "opposites" in the Mishnah and in the Homily. See chap. 2, nn. 32−35. If Melito employed a liturgical text of Passover eve, his Homily would attest the additional clauses in the Mishnah. But it is difficult in liturgical texts to distinguish between additions and original clauses, especially when the items comprise stereotyped phrases, as in this case.

Second, some texts, including the K MS and the Columbia MS to BT, read "who did for us and for our ancestors all these miracles." But the C, P, Paris, and Y MSS and the L MS to PT read "who did for us all these miracles," without mention of the "ancestors." Some texts, such as the Naples edition, have both clauses but reverse the order: "for our ancestors and for us." This movement may reflect the fact that the second reference is not original. See also Goldschmidt, pp. 54, and 126, variants to the haggadah text.

On the purpose of Gamaliel's teaching and the significance of the symbolic interpretations in clause C, see also chap. 4, nn. 15−19 and chap. 7, nn. 8−10, and texts thereto. The explanation of unleavened bread in C.3 has posed some difficulty, and the haggadah provides a different interpretation based on Ex. 12:39 and Deut. 16:3, viz., we eat unleavened bread because the Israelites in their haste to leave Egypt did not have time for their bread to rise (Goldschmidt, p. 125). The Mishnah's explanation may be similar to the thought in Ezekiel the Greek Poet, ll. 189−190, as set out by Jacobson, pp. 128−129. He points out that "in Greco-Jewish, Rabbinic and New Testament texts leaven is commonly used allegorically of that which is evil or impure." In Ezekiel the meaning is: "do not eat leaven, for God is now giving you release from your troubles. That is, . . . you should refrain from eating it, as a sign of your present deliverance." See I Cor. 5:6−8; Matt. 16:11−12; *TDNT*, "Zumē," 2:905 (references to Plutarch); and cp. Tabory (1981), pp. 72−77.

14. On the meaning of the term "redemption" and the relationship of clause C to D, see Albeck, 2:456; Lieberman *TK*, 4:654; Goldschmidt, p. 56, esp. n. 20; Heinemann (1960−61), p. 409; Gereboff (1979), pp. 48−49; and Halivni, 3:990−992, which suggests that the phrase "and [he] does not seal" was added after Tarfon, perhaps on the basis of M. Ber. 1:4, to accentuate the difference between Tarfon and Aqiva and below, chap. 4, text to n. 26, and chap. 6, nn. 22−26 and text thereto. The extra clause in D, "to eat . . . herbs," is found in the C, Paris, and Y MSS, the Unk and Naples editions, and the L MS to PT but not in the K and P MSS. (See also Rabbinovicz, p. 363, n. 20/30.) While the extra language appears to be an expansion, see Gereboff (1979), pp. 48−49, for reasons to consider it original.

15. So the C, P, and Paris MSS and the L MS to PT, with slight variations among the readings.

16. On the theme of Hallel in this Mishnah, see n. 18. On the relationship of D to E, see the references in n. 14. In addition to the clause cited in n. 15, MSS contain several other variants.

17. The variation in the tense of the second verb results in different constructions of clauses A−B. The first reading, the participle form, MBRK, is in the P and Paris MSS, the Unk and Naples editions, the L MS to PT, and essentially the Y MS (which has BRK with the prefix M added above, slightly to the right of the B). The second reading, the

conjunction + past tense, is represented by WBYRK, in the K MS, and WBRK, in the C MS. As Tabory points out (pp. 218–220), where both verbs are in the past tense, as in A, they generally belong to the protasis and precede the apodosis, here in B. (Cp., however, M. 10:9.) While he believes the word "the fourth [cup]" is interpolated, it may be original to the Mishnah, an elliptical continuation and close of the protasis. Since the "four cups" are mentioned in M. 10:1, we should not consider the mention of the fourth cup in M. 10:7 as postmishnaic; indeed it is appropriate for it to be mentioned. While one may speculate on the prehistory of the tradition, we should consider the reference an original part of the Mishnah's text. On the four cups, see chap. 5, nn. 49–56 and text thereto.

The Naples edition, in A, adds to the object of the second verb an anticipatory objective pronoun and a word in construct form with "his food": "[over] it the blessing of [his food]." This apparently has been generated by attraction of the similar phrase in clause B, "he says over it the blessing over the song." But there the verb is "says" (W'WMR) and not "say a blessing" (WMBRK); hence here it is awkward and redundant. See chap. 4, n. 49; and cp. M. 10:9.

18. On the identification of the "blessing over the song," see Meiri, pp. 250–251; Friedmann, pp. 65–70; Kasher, pp. 181–183; Goldschmidt, pp. 64–68; Elbogen, pp. 64–65, 86–87, 413–414, n. 3, and the reference there to Wieder, esp. pp. 69–70; esp. Heinemann (1960–61), pp. 107–108; Tabory, pp. 218–219, 226; Hoffman, pp. 120–122; and Halivni, 3:996–997. See also chap. 4, text to n. 27 below.

Tabory, pp. 207, 212–215, has a novel and brilliant (but I believe incorrect) interpretation of clause B. He suggests that the Hallel is referred to first not in M. 10:6 but here, in M. 10:7B. He bases this primarily on the usage of the Hebrew word GWMR, which we have translated as "finishes," and which he claims must be rendered simply as "to say" or "to recite." His motivation is that we should not understand the word according to its amoraic usage. He is correct that GWMR is later used to denote saying the complete Hallel—in contrast to the abbreviated version—and that these two types of recitations are known only in amoraic Babylonian sources, not in tannaitic sources (see Lieberman *TK*, 4:651–652, 872). But this is beside the point. The word GWMR is used here not in its amoraic sense of saying the complete text of Hallel but in the sense of finishing something started earlier—earlier in the celebration, as prescribed in M. 10:6. First, contra Tabory, it is reasonable to assume that the Houses in M. 10:6 deal with the Hallel. Hallel is mentioned at the close of M. 10:5. Moreover, the Tosefta places its citation and expansion of the Houses' dispute in M. 10:6 at T. 10:9C—after it mentions and treats details of the Hallel in T. 10:6, 9A and 9B. Second, T. 10:8, p. 197, line 18 provides an exact parallel to the Mishnah's usage of GWMR: Those who go to the house of assembly to read the first portion of Hallel, go home to eat and drink, and then "return and finish the Hallel." (The second instance of GWMR at l. 18 can be explained in terms of the context and the attraction of the first instance; see Lieberman *TK*, 4:651.)

19. See chap. 5, nn. 60–61 and text thereto.

20. See the usage of MPTYRYN in M. Meg. 4:1, 2, 10; Baneth, p. 256, n. 72; and the discussion in chap. 5, n. 62 below and text thereto.

21. See chap. 4, nn. 37–38 and text thereto.

22. *Piggul* is an offering prepared with the intention of eating it after its proper time. *Notar* is food left over after its proper time. Clause A makes use of the rule concerning

imparting uncleanness to hands in order to prevent the undesired result of an individual eating the offering after midnight. See Leiman, pp. 102–120, and chap. 4, n. 38 below.

23. See: on B–C, chap. 4, nn. 34, 40 below and texts thereto; and on A–C, chap. 4, text to n. 28.

24. I use the abbreviation Erf to denote the Erfurt MS, as cited in Lieberman's text.

25. See M. 10:1; chap. 5, nn. 46–48, esp. 52–54, and texts thereto.

26. See M. 10:2.

27. See chap. 4, nn. 29–32 and text thereto; and chap. 5, nn. 55–56, and text thereto.

28. For the word translated as "townspeople," see Kutscher, pp. 19–20; Bendavid, 1:18–19; and M. Qid. 2:3 and T. Qid. 2:2, p. 282, ll. 4–6. On B, see chap. 6, n. 7 and text thereto. On "finishing" the Hallel, see n. 18 above.

29. See Pardo, loc. cit.; Lieberman TK, 4:654; and chap. 5, n. 62 below.

30. See M. 10:6.

31. See M. 10:3.

32. See M. 10:8; and, on the definition of afiqimon, chap. 5, n. 62, and Lieberman TK, 1:57–58.

33. See: on B–D, chap. 6, nn. 10–16 and text thereto; on the removal of the table (which is portable), Lieberman TK, 4:656, Zevulun and Olenik, pp. 10–11, 10*, and Tabory (1979), esp. p. 212.

34. See M. 10:9.

4. The Mishnah's Response

1. Some scholars suggest that Jews continued to offer a passover sacrifice until the beginning of the second century. Their argument is not convincing. See Appendix A.

2. For how this accords with the Mishnah's overall characteristics, see chap. 1, text to nn. 3–5.

3. See chap. 2 and in particular: Gutman, pp. 52, 151; Jubilees 49:12, on which see Charles, p. 80; Temple Scroll 17:8, on which see Yadin, 1:80; Philo, Special Laws, 2:145, vol. 7, pp. 394–395, on which see p. 627 and Daniel ed. p. 319, n. 5. The different expressions—"that same night," "in the evening," and "at sundown"— undoubtedly contributed to the formation of the several positions.

The medieval rabbinic commentaries noticed the synchronization, and Lieberman has elucidated it. See, e.g., Tosafot to b. Pes. 99b, s.v. ʿD ŠTHŠK and to b. Zev. 57b, s.v. WʾYBʿYT . . . ; Tosefot R. Judah Sir Leon, to b. Ber. 27a, vol. 1, pp. 318–319; esp. Meiri to b. Ber. 9a; Heller and Solomon Haedani to M. Pes. 10:1; and Lieberman TK, 4:509–511, 600–601. See also n. 4.

4. See Lieberman TK, 4:509–511; and below. On the issue of the "evening," see Jeremias (1932), pp. 78–86; Epstein (1957), pp. 327–330; Albeck, pp. 138–139; Kasher, pp. 151–154; and Chenderlin, pp. 369–393, esp. 370–373.

The time to slaughter and eat the sacrifice is subject to discussion in other early rabbinic sources. See, e.g., Mekilta Ba, chap. 5, chap. 6, pp. 18, ll. 1–3, and 19, ll. 1–8, Lauterbach ed. 1:43, 45–56; Mekilta DRŠBY to Ex. 12:8, p. 13; M. Zev. 5:8; Sifra Emor, chap. 11.1, p. 100b; Sifre Deut. sec. 133, p. 190; and Midrash Tannaʾim to Deut. 16:6, p. 92.

On the Mishnah cp. Baneth, p. 237, n. 5.

5. Lieberman *TK*, 4:510. But cp. the analysis in the text to n. 10 below.

6. See Lieberman *TK*, 4:511, 600—601. The word "them" refers to the three items in A, for D more appropriately glosses a general rule than a report of a master's action, C. Moreover, C may be an interpolation, for it is not directly connected to D, and elsewhere it circulates independently. It probably originated in the context of a verse. See Neusner (1971), 1:212—213, 231, 245, 257—258 (to which see Rabbinovicz to b. Pes. 115a, and Lieberman *TK*, 4:510, n. 92), 265, 280—281, 298.

7. The third item, "the passover offering," is missing in the London MS.

8. On the text of this Mishnah, see chap. 3, nn. 6—9.

9. See chap. 3, n. 9; chap. 7, nn. 43, 61, and text thereto; and Lieberman *TK*, 4:654. Lieberman's understanding of the clause is supported by the usage elsewhere in the Mishnah and the Tosefta, e.g., M. Tamid 7:2 and M. Sot. 7:6. See also M. Sot. 5:5; M. Eruv. 10:11—15; M. Hag. 3:8; M. Bekr. 6:2; and cp. M. Sheq. 1:3 and M. Yoma 2:3. In addition note the usage of BMQDŠ without HYW to contrast Temple practices with the present ones, especially when the latter continue the former in new ways. See M. R.H. 4:1, 3 (actions attributed to R. Yoḥanan ben Zakkai); and cp. M. Git. 5:4, M. San 9:6, and T. Ber. 6:22, p. 39, ll. 101—102. Note also the usage of WBMQDŠ, with the conjunctive prefix W-, to contrast two practices, e.g., M. Sot. 7:6. See Kosovsky, p. 1562, and Kosovsky (1932—1961), 6:84—85, and in general Albeck, 2:489—490, and 3:387. On the Mishnah's use of the present tense and narrative style to describe actions, see Neusner (1974—1977), vol. 21; Neusner (1980), pp. 202—207; Neusner (1981), chap. 3; and esp. chap. 7 below, text to nn. 27—44. Cp. Baneth, p. 241, n. 19.

10. See nn. 4—7 above, esp. n. 7. The baraita is also cited in b. Pes. 120a. See as well Sifra Emor, chap. 11.4, p. 100b, and Maimonides, *Mishneh Torah, Ḥameṣ*, 6:1.

11. The exposition also reflects the character of that part of Midrash designed to find biblical support for later practices and notions and to indicate that logic alone is not sufficient to derive them. See Neusner (1974—1977), 7:187—231, and Bokser (1980), pp. 456—457, n. 67.

12. Support for this interpretation of the verse comes from several quarters in addition to the context. It is reflected in the practice of the Samaritans, in the accounts of Ezekiel the Poet, Philo, and Josephus, and in the biblical exegesis of Abraham ibn Ezra (twelfth century). For the Samaritans, see chap. 2, n. 9. Jeremias (1932), pp. 49—51, 89—96, esp. 96—110, and Stein, p. 14; for Ezekiel the Poet, see chap. 2, n. 7 and text thereto; for Philo, see *Sacrifice of Abel and Cain*, no. 63, vol. 2, pp. 140—43, the references in chap. 2, n. 20, and in general *Special Laws*, 2:145—148, vol. 7, pp. 394—397; for Josephus, see *Antiquities* 2:312—313, vol. 4, pp. 300—301, where he drops the question and employs the answer as an explanation for the several procedures; for ibn Ezra, see commentary to Ex. 12:24 and 26. Cp. Naḥmanides to Ex. 12:24, vol. 1, p. 335. See also Mekilta DRŠBY to Ex. 12:26, p. 26, ll. 20—22.

13. See chap. 3, nn. 10—12, and chap. 7, text to n. 62, esp. concerning substitutions, additions, and other changes in the questions. See Harris, on the importance of questions, and Fishbane, pp. 79—83, 147—148, on the pedagogic dimension.

14. Alon suggests that the reference to "roasted [meat]" refers to a nonsacrificial animal roasted to resemble the passover lamb. See n. 17 and text thereto below. If he is right, then the third question also responds to an actual detail of the rite in effect post-70.

The compelling need to connect the seder to the second and third instances of the biblical device of the question is reflected in Mekilta's selection of comments. First, Mekilta *Pisha*, chap. 17, to Ex. 13:8, p. 66, l. 9, Lauterbach ed. 1:149, in the context of the law of unleavened bread and the child's inquiry (s.v. "And you shall tell your child," WHGDT LBNK), has "at a time when unleavened bread and bitter herbs are placed before you upon your table." Second, Mekilta *Pisha*, chap. 18, to Ex. 13:14—16, pp. 73—74, Lauterbach ed. 1:166, presents a version of the typology of the four children. But, third, Mekilta to Ex. 12:25—27 lacks all reference to this theme. To Ex. 13:8 cp. Mekilta DRŠBY, p. 40, Hoffmann ed. p. 33, n. 4.

The problem that the loss of the sacrifice posed to the use of the question may be dealt with in a different way in M. Pes. 9:5 and T. Pes. 8:10, p. 188, ll. 58—59. These passages claim that the items now unavailable applied only during the "Egyptian Passover," that is, the first Passover evening gathering in Egypt, and never later. Cp. Zeitlin, pp. 435—440, who suggests that the dipping of the herbs replaces the dipping or spreading of the blood of the paschal lamb, as prescribed in Ex. 12:22.

15. On the text of this Mishnah see, chap. 3, n. 13.

16. Edels, ad loc.; Friedmann, pp. 54—57; and see Neusner (1980), pp. 227—228, 241. Cp. Urbach (1961), p. 148. On the interpretation of this Mishnah, see also Hoffmann (1913), p. 17; Kasher, pp. 113—114, 133 [n.b. his "critical" text of the Mishnah, pp. 128—129, is not based on all the Mishnah MSS]; Goldschmidt, pp. 51—53; Safrai, pp. 300—301; and cp. Stein, pp. 41—42, Zeitlin (1973), p. 540, and Tabory, pp. 243—249.

On the notion of "intent" see also: Mekilta *Pisha*, chap. 11, p. 36, Lauterbach ed. 1:83; M. Pes. 5:2—4, 6:5; T. Pes. 4:2—9, pp. 159—163, ll. 11—60, esp. 11—12, 5:4—5, pp. 167—68, ll. 19—27; Lieberman *TK*, 4:555—559, esp. 550, ll. 11—12, and 554, ll. 26; M. Zev. 1:1, 4, and Maimonides, ad loc.; M. Yad. 4:2; and Meiri to b. Pes. 108a, p. 230a; Neusner (1973), 1:129—132, 2:158, 161, 324—325; Albeck, 2:449; and Levine, pp. 164—208.

17. Alon, pp. 164—166, followed by Goldschmidt, p. 12, n. 10, and 51, n. 1; and Safrai, p. 299.

18. See chap. 3, text to n. 22; Bokser (1981) and (1983). The analysis here, in addition to the text to n. 19 below, explains why I cannot accept Tabory's historical reconstruction of this Mishnah.

19. See chap. 3, n. 7.

20. On these *mishnayot*, see chap. 3, nn. 13—16, and Goldschmidt, pp. 54—58.

21. See chap. 2, text to nn. 5, 6, 9, 14, 17, and 23. On these expert singers, their relationship to the Levites with whom they are identified in Chronicles, and the function of their songs, see chap. 2, n. 5, to which add: *EnM*, "MŠWRR," by Jacob Liver, vol. 5, pp. 498—506, esp. 501—504; Segal, pp. 17—19; Heinemann (1964), pp. vi, 79; and Japhet, pp. 197, 204, 396. In biblical times, songs undoubtedly were secondary to sacrifices, and singers were minor officials. But apparently in First Temple times, psalms already accompanied sacrifices, with singers coordinating their recitation with sacrifices. See Kaufmann (1960), pp. 109—110, 309—311; and esp. Sarna, pp. 291, 293—294.

22. See also T. Pes. 4:11, p. 163, l. 69, and 8:22, p. 188, l. 72; and Lieberman *TK*, 4:561—562, 630. In T. Pes. 4:11, it is clear that the Levites and not the Israelites are the singers in the temple. But the subject of M. Pes. 5:7 is not explicit. Since the Tosefta's

language is very similar to the Mishnah's, we may confidently rely on the former to throw light on the latter. See also T. Suk. 4:17, p. 276, l. 58, and Lieberman *TK*, 4:902; M. Suk. 5:4 and T. Suk. 4:7, p. 274, ll. 26–27; T. Bik. 2:10, p. 292, ll. 58–59; T. Yoma 2:8, p. 234, ll. 72–75; T. Arak. 2:1, p. 544, ll. 14–15, and Lieberman (1950), pp. 142–143 and n. 22.

Rabbis required people to recite the Hallel on the various festivals. See T. Suk. 3:2, p. 266, ll. 6–9, and Lieberman *TK*, 4:871–872. They also transferred the daily recitation of the Levitical songs to individual Jews. Hence the dissociation of the Hallel from the experts may form part of a wider rabbinic effort to enable Jews to function without the Levites. See Elbogen (1972), pp. 64–65; Liver, pp. 69–70; and, in general, cp. Tabory, pp. 202–237.

23. See T. Taan. 3:3, p. 337, ll. 14–15, and Lieberman *TK*, 5:1104; and cp. T. Sot. 15:7, p. 241, ll. 59–60, and Lieberman *TK*, 8:764. On the increased importance of hymns and choral music after the temple's destruction, see Werner (1943), pp. 339–352, idem (1970), pp. 24–25, 131; Bayer, pp. 90–131; esp. *EnJ*, "Music," vol. 12, pp. 566, 571; Elbogen (1972), pp. 375–378, 473, esp. 475, n. 5; and Sarna.

The Qumranites, in what may be an analogous situation, increased their use of blessings and hymns to help replace the sacrifices that they could not bring. See Schiffman, pp. 78–79, and chap. 5, n. 16 below. The Early Church may provide an additional example. See Wellesz, pp. 34–35, 146–156.

24. Meiri to Pesaḥim, p. 250.

25. Friedmann, pp. 71, 72. See also Albeck, 2:139–140.

26. For another example of a psalm of thanksgiving, see T. Bik. 2:10, p. 292, ll. 58–59, and esp. Lieberman *TK*, 2:850, and n. 79. See Goldschmidt, pp. 61–62; Ginzberg, pp. 159–171, esp. 168; Weiser, pp. 31, 83–86, 705–713; Greenberg, esp. pp. 78–79; and Tigay.

On the principle that words on lists appear in the order of their length, see Friedman. While Tabory makes this same observation (p. 243, n. 1), he does not consider the possibility that the sequence was changed intentionally to provide a basis for the thanksgiving. This idea would tend to vitiate his reconstruction of the text, pp. 243–247. Cp. also Urbach (1961), pp. 147–148.

27. On M. 10:7 see chap. 3, nn. 17–18.

28. On the text of M. 10:9, see chap. 3, nn. 22–23. The blessing pattern thus consists of: a form of the verb "to say," ʾMR + the construct form of the noun, "blessing," BRKT + the specified blessing, e.g., *hashir* or *hazevaḥ* or *hatanim*. The formulation in line A for the "blessing over the food" follows a different pattern. It consists of: a form of the verb "to bless," BRK + a form of the preposition "over," ʿL + the name of the food. This pattern is regularly used in regard to a food, but as M. 10:2 indicates, other usages are also found. See Kosovsky, 1:411; and Kosovsky (1932–61), 2:176. As pointed out in chap. 3, n. 17, the Naples edition of the Mishnah, in M. 10:7A, has the anomolous reading MBRK ʿLYW BRKT MZWNW which may have been generated by the pattern in 10:7B.

29. See, e.g., Lev. 23:40, and Deut. 16:11, 14, 15.

30. See Lieberman *TK*, 4:649; chap. 2 above, nn. 5–6 and text thereto; chap. 5 below, nn. 49–56 and text thereto; and Bloch, pp. 148–152. For additional possible evidence concerning the need to supply new means to be "happy," see Goldberg,

p. 345, n. 9; Jacobson (1976), p. 204; and cp. Winston, p. 316. In general cp. Kaufmann, 1/1–3:585; T. Pes. 5:3, p. 167, l. 17; and Japhet, pp. 212–217.

Since Jubilees' account of the festivity mentions wine, we know that even before 70 C.E. people drank wine to become happy, as was only natural. This is what is claimed by Psalm 104:15, to which we can add Deut. 14:26, Koh. 8:15, and Zech. 10:7. Nevertheless, even in Jubilees the wine accompanies the sacrifices, and we are not informed whether the author of that passage would have assumed that proper festivity could take place without the sacrifice and the meal. Therefore, as the baraita cited immediately below indicates, some rabbinic circles might assume that this use of wine is novel. See esp. chap. 5, n. 55.

31. MSS and medieval citations lack this clause, found in the printed editions. See Rabbinovicz, p. 329, nn. 300, 400; Columbia MS; and Isaiah the Elder, loc. cit.; and cp. Lieberman *TK*, 4:649.

32. Fredman, pp. 82–83.

33. See Albeck, 2:137–142, esp. 140, n. 9, and 457, who suggests that M. Pes. 10:9–10 are not an integral part of chap. 10 but a supplement; Lieberman *TK*, 4:647, and the references there, esp. to Meiri, pp. 1, 206. Safrai, p. 297, suggests an alternative "original" location, in chap. 7. These suggestions may have been overly influenced by amoraic comments and interests. See Epstein, pp. 13–14.

34. In addition, several amoraic pericopae attest to the present sequence. This includes b. to M. Pes. 10:8, which associates the Mishnah's rule on the sacrifice with eating of *maṣṣah*, and b. and y. to M. Pes. 10:9, which analyze the logic of the dispute between Aqiva and Ishmael. On the y. see Lieberman (1934), p. 524, and Fraenkel and Meir Marim, ad loc.

35. Neusner (1974–1977), 13:3; see also pp. 2, 7. I thank Professor Joel Gereboff for stressing the significance of the analogy between M. Pesaḥim 10 and the conclusions of Miqvaot and Negaʿim.

36. See Neusner (1974–1977), 6:3, 17, 269; Neusner (1980), pp. 202–207.

37. See chap. 5, n. 62 below.

38. See Albeck, 2:457 and ad loc.; y. Pes. 10:9, 37d, on which see Lieberman (1934), p. 524; the reference to *piggul* and *notar* in M. Pes. 10:9; cp. M. Zev. 5:8 and Solomon Haedani to M. Pes. 10:8.

The place of M. 10:8–9 may be further attested by the way in which T. 10:11–12 may develop the Mishnah's point. Both require an individual to stay awake—in the Mishnah to eat the sacrifice, and in the Tosefta to study the meaning of Passover and its laws. This analogue constitutes an example of the transference of notions from the sacrificial rite to later times, a subject to be discussed later. The Gemara, b. Pes. 119b–120a, already made a related association. As with the passover offering, so with the unleavened bread, one should complete the eating within a fixed period of time.

39. See nn. 3–7, 28, and 34 above and texts thereto.

40. I thank Professor Gary G. Porton for the suggestion that one can interpret the Aqiva-Ishmael dispute on the basis of my proposition. See y. Pes. 10:9, 37d, to which see Lieberman (1934), p. 524; b. Zev. 37a, Rashi ad loc., s.v. TRY TN'Y; Lieberman *TK*, 4:956; and Porton (1976–1982), 1:70–71. See also M. Pes. 6:4; T. Pes. 5:2–3, p. 167, ll. 9–19, and 8:7, p. 185, ll. 27–28; and Lieberman *TK*, 4:624.

5. A Jewish Symposium?

1. *OxCD*, "Symposium," by Michael Coffey.

2. Ibid., "Symposium Literature," by Michael Coffey. See also *OxCD*, "Athenaeus (1)," by W. M. Edwards and Robert Browning, and "Plutarch," by D. A. Russell; Tabory, pp. 252–256; and n. 3 below.

3. Plutarch, *Table Talk*, II, Proem, 629C–D, vol. 8, pp. 107, 109 (emphasis added). See also: *Table Talk*, I, Quest. 1, 612F–613C, vol. 8, pp. 8–23; III, Proem, 645B–C, vol. 8, pp. 200–203; IV, Proem, 686B–D, vol. 8, pp. 452–55; VII, Proem, 697C–E, vol. 9, pp. 4–7; VII, Quest. 7, 710B–711A, vol. 9, pp. 72–77; VII, Quest. 9–10, 714–716C, vol. 9, pp. 90–102; VIII, Proem, 716D–717A, vol. 9, pp. 108–111.

4. See Beer, pp. 64–74; Stein; chap. 1, nn. 7, 31, and 36 and texts thereto; and esp. Hengel, 1:243–247.

5. Stein, pp. 18, 25. Raphael, pp. 86–92, provides an interpretive review of the symposia parallels and of Stein's article, implicitly criticizing Stein's historical evaluation.

6. Stein, p. 25.

7. Ibid., p. 44.

8. Ibid., p. 15, emphasis added.

9. Undoubtedly, as noted by several scholars, the upper classes are likely to be the regular participants at such meals. See, e.g., Lieberman *TK*, 1:62, 63; Stein, pp. 16, 17–18, 28, 31; in general, Bahr, and Lietzmann; and nn. 46–48 below.

10. See chap. 1, n. 32 and text thereto; 1 Sam. 16:3–5; *EnM*, "ZBH," by J. Licht, esp. col. 902; *EnJ*, "Cult," by B. Levine; cp. Milgrom (1976); De Vaux, pp. 468, 469–470, and chap. 17; Ringgren, pp. 155, 158, 171; Weinfeld, pp. 212, 217–224.

11. See chap. 1, text to n. 24; chap. 2, n. 2; and Kaufmann, 1/1–3:131, 543, 2/4–5:488.

12. See also Philo's comment on this passage, cited in chap. 2, n. 21.

13. See chap. 1, nn. 28–30 and text thereto. Even a review of the evidence from a traditional religious perspective does not fail to see that the Passover eve celebration in Temple days was not prominent outside of Jerusalem. See Bloch, pp. 134–136, who explains this fact by proposing that in Temple times rabbinic Judaism did not have a large following.

14. Josephus, *Antiquities*, 14:214, vol. 7, pp. 562–563. See also 14:257–258, vol. 7, pp. 586–587; and Smallwood, pp. 133–135. On Isa. 30:29 see Luzzatto, ad loc., p. 358.

15. On the general problem see Hengel, 1:243–247; M. Smith (1971), esp. pp. 351–352; Neusner (1973) *Purity*, p. 71 and n. 1; n. 14 above; and n. 43 below and text thereto.

16. See chap. 1, n. 21 and text thereto; Neusner (1971) *Pharisees*, 1:297–300, who points out that 297 of 341 pericopae, or 67%, deal with purity and tithing; Neusner (1973) *Purity*, pp. 70–71; and n.b. the additional comments on the NT, in Neusner (1973, 1979) *Politics*, pp. xii–xv, and Appendixes I–II by Morton Smith and J. A. Ziesler. Cp. Geiger, pp. 82–83, and Rabin, pp. 30–35.

17. Licht, 1QS, 6:2–8, pp. 138–144. The translation is based on Vermes (1975), pp. 80–81. See Licht's notes and Lieberman *TK*, 5:1072, n. 15.

18. See also Rule Annex, IQSa, 2:17–22, in Licht, pp. 266–267, 270; Licht, 1QS 9:3–5, pp. 187–189, and 10:1–17, 22, and esp. 69, pp. 201–218. Schiffman (1979) forcefully argues that the Qumran meals were messianic in character and not cultic. Cp. Schürer, 2:567, 579, n. 16, and esp. 582. On the communal meal and cultic notions, see also Kuhn, esp. 70–71; Van der Ploeg; F. M. Cross, pp. 62–67, 177–179; Sutcliffe; Gärtner, pp. 9–15, 44–46, 99–101, 121; Delcor; and esp. Hengel, 1:243–247. On the study of Scriptures, see Schiffman; and Bokser (1980), pp. 437–438, 455, n. 58. On prayer and liturgy, see Licht, pp. 210–211, 214, 215; Baumgarten (1953), esp. pp. 154–155, 157; Baumgarten (1975), pp. 75–87, esp. 83–84; Talmon (1960); Talmon (1978); as well as Werner (1957), esp. 26–28, 32–35; Bayer, pp. 117–121, 125–131; and Gerson-Kiwi; and n. 32 below and text thereto. In general see Hengel, 1:218–247; *InDBS*, "Essenes," by O. Betz; *InDBS*, "DSS," by G. Vermes; and Schürer, 2:555–590.

19. Bokser (1977).

20. *On the Contemplative Life*, nos. 73–74, vol. 9, pp. 156–159, and see p. 157, n. b, there.

21. Nos. 81–82, vol. 9, pp. 162–165. See also no. 25, vol. 9, pp. 126–127; and Daumas and Miquel, pp. 51–52, 141, n. 3, 126, n. 2.

22. No. 40, vol. 9, pp. 136–137.

23. No. 48, vol. 9, pp. 140–141.

24. Nos. 57–58, vol. 9, pp. 146–147.

25. No. 64, vol 9, pp. 150–151.

26. On the Therapeutae see Geoltrain, pp. 11–29; Daumas and Miquel, pp. 11–26; Hengel, 1:247, 2:165, n. 887; Vermes (1976), pp. 21–22, 30–36; Schürer, 2:591–597; and esp. Winston (1981), pp. 41, 313–14, n. 98. On the meal and the group's allegorical exegesis see esp. Geoltrain, pp. 19–24; Daumas and Miquel, pp. 51–55, and nn., esp. p. 109, n. 2; and Delcor, pp. 408–409. On the date of the gatherings, see Philo, 9:523, Colson's note to no. 65; Stein's references, p. 21, n. 33; Werner (1957), p. 33, n. 35; Geoltrain, pp. 24–25, and 59, n.; Daumas and Miquel, pp. 50–51, 124–125, nn. 1–3; Delcor, pp. 415–416; Baumgarten, pp. 39–42; Bokser (1977); Schürer, 2:595; and Winston (1981), p. 320, n. 38.

27. See Schürer, 2:475, n. 63; Bokser (1977); Bokser (1980), pp. 430, 440–441; Bokser (1981); Scholem, p. 34; chap. 2, text to n. 22 above; and nn. 32–38 below and text thereto.

28. *Special Laws* 2:145–148, vol. 7, pp. 395–397. See Philo, ibid., 2:145–149, vol. 7, pp. 395–397, Daniel ed. pp. xxxiii–xxxv, 318–322, and notes, esp. 320, n. 2, 321, n. 7, 322, nn. 2, 3. Concerning the comparison, "as priests with pure hands," see Daniel ed. pp. 319–320. Concerning the notion that on Passover the whole people act as priests, see the additional references in chap. 2, nn. 16–17 and text thereto; Daniel ed. pp. 330–335, and Goodenough (1929), pp. 65–66. On Philo's differentiation between the Jewish feast and the banquet and symposium, see chap. 2, nn. 18–20 and text thereto.

29. On Philo's philosophical spiritualizing, see Winston (1981), pp. 30–35, 355, n. 289, esp. the reference to Thompson.

30. As indicated above, text to n. 11, the process of transference is already present in the Bible.

31. Stein, pp. 20–22, 40.

32. Talmon (1960), p. 476. See ibid., passim, and Talmon (1978).

33. Neusner (1973), p. 108; and see pp. 45–46, 72–73, 78, 112. On ethicizing tendencies, see also Attridge, pp. 165–176, esp. 168–169, 176, 183, 184; Urbach (1969), pp. 323–324, 339; and cp. Hengel, 1:174.

34. Neusner (1973), p. 129. See also Neusner (1974–1977), 22: esp. 293–303, who examines early rabbinic notions of purity and temple, pointing out that by the latter part of the second century some rabbinic circles had adopted the notion of ''community'' as a new source of primary comparisons. See also Neusner (1980), pp. 287–290; and Bokser (1981), who traces these variations into the third century.

35. Fiorenza, pp. 167–168. See also Baumgarten (1953), esp. pp. 153–154, 157; and the references in n. 17 above.

36. Fiorenza, p. 168. See also Neusner (1973) *Purity*, pp. 69–71; and Neusner (1980), pp. 35–44, esp. 40; and cp. McKelvey, esp. pp. 42–57, 179–187, n.b. 45–53, and Thompson, who suggests that the metaphysical background of Hebrews leads to the charge that sacrifices are not only replaced but impotent. See n. 29 above and text thereto.

37. Fiorenza, p. 168.

38. Ibid., pp. 176–177. I may relate this last point to the discussion, in chap. 2, text to nn. 31–38, concerning Jesus as an eternal and final sacrifice. See also Williams, pp. 230–233. It is not surprising, though, that the Book of Acts represents early Christians as continuing to worship in the temple, for Acts, along with Luke, does not, in general, describe Jesus' death as an expiation and salvation. See Feinde, Behm, Kümmel, pp. 104, 129–130, as well as 98–100, 114–115, 120–121; *InDBS*, ''Acts of the Apostles,'' by W. C. Robinson, esp. pp. 7–8; *InDB*, ''Lord's Supper,'' pp. 158, 159; and cp. Townsend (1981) and Townsend.

39. As mentioned earlier, this is not to deny the role that the general Hellenistic culture may have had in the particular ways in which the groups expanded the meal. See n. 15 above and n. 43 below and texts thereto.

40. See chap. 1, nn. 11–23 and text thereto. There is a biblical precedent even for extending the locus of purity outside of the temple. The biblical law of the menstrual woman applies not just in the temple. Since it was discussed by the Pharisees at a relatively early period, it may have provided a model for extending the realm of purity outside of the cult. Verses such as Ex. 19:6, Lev. 11:43–47, Deut. 7:6 and 26:19, which speak of the whole nation being priests or holy, would support this wider perspective. Historical questions, however, remain: Why was this equation made at a certain time? Similarly, why did certain Jews make the equation and not others? See Neusner (1974–1977), 16:2–9 and 22:99–109.

41. See chap. 1 above.

42. See nn. 11, 17, 25; Goodenough (1929), pp. 65–66; and Zeitlin, pp. 432–433.

43. See chap. 1, n. 36, and n. 15 above and texts thereto; and M. Smith. On the decreased importance of a central temple and the rise of local means to relate to the divine as characteristic of Hellenism, see Smith.

44. See text to nn. 22–25, above, and Josephus, cited below, text to n. 64.

45. See chap. 1, nn. 34–35 and text thereto; and, e.g., Neusner (1973) *Politics*. See n. 46.

46. See n. 9, above, to which add Jacobson, p. 135.

47. See chap. 3, nn. 2–3.

48. Concerning reclining, see Friedmann, pp. 15–24, and his biblical references, including 1 Sam. 28:23 and Ezek. 23:41; Kasher, pp. 68–76, cp. 115–116; Plutarch, *Table Talk*, I, Quests. 2 and esp. 3, 615D–619F, vol. 8, pp. 24–29 and esp. 45. Rabbinic sources frequently mention reclining on a couch: M. Ber. 6:6; T. Ber. 4:8, p. 20, ll. 22–30 (an upper-class dinner etiquette; Lieberman TK, 1:62–63), 4:11, p. 20, l. 36 (Erfurt MS), 4:20, p. 25, l. 98, 5:5, p. 26, ll. 12–15 (the order of the couches; Lieberman *TK*, 1:75–76); T. Ter. 10:9, p. 161, ll. 27–28. See also T. Dem. 3:7, p. 74, ll. 23–24; T. Shab. 21:17, p. 56, ll. 23–24 (couches for reclining at a meal). Non-Jewish sources, archaeology, and ancient art throw light on the dining arrangements, including the use of couches. See Zevulun and Olenik, pp. 8–41, 6*–23*; von Gall; Richter, pp. 52–72, 91–95, 105–110, esp. 63–64, 107; Goodenough, 9:105, 182, 228–233; 11:pl. IV, figs. 90, 166; Krauss, 2, i:31–50; Krauss (1910–1912), 3:42–46, and nn.

Workers normally ate in an unleisurely manner and the poor probably did not make use of luxurious couches: T. Dem. 5:7, p. 86, l. 36; Lieberman *TK*, 1:253; M. Ned. 4:4; M. Neg. 13:9; M. San. 2:1, 3, 4. See Kosovsky (1932–1961), 5:168; n. 9 above; and cp. Baneth, pp. 237–238, n. 7; Friedlander, 2:132, 150, 154–155; Krauss, 2, i:31–32; *InDB*, "Banquet" and "Meals"; *EnM*, "MTH," by Magen Broshi; and cp. Tabory, pp. 7–17, esp. 9.

49. See chap. 4, n. 30, above, and text thereto; cp. Tabory, pp. 26–35. See also Cowley, no. 30, l. 21, and no. 31, l. 20; Porten, p. 289; Goodenough, 6:132–141 and his references, esp. Plutarch, *Table Talk*, passim, vols. 8–9, esp. I, Quests. 6–7, 623D–625C, vol. 8, pp. 68–79, and VI, Quest. 7, 692B–693E, vol. 8, pp. 486–495; and Clement, *Paidagogos*, 2:2, nos. 19–34, pp. 110–124. In addition, as Goodenough, M. Smith (1974), pp. 815–829, and Porton have noted, Palestinian Jews and non-Jews used wine motifs for diverse purposes, and some people participated in a wine-dionysiac cult. Furthermore, the emerging Church found wine an important element in its interpretation of the Last Supper, in Matt. 14, Mark 26, Luke 22, and 1 Cor. 11. See *InDB*, "Wine," by J. F. Ross; *TDNT*, "Oinos," by H. Seesemann, 5:162–166; Daube; and Lietzmann, pp. cited in n. 51 below.

50. On the meaning of M. 10:7, see chap. 3, n. 18.

51. Two factors are thus at work. As T. Ber. 4:8 (p. 20, ll. 24–25, 27–28), 4:12 (pp. 20–21, ll. 37–38), and 5:3 (p. 26, ll. 6–15) make clear, rabbinic circles, like other people in antiquity, customarily drank wine at meals. At the same time, Pharisees and later rabbis used wine for religious purposes. The dispute between the Houses of Hillel and Shammai concerning the sequence of blessings "over the wine" and "over the day" attests that wine was used liturgically already in the first century. See Goodenough, 6:136, and Neusner (1971) *Pharisees*, 2:145–146, and cp. 42–45. On religious and other uses of wine see: Lieberman *TK*, to the cited passages of Tosefta, esp. 1:62, 75, l. 17; Elbogen, pp. 179–187; Goodenough, 5:99–197, 6:3–217, esp. 61–93, 126–173, and 12:123–131, who surveys the sources in detail; *EnM*, "YYN," by H. H. Beinart, esp. cols. 680–682; Brown; Lietzmann, pp. 161, 165–171, 267–269, 273–

274, 316–319, 335–365, 320–324; 620–652, esp. 626–629; Stein, passim, esp. p. 17; Sutcliffe, p. 51; Bahr, pp. 181–182, and the references he cites. See also the references in n. 49; Loew, 1:48–189, esp. 147–149; Feliks, pp. 17–24; Daube (1974); and *EnJ*, "Symbolism," by E. R. Goodenough, esp. cols. 569, 570; and esp. Tabory, pp. 24–89a, n.b. 47, 48, 214.

52. Stein, pp. 25–26. See also Friedmann, pp. 25–27, 73–74; the reference to Tabory, at end of n. 51 above; chap. 4, par. 4, and nn. 29–30 and text thereto.

53. See M. 10:1, 2, 4, 7, and T. 10:2; Jastrow, s.v. "MZG"; and the references in n. 51.

54. On this passage see chap. 3, n. 25; Plutarch, *Table Talk*, IV, Quest. 6, 672B, vol. 8, pp. 366–367, VI, Quest. 7, passim, esp. 693C, vol. 8, pp. 486–495, esp. 492–493; and Clement, *Paidagogos*, 2:2, no. 30, pp. 119–120. Cp. Lieberman *TK*, 4:648.

55. See chap. 4, nn. 29–31 and text thereto; b. Pes. 108a–109a, which cites a version of Tosefta's baraita and additional baraitot. One of the latter, presented in chap. 4, focuses on the new use of wine to replace meat. Another text there, 108b–109a, combines two earlier pericopae. The first treats the four cups and emphasizes that they are necessary to provide "happiness." The second deals with happiness and mentions that one of several ways to attain it is by drinking wine. (See Rabbinovicz, and the analogous version of Tarfon's comment in y. Pes. 10:1, 37c. The conflation in the text produced certain exegetical problems. Cp. to b. Pes. 108b, Rashbam, WKY MH TWᶜLT, with Moshe Halavah, p. 146b; and Halivni, 3:980–982.) See also Mekilta *Pisḥa*, chap. 9, p. 30, Lauterbach ed. 1:68; Mekilta DRŠBY to Ex. 12:16, p. 18; and Bloch, pp. 148–152.

56. Amoraic (and postamoraic) interpretations are found in b. Pes. 109b–110a, the comment of Rabina, and 117b, bottom, and esp. in y. Pes. 10:1, 37c, and Gn. R. sec. 88, p. 1081. The latter, for example, contain the notion that the four cups symbolize aspects of divine retribution against Israel's enemies or aspects of the redemption of Israel. See Friedmann, pp. 25–26; Lieberman (1934), pp. 517–18; Daube (1974), p. 17; and Bokser (1984) nn. 18–21 and text thereto. In addition to the references cited in n. 49, see also Azulai, to b. Pes. 108b, 1:110–111; Meiri, p. 252; Kasher, pp. 82–95; Goldschmidt, pp. 5–7, 61. Cp. Fredman, pp. 81–84, who also emphasizes that the meaning of the drinking of wine is imparted through the ways in which it is prescribed and defined in the course of the rite.

57. On the text of this Mishnah, see chap. 3, nn. 6–9.

58. See chap. 4, nn. 8–10 and text thereto.

59. On the text of this Mishnah and esp. the reading of this clause, see chap. 3, nn. 10–12 and the references there, in particular to Goldschmidt, p. 12.

60. On the text of this Mishnah, see chap. 3, nn. 17–19.

61. Therefore, the plain meaning is not that the wine will totally prevent an individual from saying the hymns but rather that it may cause a person to say them in an inappropriate manner. Rashi (1905), 1:104, no. 90, and 2:193, no. 45, likewise rejects the former interpretation: "they prohibited drinking [additional wine] only between the third and fourth cup so that one should not become drunk and be unable to understand when one says Hallel." Cp. Ratner, p. 134. After analyzing M. 10:7 in this manner, I found that Lewy, pp. 20–21, offers a similar interpretation. See also Baneth, pp. 255–

256, n. 71; and cp. Stein, pp. 26, 36. Plutarch expresses a similar concern to prevent degenerate music at banquets; *Table Talk*, VII, Quest. 5, 704C–706E, esp. 704D, 706C, vol. 9, pp. 42–55. See nn. 63–67 below and text thereto.

62. See Lieberman (1934), p. 521, and *TK*, 4:655; and Liddell and Scott, p. 642, s.v. *epikwmazw*, and *epikwm-kwmiov, -os*. The explanation of "nuts, dates, and parched grain" in T. Pes. 10:11 is thus incorrect. If, however, the Tosefta refers to types of delicacies served after a meal, especially to whet one's thirst, this comment, as well, would reflect the attempt to distinguish the Passover meal from symposium manners and revelry. See Liberman *TK*, 1:57–58, and esp. Tabory, pp. 13–14, 221–222. Cp. Lieberman *TK*, 4:655, ll. 30–31, end of the first par. See also Friedmann, pp. 74–76; Lewy, pp. 18–19; Baneth, pp. 243, 256, n. 73; Finkelstein, pp. 29–30; Albeck, 2:457; Zeitlin (1964), p. 231; Kasher, pp. 171–174. Cp. Werner, pp. 205–206, Werner (1976), p. 12, to which see, however, the critical comments of Hall, esp. pp. 30–31, and cp. Hall (1979), pp. xxvii, 35, n. 32; and Daube (1968). Daube's interesting interpretation apparently follows the revised reading of the passage, in b. Pes. 119b–120a, which replaces the word "passover offering" with "unleavened bread," or else, disregarding the word PSH, the "passover offering," follows the late interpretation of the text that takes *afiqimon* as unleavened bread and thus renders the passage as: "They do not eat anything after the *afiqimon*." It similarly assumes that the hiding of the *afiqimon* (or *afiqomon*) is an ancient practice. But this custom apparently is late and developed from the practice of "playing with a piece of *massah*," mentioned in T. Pes. 10:9. The latter was designed to keep the child awake and attentive and also has parallels in the symposia literature. See Fischel, pp. 12–13.

63. See nn. 22–25 above and text thereto, and chap. 2, nn. 18–20 and text thereto.

64. Josephus, *Wars*, 6:423, vol. 3, pp. 499.

65. See n. 61 above, to which add *Table Talk*, VII, Quest. 7, 710B–711A, vol. 9, pp. 72–77.

66. Clement, *Paidagogos*, 2:4, nos. 40–41, 44, pp. 129–130, 133. Sec. 44 is cited by various modern writers, e.g., Werner (1943), p. 349; Idelsohn, pp. 93–94, and cp. 92–100; Wellesz, pp. 92–93. In general see Stein, pp. 26, 36, 44; and esp. Wellesz, pp. 52–97, in particular 79–85, on the notion that music has a pernicious effect on morals and is associated with pagan religious ceremonies, and on the role of dinner music, often performed by women; and Friedlander, pp. 337–365, esp. 348–351, 363–365.

It should be noted that the Mishnah's dissociation of the Passover rite from certain features of the symposia may also form part of a general rejection of these features of the common Hellenistic culture. Rabbinic circles, for example, reflect an ambivalent attitude toward music. In the early period, instrumental music was deemphasized as part of the response to the temple's destruction. See chap. 4, n. 23, above. In addition, perhaps later, we find references to the degenerate nature of music or certain types of music. See *EnJ*, "Music," esp. cols. 579–580; *EnJ*, "Se͑udah," by M. Ydit; Lieberman, in Mekilta DRŠBY, p. 250, n. to Ex. 29:21; and y. Meg. 3:2, 74a and its analogue in b. Git. 7a. The latter version may have been mooted so as not to appear to criticize the exilarch too openly (Saul Lieberman, class lecture, Jewish Theological Seminary of America, New York, December 2, 1969). Cp. M. Beer, pp. 157–158; Neusner (1966–1970), 2:98–107, esp. 103–104, and 3:54–58. See also M. Sot. 9:11,

T. Sot. 15:7 (p. 241, ll. 59–60), esp. Lieberman *TK*, 8:764, and b. Sot. 48a; and T. San. 12:10 (Zuckermandel ed. p. 433, ll. 27–28), to which cp. Goldin (1976), pp. 44, n. 40.

67. See, for example, Winston (1981), p. 312, n. 86.

68. I do not deal with the issue of where during the rite the actual meal took place. Some scholars believe that in an early stage of the ritual, the participants ate the meal before the exposition. Such a variation might also affect the degree to which the Passover celebration is similar to—or different from—the symposia. See, e.g., Hoffmann; Lieberman *TK*, 5:654; Safrai; and esp. Tabory, pp. 16–22, 247–249, and Goldschmidt, p. 10, and n. 1. Tabory (1981) suggests that the pre-70 sacrificial meal constituted the main and only meal and that it lacked the symbolic elements of the later rabbinic rite. See chap. 7, n. 25 below.

6. *The Perspective of Early Rabbinic Judaism*

1. On the biblical pattern, see chap. 4, nn. 12–14 and text thereto; and, in general, Goldschmidt, pp. 10–11 and his references, esp. in nn. 3–7; and cp. Friedmann, p. 50. See n. 3 below. The child's question in Deut. 6:20 does not specifically deal with Passover. See also Halivni (1981), pp. 67–69.

2. On this Mishnah, see chap. 3, nn. 10–12.

3. The baraita containing the typology of four children appears in Mekilta *Pisha*, chap. 18, p. 73, Lauterbach ed. 1:166–67; y. Pes. 10:4, p. 37d; and the Passover haggadah. In addition to the references in Goldschmidt, cited in n. 1, see Urbach (1961); Bahr; Francis; Fischel (1975), pp. 69–70. This typology may be a popular philosophical or wisdom pattern that, through the common feature of a child's question, became imposed on the biblical text. See, in particular, Fischel (1975) and Francis.

4. See also M. Avot 3:17; T. Hag. 2:1, p. 380, l. 3; M. Parah 12:10, T. Parah 12:8, p. 640, ll. 23–25, and Neusner (1974–1977), 9:196, 213; M. Arak. 1:1; M. Yad. 4:7; and Kosovsky (1932–1961), 3:475–476.

5. T. Hag. 1:2, pp. 374–376, ll. 5–22. On these two examples, see Bokser (1979), pp. 16–18, and Bokser (1980), pp. 100–101 and nn., both of which also refer to additional examples. See in particular: T. San. 7:9, p. 426, ll. 32–34; T. Miq. 2:10, p. 655, l. 1 (to which see Lieberman *TR*, 4:9); M. Toh. 3:6 and T. Toh. 3:7, 9, 11, p. 663, ll. 6, 12, 16–17 (to which see Lieberman, *TR*, 4:57, and Neusner [1974–1977], 11:72, 85); M. T.Y. 4:7.

In the T. Hag. 1:2 passage, note especially the criterion for inclusion in the group to eat the paschal lamb. Other criteria are also offered there in T. Hag. 1:2, and in Sifre Zutṭa, to Num. 15:38, p. 288, l. 23. See also T. Pes. 4:2, p. 159, l. 13, and Lieberman (1968), p. 16, nn. 16, 18. Again, this reflects the overall rabbinic concern to delineate those who can be included in the law, here specified in terms of Passover. It is from this perspective that the biblical pedagogic device is formulated and adapted.

6. See also Kosovsky, and Kosovsky (1932–1961), s.v. MLMD; esp. M. Ned. 4:3; M. Sot. 3:4, M. Sot. 9:14; and T. Sot. 15:8, p. 242, l. 79 (to which see Lieberman *TK*, 8:768, and Lieberman, pp. 20–21); M. Qid. 4:13–14; T. Qid. 5:10, 15, 16, pp. 297–298, ll. 53–54, 66–67, 74–75. Cp. M. Tamid 3:6, M. Edu. 1:4; M. Yad. 4:3.

7. In the light of this discussion, see T. 10:7 which refers to a parent who recites Hallel on behalf of male and female children, and which delineates certain procedures. Here the tannaitic interests are even more prominent.

8. The text also supplies four answers, each ostensibly tailored to a different child. To some degree, this half is in accord with the Mishnah, line F. On the four types of children, see n. 3. See also Halivni (1981), pp. 67–70.

The fact that the pattern of M. Pes. 10:4 does not accord with that of the fourfold typology finds support from (and helps explain) certain difficulties in b. Pes. 116a, in the Gemara following M. Pes. 10:4. One Amora formulates one of the "questions" and mentions a "requirement to dip twice." This comment generates the question, "How can we speak of a 'requirement' in regard to a child?" The child will not understand the obligation behind the practice he or she may observe. But the confusion may result from two different points of reference. The first Amora apparently assumes that the person who asks the question need not be a child, while the second master, who finds the reference to a "requirement" problematic, assumes that the reference is to a child. See Rabbinovicz, p. 361, n. 90, and Halivni (1981), p. 67, n. 3.

9. See Mekilta DRŠBY, to Ex. 13:3, 8, pp. 38, 40, for related texts that also formulate the issue from the perspective found in the Mishnah.

10. On this text see chap. 3, nn. 31–32.

11. For a simlar reason one cannot assume that C–D generated B. The autonomous nature of B is confirmed by the existence elsewhere of different versions of the law in B. Mekilta DRŠBY, to Ex. 13:3 and 8, pp. 38, 40, formulates it in terms of "between him and himself, between him and others." Mekilta *Pisha*, chap. 18, cited at n. 15 below, formulates it in terms of a fraternity of sages and students. Both passages circulate without an analogue to the Gamaliel story in C. See esp. Kanter, p. 62.

12. Goldschmidt, p. 118. See Lewin, pp. 154–155.

13. See: on the Tosefta's formulation, Lieberman *TK*, 4:655; on the term HLKH and HLKWT, Halivni, 1:672–673, Bokser (1980), pp. 448–449, n. 96, and n. 14 below and text thereto; and on the additional variation of "all that night" vis-à-vis "until the cock's call," Halivni, l:xi. Cp. Stein, pp. 33–35; Goldschmidt, pp. 19–20; and esp. Kanter, p. 62. After making this observation, I found that Tabory, p. 214, also suggests that "study of halakhot" is especially appropriate to rabbinic circles. But he does not treat the alternative usage in the haggadah.

14. P. 354, ll. 13–15. See Lieberman *TK*, 5:1167–1169 and the references there to parallels; and additional instances in T. San. 7:10, p. 427, ll. 1–3, "engaged in halakhah," 'SWQYN BHLKH, to which see Lieberman *TR*, 2:159; M. Shab. 1:4 and T. Shab. 1:16, p. 4, l. 36; M. Ned. 4:3; T. Sot. 7:21, p. 200, ll. 207–226, to which see Lieberman *TK*, 8:691–692; T. Zav. 1:5, p. 676, l. 33, to which see Lieberman *TK*, 4:119; and Kosovsky, 3:1390–1391, s.v. 'SQ, and Kosovsky (1932–1961), 5:385–386, s.v. 'SQ.

It should be noted that my analysis of Gamaliel's story underscores the redactional function of the pericope in illustrating the study of *halakhot*. It is theoretically possible that the story originally did not speak of "halakhot" but that the redactional needs caused the editor-compiler to use this language to replace some other formulation. Cp. Kanter, p. 62.

15. Mekilta *Pisha*, chap. 18, pp. 73–74. The text in Mekilta, Lauterbach, 1:167, is

substantively the same. See Lieberman's citation, *TK*, 4:655 and Lieberman (1934), pp. xxii–xxiii. On the use of the pericope at Ex. 13:14, see Mekilta, Friedmann ed., p. 23a, n. 28.

16. On the term BYT HMDRŠ see Goodblatt, pp. 93–107. In contrast with the observation presented in the text, the Tosefta breaks with the biblical setting in the opposite direction as well. T. Pes. 10:6–9a refers to townspeople who go to a synagogue (literally "house of assembly") to participate in the Hallel recitation, and to an adult who recites Hallel for minor children. A limited rabbinic setting is thus not the only frame of reference. In this light see Epstein (1957), pp. 333–334.

17. See Goldschmidt, pp. 13–19, esp. 14, 18, 30; Urbach (1961), pp. 144–145; and esp. Safrai, p. 301. Cp. Hoffmann (1924), pp. 20–22; Hoffmann (1972), pp. 2–3; and Tabory (1977–1978) which should be compared with his earlier study, Tabory, pp. 207–211. See also Hall (1979), p. xxvii, and now Halivni (1981), pp. 69–70.

18. In addition to Goldschmidt, see Tabory, pp. 238–39; Alt, on the function of such biblical passages; and Fishbane, pp. 121–140.

19. See von Rad, pp. 3–13, 55–57; and esp. Weinfeld, pp. 32–33, and Goldschmidt, p. 30, who previously explained the choice of Deut. 26 on the basis of its formulaic nature. This suggestion is confirmed by recent research in liturgy, e.g., Heinemann (1964), Greenberg, pp. 88–90, and Tigay, pp. 372–78. See also Halivni, 1:671–672; Lieberman *TK*, 2:850, n. 79; and Hoffman, p. 20. Cp. Friedmann, pp. 50–52; Kasher, pp. 19–23; and Daube, p. 434.

20. On Philo, Therapeutae, and Qumran, see chap. 2, nn. 15–23 and text thereto, and chap. 5, nn. 18, 26 and the references there, esp. to Schiffman, pp. 22–76, n.b. 20–21, 75–76. On the significance of the changed role of study and exposition, see Hengel, 1:169–75; Neusner (1971); Neusner (1973) "Written"; Bokser (1977); Bokser (1980), pp. 433–434, 437–441, and nn., esp. n. 65, and the references there, esp. to Porton (1979), Le Déaut, pp. 269–270, and cp. Urbach, pp. 171–181, esp. 178. In general see Schürer, 2:337–355. In light of this discussion, the reference in Goldschmidt (p. 30) to M. Yoma 1:6 is especially appropriate. The Mishnah assumes that a high priest might not be able to expound the Scriptures. Rabbis thus expounded the Bible and wanted all Jews to be able to participate in this encounter with the text.

The fact that Philo, the Therapeutae (according to Philo's description), Qumran, and early rabbinic authorities engaged in study and made study a holy and special activity points to another instance of the process of transference and its contribution to religious developments. To be sure, the fact that these individuals or groups chose to emphasize study may also reflect the common Hellenistic emphasis on learning found especially among philosophical and intellectual circles. What remains significant is the end to which the Jewish groups put their learning and the fact that they, and not other Jews, chose to pursue and devote themselves to this activity.

21. Sifre Deut., sec. 301, p. 319, presents a relatively early example of this type of exposition, and one version of it has been included in the haggadah (Goldschmidt, pp. 120–122). See also Midrash Tannaim to Deut. 26:5–9, pp. 172–173; and Midrash Leqaḥ Ṭov to Deut. 26:5–9, pp. 45b–46a (= 90–91). On early exegesis of this section, see Tabory (1977–1978), and Halivni (1981), p. 70.

22. On this Mishnah, see chap. 3, nn. 14–16; Goldschmidt, pp. 55–58, esp. 56, n. 20; Heinemann (1960–1961), pp. 406–407; and Gereboff (1979), pp. 48–49.

Goldschmidt and Heinemann apparently are unaware of the reading in the Parma MS.

23. Loewenstamm, p. 21.

24. Jubilees 49:6. See chap. 2, text to n. 6., and Loewenstamm, pp. 80–94.

25. As Heinemann (1964), pp. 149–150, observes, it is natural for a person to think of the future when mentioning a past act of God. Cp. Schürer, 2:512.

26. To be sure, one of the functions of a ritual is to heighten this contrast between the way things should be and the way they actually are (the current reality), making people think about and, in a limited way, experience the ideal. See chap. 7 below; and Bokser (1984).

27. See Heinemann (1964); Kadushin; Bokser (1980), pp. 48–53, 124–128; esp. Bokser (1981) and Bokser (1982), and references there. On the system of blessings at Qumran, see Talmon (1960) and above, chap. 5, n. 32, and text thereto.

7. *From Form to Meaning*

1. Von Rad, p. 5.

2. Goldin (1965), p. 277.

3. See chap. 6, n. 17.

4. Ludwig, p. 27, also pp. 31, 44.

5. See, e.g., M. Ber. 5:4 and T. Ber. 1:10–12, pp. 4–5, ll. 41–64; and Urbach (1969), pp. 599–610, 622–623. This is not to deny the fact, mentioned in chap. 5, n. 26, that rituals may be designed precisely to highlight the disparity between reality and the ideal, reminding people of the way things should be. See Smith (1980) Bare; and the discussion of Victor Turner's observations, below.

6. Goldschmidt, p. 122. See Goldin, p. 414.

7. Those Jews in antiquity who hoped for another Moses to alleviate their situation did so as part of an apocalyptic, active eschatological hope. Early rabbinic Judaism, surely after 135 C.E., was antipathetic to such a view. At most, early rabbinic circles spoke of a human leader who would help them in their redemption. See Saldarini; esp. Vermes (1973), pp. 94–99; Schürer, 2:510–554; Goldin; Callan; and the insightful comments of Laytner.

8. Urbach (1969), pp. 587, 591, 593, 622–623, also points to a shift in notions concerning redemption.

9. The perspective of this type of symbolic explanation is similar to that of allegory, as described by Goldin (1965), pp. 283–285: "I refrain from referring to allegorizing exercises . . . because . . . allegorical interpretation has little to teach us about what we would call adaption. . . . In allegorical exegesis the traces of the original Word tend to get erased. In allegory we create a dichotomy between the explicitly scriptural statement and its presumptive intent. . . . Soon we discover . . . that such exegesis tends to remove original practice from circulation, threatens to push the past into the expendable archaic, and the present becomes not an adaption but an emancipation." After quoting from Philo, Goldin observes, "Allegory . . . rationalizes [and] excuses."

10. See chap. 3, n. 13, on the text of this passage; and text to nn. 29–34 below for a full discussion of the mythic dimension of the rite. Tabory (1981) also points to the sacrificial nature of the pre-70 rite and the significant differences between it and the rabbinic ritual meal. See n. 25 below.

11. See Turner (1977), p. 214; and esp. Turner, pp. 102, 127–128.

12. Turner (1974), p. 53; see also p. 273.

13. Turner, p. 167. See also Turner (1974), p. 53; and P. Brown (1981), pp. 42—44, describing how those of low status in medieval times, e.g., women and the poor, find in pilgrimages a role that they normally lack in regular institutional settings.

14. Fredman, p. 10. See also Turner, pp. 94—97.

15. "Pilgrimages as Social Processes," in Turner (1974), pp. 166—230. Tabory (1981) also notes the fellowship dimension of the sacrificial Passover meal. See n. 25 below.

16. P. Brown (1981), p. 42.

17. See, e.g., Turner (1974), p. 173. It would be interesting to analyze all the Jewish materials on pilgrimage from Turner's perspective. See, for example, 1 Sam. 1; 1 Kings 12:26—33; Safrai (1965); and Haran (1970).

18. Philo, *Special Laws*, 1:69—70, vol. 7, pp. 138—140; and cp. Turner (1974), pp. 167—169. See also Amir.

19. P. Brown (1981), p. 42, who quotes from William A. Christian, Jr., *Person and God in a Spanish Valley* (New York, 1972), p. 70.

20. P. Brown (1981), p. 42, and p. 146, n. 96, citing Prudentius, *Peristephanon*, 11:191—92; 199—202, from *Prudentius*, trans. H. H. Thomson, Loeb Classical Library (London, 1961).

21. Josephus, *Antiquities*, 4:203—204, vol. 4, pp. 572—573. Cp. Shalit ed., 2: [Hebrew number] 82, n. 113a. See the additional references in chap. 2, n. 23; and the citation of Philo, immediately above, text to n. 18.

22. See Urbach's observations, cited in n. 8.

23. I refer to Jubilees 49:15, cited in chap. 2, text to nn. 6—7. See also Turner (1974), p. 197; and esp. Turner (1977), pp. 202, 208, 210.

24. Cp. Philo, *Questions and Answers on Exodus*, 1:3, Sup. 2:8—9.

25. See Bokser (1984). Fredman devotes her book to the notion that the seder and especially its main symbol, the unleavened bread, represent the Diaspora experience. See my citation, text to n. 31 below. She does contrast the rabbinic rite with its antecedents, e.g., pp. 3, 135—138, but discusses the latter very briefly. I first became sensitive to the importance of the difference when I considered the nature of a pilgrimage festival, as presented in P. Brown (1981), and in Turner's article on "Pilgrimage" (Turner [1974]). I also found Turner (1977) helpful for its two typologies of sacrificial rites.

Later I found that Laytner, pp. 46—47, also points to M. 10:4 and notes that the haggadah stresses the mythic and not just the historical nature of the exodus experience. But he makes too sharp a differentiation between the rabbinic and the prerabbinic rites in this regard. One cannot deny the mythic quality in the Exodus and Deuteronomy accounts, as I discuss below, text to nn. 27—28. I have therefore formulated the dichotomy in terms of predominant interest and the stress on one or the other of the perspectives. I have similarly sought to describe how the historical understanding of the exodus as a past event in the Second Temple period might have formed part of a wider experience.

See now Tabory (1981), who also points to the sharp difference between the pre- and the post-70 meals. He brilliantly suggests that while the rabbinic rite is a ritual meal consisting of a regular meal and the eating of symbolic elements, the pre-70 rite essentially constituted a sacrificial-fellowship meal: "The original custom, which prevailed throughout the period of the Second Temple, was to consider the obligatory foods as the main meal and no other meal was eaten besides it. This contention is based, in part, on the theory of sacrificial meals which has been presented by many scholars. According to this theory, the Passover sacrifice was a thanksgiving meal eaten, in the presence of G-d, by a group of people who stressed, by their communal meal, their common heritage. The bread of this meal was maẓẓah, the meat was that of the sacrificial lamb, while the prescribed vegetable was lettuce, which was considered a bitter herb'' (English Summaries, p. 17). Tabory's analysis complements the argument here and in Bokser (1977). But again one must also take note of the pre-70 mythic dimension, albeit of a different form from that of the rabbinic rite, and consider the impact of the change of location—from a national shrine to an individual home—on the nature of the fellowship meal.

26. See chap. 1, n. 2, and text thereto. The comments here provide the specifics to my observation, in chap. 5, concerning the use and interpretation of the meal in the Passover context. Whether or not the choice of a meal was reinforced by the contemporary popular uses of a meal, familiar from rabbinic sources and other Jewish and Hellenistic groups, the essential issue remains how the meal was adapted. The overall purpose imparts meaning on whatever symposiatic features may be found in the celebration and accounts for its initial expansion as well. See below.

27. Childs, p. 200. See also p. 203. For von Rad, see n. 1 above.

28. Childs, p. 205.

29. Neusner (1979) *Torah*, pp. 39–40.

30. Ibid., p. 40.

31. Fredman, p. 95.

32. The comment appears in b. 116a and is attributed in modern printed editions to Samuel but in the Venice first edition, Columbia MS, and other witnesses (cited in Rabbinovicz, p. 361, n. 100) to Rava.

33. The comment appears in b. Pes. 116b and is attributed in both MSS and printed editions to Rava. See n. 32; Rabbinovicz, p. 363, n. 50; chap. 3, n. 13 above; and Goldschmidt, pp. 53–54.

34. See n. 10 above.

35. Ibid.

36. See chap. 4, n. 36 above; Neusner (1981), esp. chap. 3 and chap. 6, text to nn. 22–26; and J. Fraenkel, pp. 119–121.

37. See Neusner (1980), pp. 202–212, 273–290; and "Map Without Territory: Mishnah's System of Sacrifice and Sanctuary," in Neusner (1979) *Method*, pp. 133–153.

38. Neusner (1979) *Method*, p. 138.

39. Ibid., p. 147; and Neusner (1980), p. 282.

40. See Neusner (1979) *Method*, p. 147; Neusner (1980), p. 281.

41. Neusner (1979) *Method*, p. 149; Neusner (1980), p. 284.

42. Neusner (1979) *Method*, p. 150; Neusner (1980), p. 285.

43. See chap. 3, n. 9; chap. 4, n. 9, and text thereto; and below, text between nn. 47–48, and n. 61 and text thereto.

44. See the reference in Neusner (1980), p. 202, n. 3.

45. Cp. Ludwig, p. 30, on the challenge posed by the destruction of the first temple. See also Herr.

46. See chap. 2, nn. 25 and 31—38, on the Christian materials. De Lange, p. 94, comments that he searched in vain to find a rabbinic response to these charges. We can understand this failure since rabbis dealt with the issue indirectly, without acknowledging that a change had occurred. See Kimelman for a discussion and bibliography of third-century responses to Christian polemics.

47. T. Ahilot 3:9, p. 600, ll. 16—18. In line B of Tosefta, Zuckermandel's text reads, "And the men entered . . ." The citation in Samson ben Abraham of Sens (to M. Ohalot 2:4, in Vilna ed. of BT) has "women" as does the parallel in Sifre Zutta to Num. 19:16, p. 313, and Epstein ed. p. 75, ll. 24—26. See Lieberman *TR*, 3:101; Epstein's notes; Neusner (1974—1977), 4:73; and Appendix A. The Tosefta follows the principle of M. Ohalot 2:4A. Alon believes the text refers to a roasted animal prepared in imitation of the sacrificial lamb and not to an actual sacrifice. See chap. 4, nn. 14, 17.

48. On this Mishnah see Appendix A.

49. Chap. 1, text to n. 4.

50. Ostow, pp. 15—16.

51. See, e.g., Schürer, 1:521—528; Bokser (1981); and chap. 2, n. 10 above.

52. Goldin (1965), pp. 286—287.

53. Ibid., p. 276.

54. Ibid., p. 278. See also "Revelation and Tradition as Religious Categories in Judaism" in Scholem (1971), pp. 282—303.

55. Neusner (1975), p. 194.

56. Ibid., p. 195. See also Bokser (1980), pp. 467—471, esp. 468, and 487, n. 26, on creative transmission of traditions.

57. P. Brown (1981), p. 71.

58. Goldin (1965), p. 282.

59. Neusner (1979) *Method*, p. 146, and Neusner (1980), p. 281.

60. Blau, p. viii. See also the reference to Scholem in n. 54.

61. See chap. 3, nn. 6—9, and the additional references in n. 43 above.

62. See chap. 3, nn. 10—12, and chap. 4, nn. 13—14, and text thereto.

63. See chap. 4, nn. 3, 22, 24—25, and texts thereto, and the additional references in chap. 1, n. 37; and above n. 25.

64. On the date of the Mekilta, see the references in Bokser (1980), pp. 356—357, nn. 66—67, esp. Kutscher's linguistic study, in *Lešonenu* 32 (1967—1968):103—116.

65. The passage derives from Exodus Rabbah II (the second half of the work, on Ex. 12—40), which is dated, in *EnJ*, "Exodus Rabbah," by M. D. Herr, to the ninth century. See also Shinan; and below.

66. Mekilta *Pisḥa*, chap. 5, p. 14, Lauterbach ed. 1:33—34, upon which the translation is based. If we could rely on the attribution in B.1, we would be dealing with an early second-century teaching; see Hyman, 3:913—915. Since, however, Eliezer Haqappar figures in the passage, in the tradition immediately following C, the date of the unit redactionally cannot be earlier than late second- or early third-century; see *EnJ*, "Eleazar (Eliezer) Ha-Kappar," by Shmuel Safrai. Moreover, part of the Midrash's perspective is determined by its confrontation with the biblical text. See the references in n. 64 above.

While B.2 might imply that the passover offering as a whole provided the needed merit, A and C focus on the specific detail of taking the lamb four days early. See the related comment attributed to R. Ishmael concerning the commandment to place the blood on the doorposts, in *Pisḥa*, chap. 7, p. 24, Lauterbach ed. 1:56; and chap. 11, pp. 38–39, Lauterbach ed. 1:87; and the discussion of this passage in Sanders, pp. 89–90, and the comments, pp. 104–107, 180–182. One should perhaps not place too much stress on the specific commandment mentioned. The Bible, here, Ex. 12 and Ezek. 16, determine the selection. If the specific choice is not crucial, the Midrash's overall point consists of the opening comment, viz., that *miṣvot* were required to merit redemption. Since God does not need a person's actions, whatever God requests is aimed at improving a person's interests. See M. Mak. 3:16; and Kadushin (1969), pp. 72–74. Accordingly, the passover sacrifice did have a purpose, but it did not serve that function alone. Cp. the text of Mekilta following A–C, in which a master challenges the assumption of A–C, claiming Israel did have a stock of merits. A different reason for the requirement to take the passover lamb is then supplied.

67. See the conclusion of the previous note. On the importance of circumcision in ancient Judaism, see Smith (1980) and his references.

68. Exodus Rabbah (*Bo*), 19.5, Vilna ed. pp. 36d–37a. The English translation is based on Midrash Rabbah, Freedman and Simon eds., 2:235–236. In clause C, Freedman and Simon follow the commentaries, e.g., Rashash (in Vilna ed.), and replace the verse cited with Ex. 12:50, which reports the Israelites' actions after Moses mentions circumcision. The printed edition's reading is supported by the citation of the passage in *Yalqut HaMakhiri* to Psalms, to Ps. 50, p. 137b [= p. 274].

69. See n. 65. Therefore we cannot automatically rely on the attribution, in B, to R. Simeon b. Ḥalafta, a late second-century to early third-century master, and place the whole passage during his lifetime. Note the two analogues in S. S. Rabbah, generally dated to about the sixth century and therefore considerably earlier than Exodus Rabbah. (See *EnJ*, "Song of Songs Rabbah," by M. D. Herr.) The first, 1. 1[12].3, Vilna ed. p. 12b, is analogous to G–L and, in part, C. While it is similar in depicting the function of the passover lamb, it differs in other respects. The passage is attributed to R. Abbahu, a late third-century master (see L. Levine). The second pericope, 3. 1[6].4, Vilna ed. p. 21b, is analogous to B–C and G–H, and the main part of the passage is unattributed. While we cannot provide an absolute date for the tradition in Exodus Rabbah, we can see that it represents a perspective considerably later than that of the Mekilta. Moreover, the contrast between the two highlights how Exodus Rabbah assumes the expendability of the passover sacrifice.

70. See, e.g., Urbach (1969), pp. 283, 329–330. For the plain sense of the usage, in this instance, see Childs, pp. 201–202.

71. On circumcision see n. 67.

72. Turner, pp. 131–165, observes that some religious groups try to perpetuate a state of communitas. It would be worth pursuing to what degree rabbinic structures were designed to carry out such a goal.

73. Wach, p. 42. Cp. Fredman, pp. 150–151.

74. See Sklare, pp. 114–117.

Appendix A

1. See Clark, pp. 270–271 and passim.

2. Alon, 1:164–166, followed by Safrai, p. 299, and in effect Goldschmidt, pp. 12, 51, n. 1. See above chap. 7, text to n. 48.

3. Alon, 1:165. See also Strashun to b. Pes. 74a; Halivni, 2:308–309, n. 2;

Albeck, 2:451; Safrai, pp. 299-300; Gutman, p. 146, n. 46; Kanter, pp. 71-72; Lightstone, pp. 60-61; and cp. Schürer, 1:522-523, nn. 47, 55.

4. See the discussion and references in Gereboff (1979), pp. 51-56, 69-70, n. 4. On Gamaliel's opinions, see Kanter, pp. 97-99.

5. See chap. 4, text to nn. 15-19.

6. The Erfurt MS, cited in Lieberman, supplies two instances of the bracketed phrase of "the nights of." Since it lacks a clause, it does not attest anything for the remaining instance. See Lieberman, Brief Commentary, in *The Tosefta*, ad loc., and nn. 7-10 below.

7. See Lieberman, ibid.

8. See n. 4.

9. See Lieberman *TK*, 5:957.

10. Lieberman *TK*, 5:957-960. See also Francus, *Beṣah*, pp. 36, 155-156, textual notes.

11. See Lieberman *TK*, 578-579, 5:957-960, esp. n. 39; Lieberman (1970), p. 129; Safrai, pp. 299-302, esp. n. 19; M. Beer (1961); and cp. Alon, 1:145-146, 164.

12. See chap. 7, n. 47 and text thereto.

13. See also Lieberman *TR*, 3:101; and Neusner (1974-1977), 4:73.

14. See Neusner (1974-1977), 4:348.

15. 4:300-301. See also *Antiquities*, 3:248, vol. 4, pp. 236-237.

16. See Lieberman *TK*, 5:959, n. 36; and the additional references cited in Juster, 1:357, n. 1; Clark, esp. pp. 275-277; Guttmann; and Schürer, 1:522-523. It should be noted that the instances of cultic terminology in early Christian writings cited by Clark cannot be used as evidence of a continued sacrificial rite. As demonstrated in chaps. 2 and 5 and in Bokser (1981), thinkers employ cultic language to apply one type of piety to a new context or to make a polemical argument based on the values of the old piety. See also chap. 5, n. 38.

17. Schürer, 1:524.

18. Smallwood, p. 347. See also pp. 344-355, esp. 347-348.

19. Smallwood, p. 345, n. 63. She applies this observation to two analogous references in Barnabas as well.

20. Altshuler, pp. 49-50, 63-64. See also Safrai, p. 301, n. 27.

Appendix B

1. Changes in the text of the questions have affected the text of the Mishnah. In the first question, the ʾPYLW, "even," is an addition. In the last clause, WDWRŠYM, "they expound," in the plural, is an error for WDWRŠ, the singular, found in the other MSS and in K MS for the other verbs in the passage. See chap. 3, n. 11.

2. For variants see chap. 3, n. 13.

3. See chap. 3, n. 14. ʿWLM is a mistake for ʿYRK, the reading in the other MSS. HYGYʿ ostensibly is an error for a form of YGYʿ, which is found in C, P, Y MSS, Unk edition and Columbia to BT. Since, however, Paris MS has ŠHGYʿ and L MS to PT has ʾŠR HGʿ, K MS may preserve an early variant.

4. On the variants, esp. the tense of the second verb, see chap. 3, n. 17.

5. K MS' WPTR has an extra W-, not found in other MSS. It is an error, unless the W- is an explicative to denote the result of the preceding clause. Cp. K MS to M. 10:8.

GLOSSARY

Afiqimon
: Or *afiqomon*, a mode of after-dinner revelry. A term in postmishnaic times also understood to refer to the piece of unleavened bread eaten at the end of the seder.

Amora
: Spokesperson. A term used for rabbinic masters in the postmishnaic period, in the time of the Gemara.

Apotropaic
: Providing protection, a notion applied, for example, to certain religious rituals.

Aristeas
: Letter of. A Jewish–Alexandrian Greek work, written probably in the second century B.C.E., purporting to describe the origins of the Greek translation to the Pentateuch.

Baraita
: An outside teaching formulated as if tannaitic and not in the Mishnah.

B.C.E.
: Before the Common or Christian Era, the period prior to the year 1.

C.E.
: Common Era, the period since the year 1 until the present year.

Communitas
: An anthropological term denoting an atmosphere that liberates individuals from social structures that normally separate them, thus enabling them to relate more readily to people and the divine.

Destruction
: With a capital *D*, the destruction of the Temple in Jerusalem, first in 586 B.C.E. and then in 70 C.E.

Diaspora
: The body of Jews living outside of Palestine.

Early Church
: The early Christian community in the first century.

Elephantine
: A place in lower Egypt where a Jewish garrison resided in the sixth-century B.C.E. and later.

Ezekiel, poet
: A second-century B.C.E. non-Palestinian Greek Jewish poet.

Fourth Ezra	A first-century C.E. apocalyptic work responding to the destruction of the Second Temple.
Gemara	Teaching: the body of postmishnaic teachings explaining, supplementing, and structured around the Mishnah, whose editing began in the fifth century C.E. See Talmud.
Haggadah	The literary work setting out the text of the Passover eve seder; written down first in early medieval times.
Halakhah	Pl. *halakhot*. Law or laws.
Hallel	A series of biblical psalms praising God.
Havdalah	A set of benedictions recited over wine to distinguish between the sacred time of Sabbaths and festivals and the mundane time of the rest of the week.
Hezekiah	Eighth-century B.C.E. king of Judah.
Josephus	First-century C.E. Jewish general and historian who wrote in Greek concerning the war against Rome and the antiquities of the Jews.
Josiah	Seventh-century B.C.E. king of Judah.
Jubilees	Second-century B.C.E. book from the Pseudepigrapha.
Justin	Second-century Christian writer who wrote *Dialogue with Trypho*, a polemical treatise against the Jews.
Levites	Members of the Israelite tribe that served in the temple, singing songs and assisting the priests.
Liminal	An anthropological term denoting a transitional situation in between different structured settings.
Mekilta	Tannaitic commentary and exposition of Exodus in two recensions, one attributed to the school of R. Ishmael and the other to R. Simeon b. Yoḥai.
Melito	Second-century Christian preacher from Sardis who wrote a homily on Jesus and Passover.
Midrash	Exposition and commentary on the Bible: with a capital *M*, a work characterized by this

	activity; with a lower case *m*, the activity itself.
Minḥah	Daily afternoon offering in the Temple. A term used to denote the time at which the sacrifice was brought: either the large (first) afternoon, from six and one-half hours after sunrise to sunset; or the smaller (second) afternoon, from nine and one-half hours to sunset.
Mishnah	A six-part collection of laws, further divided into a series of tractates, edited ca. 200 C.E., containing the basic teachings of early rabbinic Judaism.
Oral Torah	The notion that a fixed body of divine teachings was passed down orally in a monolithic line of transmission. Initially, it was held that the Oral Torah represented a second revelation given at Sinai along with the Written Torah; later, some held that the use of proper rules of exposition could uncover the Oral Torah in the Written Torah.
Paschal	See *passover*.
Passover	With a lower-case *p*: the sacrifice, also called the paschal offering, slaughtered on the fourteenth of Nisan and eaten at the end of the day or the beginning of the fifteenth, soon after nightfall; in biblical days, the rite associated with this offering constituted a holiday. With a capital *P*: the holiday associated with the passover offering and, in postbiblical terminology, the seven (or eight) day Festival of Unleavened Bread in general.
Pesaḥim	Passovers. The name of the mishnaic treatise on Passover.
Pharisees	A pre 70-C.E. Jewish group, forerunner of the rabbis, who believed that one could experience the divine presence both in daily life outside the temple as well as in the temple, a view reflected in such practices as eating profane foods outside of the temple in the manner in which priests ate consecrated food in the temple.

Philo	Alexandrian Greek-Jewish thinker, ca. 30 B.C.E. −45 C.E.
Pisha	Passover; the term used in certain manuscripts for the Tosefta treatise relating to Mishnah Pesaḥim and the name of the Mekilta section on Passover.
Qiddush	See Sanctification.
Qumran	A Jewish group in the late Second-Temple period that went to this location at the Dead Sea and evolved institutions independent from those of the Jerusalem Temple; the Dead Sea Scroll community.
Rabban	Our rabbi, a title generally reserved for an individual believed to be one of the patriarchs or leaders of the Jewish community in Palestine.
Samaritans	A Jewish group, originally native to Samaria (northern Palestine), that in the Second-Temple period became separate from the rest of the Jewish community, though the final break did not take place until later. Many of their practices reflect a literal understanding of the Bible.
Second Temple	The temple in Jerusalem, rebuilt in the sixth and fifth centuries B.C.E. and destroyed by the Romans in 70 C.E.
Sanctification	A benediction recited over wine, ushering in and sanctifying Sabbaths or festivals.
Seder	The order for the Passover evening ritual (a word so used first only in postmishnaic times).
Symposium	Greco-Roman banquet and drinking party.
Talmud	Learning: the Mishnah and Gemara together, though the term is sometimes used to denote the Gemara alone.
Tanna	Rabbinic master in the mishnaic period, 70−200 C.E.
Temple Scroll	A document found at Qumran though not necessarily authored by that community, which sets out a blueprint for the future, presented in the form of a divine oracle to Moses and reworking biblical materials.

Tosefta   Supplement: Tannaitic collection of teachings structured around the Mishnah, explaining, complementing, and supplementing it, and edited soon after it.

Therapeutae   A contemplative spiritual group described by Philo.

Unleavened Bread   Festival of, on which unleavened bread is eaten for seven days, beginning with the night of the fifteenth of Nisan; in postbiblical times, interchangeably used with Passover.

Wisdom of Solomon   Greek-Jewish philosophical work, written ca. 37–41 C.E.

ABBREVIATIONS AND BIBLIOGRAPHY

I. ABBREVIATIONS AND BIBLIOGRAPHY TO TERMS, TRACTATES, PARTS OF
MULTIVOLUME WORKS, SERIALS, AND OTHERS

AJS	*Association for Jewish Studies Review*
ANRW	*Aufsteig und Niedergand Der Römischen Welt*
Arak.	ʿArakhin
b.	bavil, Babylonian Talmud; *or* ben
B.C.E.	Before the Common (*or* Christian) Era
Bekr.	Bekhorot
Ber.	Berakhot
BIA	*Bar Ilan Annual*
Bik.	Bikurim
BJS	Brown Judiac Studies
B.Q.	Bava Qamma
BT	Babylonian Talmud (bavli)
CBQ	*Catholic Biblical Quarterly*
CCARJ	*Central Conference of American Rabbis, Journal of*
C.E.	Common (*or* Christian) Era
Dem.	Demʾai
Edu.	ʿEduyyot
EnJ	*Encyclopaedia Judaica.* Jerusalem, 1971, 1973.
EnM	*Encyclopedia Miqrait* [*Biblica*]. Edited by E. L. Sukenik et al. Jerusalem, 1965–(8 volumes through 1982).
Eruv.	ʿEruvin
Git.	Giṭṭin
Hag.	Ḥagigah

HR	*History of Religions*
HTR	*Harvard Theological Review*
HUCA	*Hebrew Union College Annual*
InDB	*Interpreters Dictionary of the Bible*. 4 Vols. New York, 1962. Supplementary Volume. Nashville, 1976.
IESS	*International Encyclopaedia of the Social Sciences*
JAAR	*Journal of the American Academy of Religion*
JAARSup	*Journal of the American Academy of Religion, Supplement Volume*
JAOS	*Journal of the American Oriental Society*
JBL	*Journal of Biblical Literature*
JJS	*Journal of Jewish Studies*
JQR	*Jewish Quarterly Review*
JRJ	*Journal of Reform Judaism*
JRS	*Journal of Roman Studies*
JSJ	*Journal for the Study of Judaism in the Persian, Hellenistic, and Roman Period*
JSS	*Journal of Semitic Studies*
JTS	*Journal of Theological Studies*
Ket.	Ketubot
KS	*Kirjath Sepher*
M.	Mishnah
Meg.	Megillah
Miq.	Miqvaot
M.S.	Ma'aser Sheni
Ned.	Nedarim
Neg.	Nega'im
NTS	*New Testament Studies*
OxCD	*Oxford Classical Dictionary*
PAAJR	*Proceedings of the American Academy for Jewish Research*
Pes.	Pesaḥim *or* Pisḥa
PT	Palestinian Talmud (yerushalmi)

R.   Rav, Rabbi

RQ   *Revue de Qumran*

R.H.   Rosh Hashanah

San.   Sanhedrin

Shab.   Shabbat

Sheq.   Sheqallim

Sot.   Soṭah

Suk.   Sukkah

T.   Tosefta

TDNT   *Theological Dictionary of the New Testament*. Edited by G. Kittel
            and G. Friedrich, 9 vols. Grand Rapids, 1964–1974.

Ter.   Terumot

TK   Saul Lieberman, *Tosefta Ki-Fshuṭah*, 1. New York, 1955–
            Eight vols. to date.

Toh.   Ṭohorot

TR   Saul Lieberman, *Tosefeth Rishonim*. 4 vols. Jerusalem,
            1937–1939.

VT   *Vetus Testamentum*.

y.   Yerushalmi (Palestinian Talmud)

Yad.   Yadayim

Y.T.   Yom Ṭov

Zav.   Zavim

Zev.   Zevaḥim

II. ABBREVIATIONS AND BIBLIOGRAPHY TO EDITIONS AND MSS OF PRIMARY
RABBINIC SOURCES

A. *The Mishnah*

Albeck   Albeck, Chanoch, ed. *Shisha Sidre Mishnah*. 6 vols. Jerusalem,
            1954–1959. [Reference without a volume number is to
            vol. 2: Moʿed., Tractate Pesaḥim, ad loc. or to page cited.]

Baneth   Baneth, Eduard, ed. *Mischnajot. Die Sechs Ordnungen der*

Mischna. Teil II Ordnung Mo'ed. Berlin, 1927. Reprint. Basel, 1968.

Beer   Beer, Georg, transl., ed., and intro. *Die Mishna. Seder Moed. 3 Traktat Pesachim*. Giessen, 1912.

C   Lowe, W. H., ed. *The Mishnah on Which the Palestinian Talmud Rests*. Cambridge, 1883. Jerusalem, 1967.

GM   Katsh, Abraham, ed. *Ginze Mishna*. Jerusalem, 1970.

K   *Mischnacodex Kaufmann* A 50. Jerusalem, 1968.

Maimo-   *Maimonides. Mishnah im Perush Rabenu Moshe ben Maimon.*
nides   Edited by Yosef Qapiaḥ. 7 vols. Jerusalem, 1963–1968.

Naples   *Mishah Naples*, p.e. 1492. Reprint. Jerusalem, 1970.

P   *Mishna Codex Parma 138*. Jerusalem, 1970.

Paris   *Mishna Codex Paris: Paris 328–329*. Jerusalem, 1973.

Unk   *Mishna. Sedarim Zeraim, Moed, Nashim: Unknown Edition.* Jerusalem, 1970.

Vilna   *Shisha Sidre Mishnah*. 13 vols. Jerusalem: El HaMekorot, 1955–1958. Based on Vilna ed. with additional commentaries.

Y   *The Mishnah: Order Mo'ed, A Yemenite Manuscript*. Published by Yehuda Levi Naḥum, with introduction by Shelomo Morag. Ḥolon, 1975.

B. The Tosefta

The   Lieberman, Saul, ed. *The Tosefta* with a Brief Commentary.
Tosefta   Vols. 1 [to date, four parts, through the end of Nashim]. New York, 1955–.

Tosephta   Zuckermandel, M. S., ed. *Tosephta*. Reprint. Jerusalem, 1963.

C. The Babylonian Talmud

Colum-   Columbia MS to Talmud Megillah and Pesahim. X 898–T 141.
bia

DS   Rabbinovicz, Raphaelo. *Diqduque Sofrim*. 12 vols. Reprint. New York, 1960. [Cited by page and line or footnote to tractate under discussion, ad. loc.]

Ketubot,   Hershler Moshe, ed. *Talmud Bavli. Masekhet Ketubot.* 2 vols.
Hersler   Jerusalem, 1972–1979.
ed.

Ven   *Babylonian Talmud.* Venice, p.e. 1520–1523. Reprint.
               Jerusalem, 1970–1972.

Vilna   *Babylonian Talmud.* 20 vols. New York: Otzar Hasefarim, 1965.
               Reprint of Vilna: Romm, 1895, edition with additional
               commentaries.

D. The Palestinian Talmud

Beṣah,   *Talmud Yerushalmi Masekhet Beṣah with the Commentary of*
Francus   *Eleazar Azikri.* Edited, introduced, and annotated by Israel
ed.   Francus. New York, 1967.

L   Palestinian Talmud: Leiden MS Cod. Scal. 3. Jerusalem, 1971.

Ven.   *Palestinian Talmud.* Venice, p.e. 1522–1523. Reprint. N.p., n.d.

Vilna   *Palestinian Talmud.* 7 vols. New York: *Talmud Yerushalmi*, 1959.
               Reprint of Vilna edition with additional commentaries.

E. Other Rabbinic Works

Gn. R.   Theodor, J., and Albeck, Ch., eds. *Bereschit Rabba.* 3 vols.
               Jerusalem, 1965.

Mekilta   Horovitz, H. S., and Rabin, I. A., eds. *Mechilta D'Rabbi Ismael.*
               Jerusalem, 1955.

Mekilta,   Fridemann, Meir, ed. *Mekilta D'Rabbi Išmael im Tosfot Meir*
Fried-   *'Ayyin.* Vienna, 1870. Reprint. Jerusalem, 1961.
mann

Mekilta,   Lauterbach, Jacob Z., ed. and trans. *Mekilta de-Rabbi Ishmael.*
Lauter-   3 vols. Philadelphia, 1933, 1976.
bach

Mekilta   Epstein, J. N., and Melamed, E. Z., eds. *Mekhilta D'Rabbi*
DRŠBY   *Šim'on b. Jochai.* Jerusalem, 1955.

Mekilta   Hoffman, David, ed. *Mechilta de-Rabbi Šimon b. Jochai.*
DRŠBY,   Frankfurt, 1905. Reprint. Israel, 1969.
Hoff-
mann

Midrash Rabbah	*Midrash Rabbah ʿal Ḥamishah Ḥummshe Torah veḤamesh Megillot*. 2 vols. Vilna: Romm, 1884–1887. Reprint. Jerusalem, 1961. English Translation: *The Midrash Rabbah*, translated by H. Freedman and Maurice Simon. 5 vols. Reprint. London, 1977.
Midrash Tanna'im	Hoffmann, David, ed. *Midrash Tanna'im*. Berlin, 1909. Reprint in 2 vols. Tel Aviv, n.d.
Midrash Leqaḥ Ṭov	Tovia Ben Eliezer. *Midrash Leqaḥ Ṭov to Leviticus, Numbers, and Deuteronomy*. Edited by Meir Katzenellenbogen of Padua. 1884. Reprint. Jerusalem, 1960.
Sifra	Weiss, I. H., ed. *Sifra D'Be Rav*. Vienna, 1882. Reprint. New York, 1946.
Sifre	Finkelstein, Louis, ed. *Sifre on Deuteronomy*. New York, 1969.
Sifre Num.	Horovitz, H. S., ed. *Siphre D'Be Rab. Siphre ad Numeros adjecto Siphre zutta*. 2d ed. Jerusalem, 1966.
SZ *or* Sifre Zuṭṭa	*See* Sifre Numbers. *Also*: J. N. Epstein, "Sifre Zuṭṭa Parshat Parah." *Tarbiẕ* 1, pt. 1 (1930):46–77.

III. ABBREVIATIONS AND BIBLIOGRAPHY TO NONRABBINIC SOURCES, SECONDARY LITERATURE, AND REMAINING WORKS

Alon	Alon, Gedalyahu. *Toldot Ha Yehudim BeEreṣ Yisrael BiTequfat HaMishnah Ve-Ha-Talmud*. Vol. 1. Tel Aviv, 1967.
Altshuler	Altshuler, David Aron. "Descriptions in Josephus' *Antiquities* of the Mosiac Constitution." Ph.D. dissertation, Hebrew Union College-Jewish Institute of Religion, Cincinnati, 1977.
Alt	Alt, Albrecht. *Essays on Old Testament History and Religion*. Translated by R. A. Wilson. Oxford, 1966.
Amir	Amir, Yehoshua. "Philo's Version of the Pilgrimage to Jerusalem" [Hebrew]. In *Jerusalem in the Second Temple Period*, edited by A. Oppenheimer et al., pp. 154–165. Jerusalem, 1980.
Aristeas	*Letter of Aristeas to Philocrates*. See editions of Hadas and Pelletier.

Attridge   Attridge, Harold. *The Interpretation of Biblical History in the Antiquitates Judaicae of Flavius Josephus*. HTR, Harvard Dissertations in Religion, no. 7. Missoula, 1976.

Azulai   Azulai, Hayyim Yosef. *Sefer Petah 'Ennayim*. Lvorno, 1790. Reprint. Jerusalem, 1970.

Badia   Badia, L. F. *The Dead Sea People's Sacred Meal and Jesus' Last Supper*. Washington, D.C., 1979.

Bahr   Bahr, Gordon J. "The Seder of Passover and the Eucharist Words." *Novem Testamentum* 12 (1970):181–202.

Barrow   Barrow, R. H. *Plutarch and His Times*. London, 1967.

Baum-   Baumgarten, Joseph M. "4Q HALAKAH 5, The Law of
garten   HADASH, and the Pentecontad Calendar." *JJS* 27 (1976): 36–46.

Baum-   ———. "Sacrifice and Worship Among the Jewish Sectarians of
garten   the Dead Sea (Qumran) Scrolls." *HTR* 46 (1953):141–159.
(1953)

Baum-   ———. *Studies in Qumran Law*. Leiden, 1975.
garten
(1975)

Bayer   Bayer, Bathja. "The Biblical Nebel." *Yuval* 1 (1968):90–131.

Beer, M.   Beer, M. *The Babylonian Exilarchate in the Arsacid and Sassanian Periods* [Hebrew]. Tel Aviv, 1970.

Beer, M.   ———. "Theudas of Rome and Emperor Worship in the Reign of
(1961)   Domitian" [Hebrew]. *Zion* 26 (1961):238–240.

Belkin   Belkin, Samuel. *Philo and the Oral Law*. Harvard Semitic Series, vol. 11. Cambridge, 1940.

Bendavid   Bendavid, Abba. *Biblical and Mishnaic Hebrew*. Vol. 1. Tel Aviv, 1967.

Bicker-   Bickerman, E. J. "La chaine de la tradition Pharisienne." *Revue
man   Biblique* 59 (1952):44–54.

Blau   Blau, Joseph L. *Modern Varieties of Judaism*. New York, 1964, 1966.

Bloch   Bloch, A. P. *The Biblical and Historical Background of the Jewish Holy Days*. New York, 1978.

Bokser   Bokser, Baruch M. "The Achievement of Jacob N. Epstein." In

The Modern Study of the Mishnah, edited by Jacob Neusner, pp. 13–55. Leiden, 1975.

Bokser   ———. *Philo's Description of Jewish Practices*. Center for
(1977)   Hermeneutical Studies in Hellenistic and Modern Culture. *Protocol of the Thirtieth Coloquy*. Berkeley, 1977.

Bokser   ———. "A Minor for *Zimmun* (Y. Ber. 7:2, 11c) and Recensions
(1979)   of Yerushalmi." *AJS* 4 (1979):1–25.

Bokser   ———. *Post Mishnaic Judaism in Transition: Samuel on Berakhot*
(1980)   *and the Beginnings of Gemara*. Chico, 1980.

Bokser   ———. "Maʿal and Blessings Over Food: Rabbinic Transforma-
(1981)   tion of Cultic Terminology and Alternative Forms of Piety." *JBL* 100 (1981):557–574.

Bokser   ———. "Blessings and Miṣvot, the History of the Halakhah, and
(1982)   the Beginnings of the Gemara." In *Jewish Law in Our Time*, edited by Ruth Link-Salinger, pp. 3–17. New York, 1982.

Bokser   ———. "Rabbinic Responses to Catastrophe: From Continuity to
(1983)   Discontinuity." *PAAJR*. 50 (1983): 37–61.

Bokser   ———. "Passover and the Meaning of Redemption According to
(1984)   the Palestinian Talmud." *AJS*, in press.

Bonner   Bonner, C. *Homily on the Passion*. Philadelphia, 1940.

Brown   Brown, J. P. "The Mediterranean Vocabulary of the Vine." *VT* 19 (1969):146–170.

Brown,   Brown, Peter. "The Rise and Function of the Holy Man in Late
P.   Antiquity." *JRS* 61 (1971):80–101.

Brown,   ———. *A Social Context to the Religious Crisis of the Third*
P. (1975)   *Century A.D.* Center for Hermeneutical Studies in Hellenistic and Modern Cultures. *Protocol of the Fourteenth Colloquy*, pp. 1–13. Berkeley, 1975.

Brown,   ———. *The Cult of the Saints*. Chicago, 1981.
P. (1981)

Büchler   Büchler, A. *The Priests and Their Cult*. Jerusalem, 1966.

Callan   Callan, Terrance. "Pauline Midrash: The Exegetical Background of Gal. 3:19b." *JBL* 99 (1980):549–567.

Cantala-   Cantalamessa, Raniero. *I Pio Antichi, Testi Pasquali della Chiesa.*
messa   *La Omelie di Meleto di Sardi*. Rome, 1972.

Car-   Carmichael, Calum M. *The Laws of Deuteronomy*. Ithaca, N.Y.,
michael   1974.

Chad-   Chadwick, Henry. *The Early Church*. London, 1967.
wick

Charles   Charles, R. H., ed. *The Apocrypha and Pseudepigrapha of the Old
               Testament in English*. Vol. 2: *Pseudepigrapha*. Oxford,
               1913, 1969.

Chen-   Chenderlin, Fritz. "Distributed Observance of the Passover: A
derlin   Hypothesis." *Biblica* 56 (1975):369–393.

Childs   Childs, Brevard. *The Book of Exodus*. Philadelphia, 1974.

Clark   Clark, K. W. "Worship in the Jerusalem Temple After 70." *NTS*
               6 (1959–1960):269–280.

Clement,   Clement of Alexandria. *Paidagogos. Christ the Educator*.
Paida-   Translated by Simon P. Wood. The Fathers of the Church. A
gogos   New Translation, vol. 23. New York, 1954.

Cohen   Cohen, Gerson D. "The Talmudic Age." In *Great Ages and Ideas
               of the Jewish People*, edited by Leo Schwartz, pp. 143–212.
               New York, 1956.

Cohn   Cohn, R. L. "Jerusalem." *JAARSup* 46, no. 1 (1978):1–26.

Conzel-   Conzelmann, Hans. *History of Primitive Christianity*. Translated
mann   by John E. Steely. Nashville, 1973.

Conzel-   ———. *The Theology of Saint Luke*. London, 1960.
mann
(1960)

Cowley   Cowley, A. *Aramaic Papyri of the Fifth Century*. Oxford,
               1923.

Cross   Cross, Frank Leslie. *The Early Christian Fathers*. London, 1960.

Cross   ———. "Review." *JTS* 11 (1960):162–163.
(1960)

Cross,   Cross, Frank Moore. *The Ancient Library of Qumran and Modern
F. M.   Biblical Studies*. New York, 1958.

Daube   Daube, David. *The New Testament and Rabbinic Judaism*.
               London, 1956.

Daube   ———. "The Significance of the Afikoman." *Pointer*. London 3,
(1968)   no. 3 (Spring, 1968):4–5.

Daube (1974)	———. *Wine in the Bible*. Saint Paul's Lecture, no. 13. London, 1974.
Daumas and Miquel	Daumas, F. and Miquel, P., eds. *Philon D'Alexandrie De Vita Contemplativa*. Les Oeuvres de Philon D'Alexandire, edited by Roger Arbaldez et al., vol. 29. Paris, 1963.
Davies	Davies, W. D. *Paul and Rabbinic Judaism*. 3d ed. London, 1962, 1970.
Davies (1964)	———. *The Setting of the Sermon on the Mount*. Cambridge, 1964.
Dead Sea Scrolls	See Licht, Vermes (1975), and Yadin.
De Lange	De Lange, Nicholas. *Origen and the Jews*. University of Cambridge Oriental Publications, vol. 25. Cambridge, 1976.
Delcor	Delcor, M. "Repas cultuels Esseniens et Therapeutes, Thiases et Havuroth." *RQ* 23 (1968):401–425.
De Vaux	De Vaux, Roland. *Ancient Israel*. Translated by John McHugh. New York, 1962.
De Vaux (1973)	———. *Archaeology and the Dead Sea Scrolls*. Rev. English transl. London, 1973.
Douglas	Douglas, Mary. "Deciphering a Meal." *Daedalus*. Winter, 1972, pp. 61–81.
Durk-heim	Durkheim, Emile. *The Elementary Forms of Religious Life*. New York, 1961.
Edels	Samuel Eliezer ben Judah Ha-Levi Edels ("Maharsha"). Commentary on the Babylonian Talmud. In standard editions of the BT.
Elbogen	Elbogen, Ismar. "Eingang und Ausgang des Sabbats." In *Festschrift zu Israel Lewy's Siebzigstem Geburstag*, edited by M. Brann and I. Elbogen, pp. 179–187. Breslau, 1911.
Elbogen (1972)	———. *HaTefillah Be Yisrael*. A Hebrew Revised and Expanded Edition by Yehoshua Amir, J. Heinemann, et al. Tel Aviv, 1972.
EnJ, "Chron-icles"	*Encyclopaedia Judaica*. S. v. "Chronicles, Book of." by S. Japhet.

EnJ, ———. "Cult," by B. Levine.
"Cult"

EnJ, ———. "Deuteronomy, Critical Assessment," by Moshe
"Deu- Weinfeld.
teron-
omy"

EnJ, ———. "Eleazar Ha-Kappar," by Shmuel Safrai.
"Eleazar
Ha-
Kappar"

EnJ, ———. "Exodus Rabbah," by M. D. Herr.
"Exodus
Rabbah"

EnJ, ———. "Ezekiel the Poet," by Marshall S. Hurwitz.
"Ezekiel
the Poet"

EnJ, ———. "Mishmarot and Ma'amodot[!]," by Daniel Sperber.
"Mish-
marot
and
Ma'am-
adot"

EnJ, ———. "Music," by Bathja Bayer and Hanoch Avenary.
"Music"

EnJ, ———. "Passover," by Louis Jacobs and Ernst Kutsch.
"Pass-
over"

EnJ, ———. "Philo the Elder," by B. Z. Wacholder.
"Philo
the
Elder"

EnJ, ———. "Seʿudah," by M. Ydit.
"Se
ʿudah"

EnJ, "Song of ———. "Song of Songs Rabbah," by M. D. Herr.
Songs Rabbah"

EnJ,   ———. "Symbolism, Jewish," by E. R. Goodenough.
"Symbolism"

EnJ,   ———. "Synagogue. Origins and History," by L. I.
"Synagogue"   Rabinowitz.

EnJ, "Thera-   ———. "Therapeutae," by M. Mansoor.
peutae"

EnM, "BYT   *Encyclopedia Miqrait.* S.v. "BYT MRZH," by
MRZH"   S. Loewenstamm.

EnM,   ———. "MDRŠ," by Isaac Heinemann.
"MDRŠ"

EnM,   ———. "MRWR," by Jacob Licht.
"MRWR"

EnM,   ———. "MŠWRR, MŠWRRYM," by Jacob Liver.
"MŠWRR"

EnM, "MṬH"   ———. "MṬH," by Magen Broshi.

EnM,   ———. "Neginah UZimrah," by Bathja Bayer.
"Neginah"

EnM, "PSḤ"   ———. "PSḤ," by Jacob Licht.

EnM, "YYN"   ———. "YYN," by H. H. Beinart.

EnM, "ZBḤ"   ———. "ZBḤ," by Jacob Licht.

Epstein   Epstein, Jacob N. *Introduction to Amoraitic Literature*
                          [Hebrew]. Jerusalem, 1962.

Epstein (1957)   ———. *Introduction to Tannaitic Literature.* [Hebrew].
                          Jerusalem, 1957.

Epstein (1964)   ———. *Introduction to the Text of the Mishnah* [Hebrew].
                          2d ed. Jerusalem, 1964.

Falls   See Justin Martyr.

Feeley-Harnik   Feeley-Harnik, Gillain. *The Lord's Table.* Philadelphia,
                          1981.

Feinde, Behm,   Feinde, Paul, Behm, Johannes, and Kümmel, Werner Georg.
Kümmel   *Introduction to the New Testament.* 14th rev. ed.
                          Nashville, 1966.

Feliks   Feliks, J. *Plant World of the Bible.* Ramat Gan, 1968.

Finkelstein   Finkelstein, L. "Maccabean Documents in the Passover
                          Haggadah." *HTR* 36 (1943):1−38.

Fiorenza   Fiorenza, Elisabeth Schussler. "Cultic Language in Qumran and in the New Testament." *CBQ* 18 (1976):159−177.

Fischel   Fischel, Henry A. "Elements of Graeco-Roman Symposiastic Games in the Passover Seder." In *Abstracts of the Society of Biblical Literature, 112th Annual Meeting*, edited by George MacRae, pp. 12−13. Missoula, 1976.

Fischel (1969)   ———. "Story and History: Observations on Graeco-Roman Rhetoric and Pharisaism." *American Oriental Society Middle West Branch Semi-Centennial* 3 (1969):59−88.

Fischel (1970)   ———. "Studies in Cynicism and the Ancient Near East: The Transformation of a Chria." In *Religions in Antiquity, Essays in Memory of Erwin R. Goodenough*. Studies in the History of Religions. Supplements to Numen, vol. 14, edited by Jacob Neusner, pp. 372−411. Leiden, 1968, 1970.

Fischel (1973)   ———. "The Uses of Sorites (Climax, Graduation) in the Tannaitic Period." *HUCA* 44 (1973):119−52.

Fischel (1975)   ———. "Wisdom in the World of Midrash." In *Aspects of Wisdom in Judaism and Early Christianity*, edited by R. L. Wilken, pp. 67−102. Notre Dame, Ind., 1975.

Fischel (1977)   ———. *Essays in Greco-Roman and Related Talmudic Literature*. New York, 1977.

Fishbane   Fishbane, Michael. *Text and Texture*. New York, 1979.

Fitzmyer   Fitzmyer, J. A. *The Dead Sea Scrolls. Major Publications*. Sources for Biblical Study, vol. 8. Missoula, 1975.

Flusser   Flusser, D. "A Passover Sermon and Deicide" [Hebrew]. *Davar*. 14 Nisan 5735 (1975), p. 20.

Fraenkel   Fraenkel, David. "Shireh Qorban." Commentary on the PT. In standard editions of the PT with commentaries.

Fraenkel, J.   Fraenkel, Jonah. *Studies in the Spiritual World of the Aggadic Story* [Hebrew]. Tel Aviv?, 1981.

Francis   Francis, Fred O. "The Baraita of the Four Sons." *JAAR* 42 (1974):280−297.

Francus, *Besaḥ.*   See sec. II.D. in Abbreviations and Bibliography

Fredman   Fredman, Ruth. *The Passover Seder*. Philadelphia, 1981.

Freedman   Freedman, Jacob. *Polychrome Historical Haggadah for Passover*. Springfield, Mass. 1974.

Friedlander   Friedlander, Ludwig. *Roman Life and Manners*. Translated by J. H. Freese and L. A. Magnus. 4 vols. London, 1965.

Friedman   Friedman, Shamma. "The 'Law of Increasing Members' in Mishnaic Hebrew" [Hebrew]. Lešonénu 35 (1971):117– 129, 192–206.

Friedmann   Friedmann, Meir [Ish Shalom]. *Meir ʿAyin ʿal Seder Ve-Haggadah Shel Lele Pesaḥ*. Vienna, 1895. Reprint. Jerusalem, 1971.

Gärtner   Gärtner, Bertil. *The Temple and the Community in Qumran and the New Testament*. Oxford, 1965.

Geiger   Geiger, Abraham. *HaMiqra VeTargumov* [Hebrew translation of *Urschrift*]. 2d ed. 1928. Translated by Y. L. Baruch. Jerusalem, 1972.

Geoltrain   Geoltrain, Pierre, "Le traité de la Vie Contemplative de Philon d'Alexandrie." *Semitica* 10 (1960):1–66.

Gereboff   Gereboff, Joel. "David Weiss Halivni on the Mishnah." In *The Modern Study of the Mishnah*, edited by Jacob Neusner, pp. 180–196. Leiden, 1975.

Gereboff   ———. *Rabbi Tarfon: The Tradition, the Man, and Early
(1979)   Rabbinic Judaism*. Missoula, 1979.

Gerson-Kiwi   Gerson-Kiwi, Edith. "Vocal Folk Polyphonies." *Yuval* 1 (1968):181–187.

Ginzberg   Ginzberg, H. L. "Psalms and Inscriptions of Petition and Acknowledgement." In *Louis Ginzberg Jubilee Volume*, edited by S. Lieberman et al., pp. 159–171. New York, 1946.

Goldberg   Goldberg, Abraham. "Palestinian Law in Babylonian Tradition" [Hebrew]. *Tarbiẓ* 33 (1964):337–348.

Goldin   Goldin, Judah. "Not by Means of an Angel and not by Means of a Messenger." In *Religions in Antiquity*, edited by Jacob Neusner, pp. 412–424. Leiden, 1968, 1970.

Goldin (1965)   ———. "Of Change and Adaptation in Judaism." *HR* 4 (1965):269–294

Goldin (1976)   ———. "Toward a Profile of the Tanna, Aqiba ben Joseph." *JAOS* 96 (1976):38–56.

Goldschmidt   Goldschmidt, E. D. *The Passover Haggadah* [Hebrew]. Jerusalem, 1960.

Goodblatt   Goodblatt, David. *Rabbinic Instruction in Sasanian Babylonia*. Leiden, 1975.

Goodenough   Goodenough, Erwin R. *Jewish Symbols in the Greco-Roman Period*. 13 vols. New York, 1953–1968.

Goodenough   ———. *The Jurisprudence of the Jewish Courts in Egypt*.
(1929)   New Haven, 1929.

Green   Green, William S. "Palestinian Holy Men and the Rabbinic Tradition." *ANRW* 2. 19.2 (1979):619–47.

Green (1978)   ———. "What's in a Name? The Problematic of Rabbinic 'Biography'." *Approaches to Ancient Judaism: Theory and Practice 1*, edited by William S. Green. pp. 77–96. Missoula, 1978.

Green (1981)   ———. *The Traditions of Rabbi Joshua*. Leiden, 1981.

Greenberg   Greenberg, Moshe. "On the Refinement of the Conception of Prayer in Hebrew Scriptures." *AJS* 1 (1976):57–92.

Guéraud and   Guéraud, Octave and Nautin, Pierre, ed., trans., and intro.
Nautin   *Origene. Sur la Pâque*. Christianisme Antique, no. 2. Paris, 1979.

Gutman   Gutman, Yehoshua. *Beginnings of Jewish Hellenistic Literature*. [Hebrew]. 2 vols. Jerusalem, 1963.

Gutman (1954)   ———. "Philo the Epic Poet," *Scripta Hierosolymitana* 1 (1954):36–63.

Guttmann   Guttmann, A. "The End of the Jewish Sacrificial Cult." *HUCA* 38 (1967):137–148.

Hadas   Hadas, Moses. *Aristeas to Philocrates*. New York. 1951.

Halivni   Halivni, David Weiss. *Sources and Traditions* [Hebrew]. 4 vols. Jerusalem, 1968–1982.

Halivni (1979)   ———. "The Reception Accorded Rabbi Judah's Mishnah."
                    In *Jewish and Christian Self-Definition*, vol. 2, edited
                    by E. P. Sanders, pp. 204–212, 379–382. Philadel-
                    phia, 1981.

Halivni (1981)   "Comments on the 'Four Questions' " [Hebrew]. In *Studies
                    in Aggadah, Targum, and Jewish Liturgy in Memory of
                    Joseph Heinemann*, edited by J. J. Petuchowski and
                    E. Fleisher, pp. 67–74. Jerusalem, 1981.

Hall   Hall, Stuart G. "Melito in the Light of the Passover Hagga-
                    dah." *JTS* 22 (1971):29–46.

Hall (1979)   ———. *Melito of Sardis on Pascha*. Oxford, 1979.

Haran   Haran, Menahem. *Temples and Temple-Service in Ancient
                    Israel*. Oxford, 1978.

Haran (1970)   ———. "Zevaḥ HaYamim." In *Sefer Shmuel Yevin*, edited
                    by Samuel Abramsky, pp. 170–186. Jerusalem, 1970.

Haran (1979)   ———. "Priest, Temple, and Worship" [Hebrew]. *Tarbiẓ*
                    48 (1979):175–185.

Harper   Harper, P. O. "Thrones and Enthronement Seats in
                    Sasanian Art," *Iran* 17 (1979):49–64.

Harris   Harris, Monford, "The Passover Seder on Entering the Order
                    of History." *Judaism* 25 (1976):167–174.

Heilman   Heilman, S. C. *Synagogue Life*. Chicago, 1976.

Heinemann   Heinemann, Joseph. *Aggadah and its Development* [Hebrew].
                    Jerusalem, 1974.

Heinemann   ———. "Review of Goldschmidt's 'Haggadah' " [Hebrew].
(1960–1961)   *Tarbiẓ* 30 (1960–1961):405–410.

Heinemann   ———. *Prayer in the Period of the Tanna'im and the
(1964)   Amora'im* [Hebrew]. Jerusalem, 1964.

Heller   Heller, R. Yom Tov Lippman. "Tosefot Yom Ṭov." Com-
                    mentary on Mishnah, in Vilna editions.

Hengel   Hengel, Martin. *Judaism and Hellenism*. 2 vols. Translated
                    by John Bowden. Philadelphia, 1974.

Herr   Herr, M. D. "Jerusalem, the Temple and Its Cult: Reality and
                    Concepts in Second Temple Times" [Hebrew]. In

	Jerusalem in the Second Temple Period, edited by A. Oppenheimer et al., pp. 166–177. Jerusalem, 1980.
Higgins	Higgins, A. J. B. *The Lord's Supper in the New Testament.* Studies in Biblical Theology, vol. 6. London, 1952.
Hoenig	Hoenig, Sidney B. "City Square and Synagogue." *ANRW* 2.19.1 (1979):448–476.
Hoffman	Hoffman, Lawrence A. *The Canonization of the Synagogue Service.* Notre Dame, Ind., 1979
Hoffmann	Hoffmann, David. "A Critical Article Concerning Several Mishnayot in Pesaḥim Chapter Ten" [Hebrew]. In *Beith Waad Lachachomim*, vol. 2, edited by J. Ch. Daiches, pp. 17–21. Leeds, 1902.
Hoffman (1913)	———. *HaMishnah HaRishonah.* Berlin, 1913. Reprint. Jerusalem, 1968.
Hoffmann (1924)	———. "Novellae and Notes" [Hebrew]. *Jeshurun* 11 (1924):20–22.
Hoffmann (1972)	———. "On the Passover Haggadah" [Hebrew]. *Ha-Maayan* 12 (Nisan, 1972):1–9.
Hyman	Hyman, Aaron. *Toldot Tannaim VeAmoraim.* 3 vols. Reprint. Jerusalem, 1964.
ibn Ezra	ibn Ezra, Abraham. Commentary on the Torah. In *Meḥoqeqei Yehudah.* Edited by Yehudah Leib Krinsky. Reprint. Bnei Brak, 1961.
Idelsohn	Idelsohn, A. Z. *Jewish Music in Its Historical Development.* New York, 1948.
IESS, "Food, II. Consumption Patterns"	*IESS*. S.v. "Food, II. Consumption Patterns," by Yehudi A. Cohen.
InDB, "Agape"	*Interpreters Dictionary of the Bible.* S.v. "Agape," by M. H. Shepherd.
InDB, "Banquet"	———. "Banquet," by J. F. Ross.
InDB, "Eucharist"	———. "Eucharist," by M. H. Shepherd.

InDB, "Lord's   ———. "Lord's Supper," by M. H. Shepherd.
Supper"

InDB,   ———. "Meals," by J. F. Ross.
"Meals"

InDB,   ———. "Wine," by J. F. Ross.
"Wine"

InDBS, "Acts   *Interpreters Dictionary of the Bible, Supplementary Volume*.
of the   "Acts of the Apostles," by W. C. Robinson.
Apostles"

InDBS,   ———. "Dead Sea Scrolls," by Geza Vermes.
"DSS"

InDBS,   ———. "Essenes," by O. Betz.
"Essenes"

InDBS,   ———. "Exodus, Book of," by R. E. Clements.
"Exodus"

InDBS,   ———. "Leviticus," by Jacob Milgrom.
"Leviticus"

InDBS,   ———. "Prophecy in Ancient Israel," by M. J. Buss.
"Prophecy"

Isaiah the   Isaiah the Elder of Terrani. *Piskei HaRid*. Vol. 2: *Tractates*
Elder   *ʿErubim, Pesaḥim, Yoma and Sukkah*. Edited by A. J.
                          Wertheimer et al. Jerusalem, 1966.

Jacobson   Jacobson, Howard. *The Exagoge of Ezekiel*. Cambridge,
                          1983.

Jacobson   ———. "Wisdom 18:9." *JSJ 7 (1976):204*.
(1976)

Japhet   Japhet, Sarah. *The Ideology of the Book of Chronicles and*
                          Its Place in Biblical Thought. Jerusalem, 1977.

Jastrow   Jastrow, Marcus. *A Dictionary of the Targumim, the Talmud*
                          Babli and Yerushalmi, and the Midrashic Literature.
                          New York, 1903.

Jeremias   Jeremias, Joachim. *Eucharist Words of Jesus*. 3d ed. New
                          York, 1966.

Jeremias   ———. "Die Passahfeier der Samaritaner." *Beihefte zur*
(1932)   *Zeitschrift fur Alttestamentliche Wissenschaft* 59
                      (1932).

Johnson   Johnson, Sherman E. "Asia Minor and Early Christianity."
                      In *Christianity, Judaism and Other Greco-Roman
                      Cults*, vol. 2, edited by Jacob Neusner, pp. 77–145.
                      Leiden, 1975.

Josephus   *Josephus*. 9 vols. Edited by H. St. J. Thackeray, Ralph
                      Marcus, Allen Wikgren, and Louis H. Feldman. Loeb
                      Classical Library. Cambridge, 1926–1965. [Unless
                      otherwise stated the reference is to this edition.]

                      Qadmoniot HaYehudim [=*Antiquities of the Jews*].
                      Edited, translated, introduced, and explained
                      by Abraham Shalit. Vols. 1–2. 2d ed. Jerusalem,
                      1955.

Judah Sir Leon   Judah ben Issac Sir Leon, R. *Tosefot to Tractate Berakhot*.
                      Edited by Nisan Sacks. 2 vols. Jerusalem, 1969–1972.

Juster   Juster, Jean. *Les Juifs dans l'Empire Roman*. 2 vols. Paris,
                      1914.

Justin   Justin Martyr. *Dialogue with Trypho*. In *Fathers of the
                      Church, Writings of Saint Justin Martyr*. Edited and
                      translated by Thomas B. Falls. New York, 1948.

Kadushin   Kadushin, Max. *Worship and Ethics*. New York, 1963.

Kadushin   ———. *A Conceptual Approach to the Mekilta*. New York,
(1969)   1969.

Kahle   Kahle, Paul. "Was Melito's Homily on the Passover Origi-
                      nally Written in Syriac?" *JTS* 44 (1943):52–56.

Kanter   Kanter, Shamai. *Rabban Gamaliel II: The Legal Traditions*.
                      BJS, vol. 8. Chico, 1980.

Kasher   Kasher, Menachem M. *Hagadah Shelemah: The Complete
                      Passover Hagadah*. 3d ed. Edited by S. Ashknage.
                      Jerusalem, 1967.

Kaufmann   Kaufmann, Yehezkiel. *History of the Religion of Israel*.
                      8 vols. Jerusalem, 1937–1960.

Kimelman   Kimelman, Reuven. "R. Yoḥanan and Origen on the Song
                    of Songs: A Third Century Jewish-Christian
                    Disputation." *HTR* 73 (1980):567–598.

Kosovsky   Kosovsky, C. Y. *Thesaurus Mishnae*. 4 vols. Jerusalem,
                    1960.

Kosovsky   ———. *Thesaurus Tosephthae*. 6 vols. Jerusalem, 1932–
(1932–1961)   1961.

Kraabel   Kraabel, Alf Thomas. "The Diaspora Synagogue: Archaeo-
                    logical and Epigraphic Evidence Since Sukenik."
                    ANRW 2.19.1 (1979):477–510.

Krauss   Krauss, Samuel. *Qadmoniyot HaTalmud*. 2 vols. in 4 parts.
                    Berlin, 1914, 1923; Tel Aviv, 1929, 1945.

Krauss   ———. *Talmudische Archaeologie*. 3 vols. Leipzig, 1910–
(1910–1912)   1912.

Kuhn   Kuhn, K. G. "The Lord's Supper and the Communal Meal
                    at Qumran." In *The Scrolls and the New Testament*,
                    edited by Krister Stendahl, pp. 65–93. New York,
                    1957.

Kutscher   Kutscher, E. Y. *Words and Their History* [Hebrew]. Jeru-
                    salem, 1965.

Lampe   Lampe, G. W. H. *A Patristic Greek Lexicon*. Oxford, 1961.

Lauterbach   Lauterbach, Jacob. "Breaking of the Bone of the Pascal
                    Lamb" [Hebrew]. *Haẓofeh* 9 (1925):235–241.

Laytner   Laytner, Anson. "Remnants of a Dissenting Tradition."
                    Conservative Judaism 34, no. 4 (1981):42–48.

Le Déaut   Le Déaut, Robert. "Apropos a Definition of Midrash."
                    Interpretation 25 (1971):259–282.

Le Déaut   ———. *La Nuit Pascale*. Analecta Biblica, vol. 22. Rome,
(1963)   1963.

Leiman   Leiman, Sid Z. *The Canonization of Hebrew Scriptures*.
                    Hamden, Conn., 1976.

Levey   Levey, Samson H. "Ben Zoma, the Sages, and Passover."
                    JRJ 28, no. 2 (Spring 1981):33–40.

Levine	Levine, Howard I. *Studies in Mishna Pesachim, Baba Kama, and the Mechilta* [Hebrew]. Tel Aviv, 1971.
Levine, L.	Levine, Lee. "R. Abbahu of Caesarea." In *Christianity, Judaism and Other Greco-Roman Cults. Studies for Morton Smith at Sixty*, edited by Jacob Neusner, 4:56−76. Leiden, 1975.
Lewin	Lewin, B. M., ed. *Otzar HaGaonim*. 13 vols. Haifa and Jerusalem, 1928−1943. Vol. 3. *Tractates Erubin and Peashim*. Jerusalem, 1930.
Lewy	Lewy, Israel. "Ein Vortag über das Rital des Pesach-Abends." *Jahres-Bericht des Judisch Theologischen Seminars*. Breslau: Fraenckel'-scher Stiftung, 1903−1904.
Licht	Licht, Jacob, ed. *The Rule Scroll 1QS, 1QSa, 1QSb*. Jerusalem, 1965.
Liddell and Scott	Liddell, H. G., and Scott, R. *A Greek-English Lexicon*. Oxford, 1968.
Lieberman	Lieberman, Saul. *Greek in Jewish Palestine*. 2d ed. New York, 1965.
Lieberman (1934)	———. *Ha Yerushalmi Kiphshuto*. Jerusalem, 1934.
Lieberman (1946)	———. "Palestine in the Third and Fourth Centuries." *JQR* 36 (1946):332−34.
Lieberman (1950)	———. *Hellenism in Jewish Palestine*. New York, 1950.
Lieberman (1968)	———. *Siphre Zutta*. New York, 1968.
Lieberman (1970)	———. "Response to the Introduction by Professor Alexander Marx." In *The Jewish Expression*, edited by Judah Goldin, pp. 119−133. New York, 1970.
Lieberman *TK*	———. *Tosefta Ki-Fshutah*. 1− , New York, 1955− .
Lieberman *TR*	———. *Tosefeth Rishonim*. 4 vols. Jerusalem, 1937−1939.
Lietzmann	Lietzmann, Hans. *Mass and Lord's Supper*. 11 fasc.

	Translated by D. H. G. Reeve. Introduction and supplementary essay by Robert D. Richardson. Leiden, 1979.
Lightstone	Lightstone, Jack N. "Ṣadoq the Yavnean." In *Persons and Institutions in Early Rabbinic Judaism*, edited by W. S. Green, pp. 49–147. Missoula, 1977.
Liver	Liver, Jacob. *Chapters in the History of the Priests and Levites* [Hebrew]. Jerusalem, 1968.
Liver (1963)	———. "The Half-Shekel Offering in Biblical and Post-Biblical Literature." *HTR* 56 (1963):173–198.
Loew	Loew, Immanuel. *Die Flora der Juden*. 4 vols. in 5 parts. Vienna, 1924–1934.
Loewenstamm	Loewenstamm, S. S. *The Tradition of the Exodus in Its Development* [Hebrew]. 2d ed. Jerusalem, 1965.
Ludwig	Ludwig, Theodore M. " 'Remember Not the Former Things': Disjunction and Transformation in Ancient Israel." In *Transitions and Transformations in the History of Religions. Essays in Honor of J. M. Kitagawa*, edited by F. E. Reynolds and T. M. Ludwig, pp. 25–55. Leiden, 1980.
Luzzatto	Luzzatto, Samuel David. *Sefer Yishayahu. Il Profeta Isaia*. Padua, 1855. Reprint. Jerusalem, 1966.
MacMullen	MacMullen, Ramsay. *Enemies of the Roman Order*. Cambridge, 1966.
Maimonides, *Mishneh Torah*	Maimonides Moses. *Mishneh Torah* with Commentaries. Jerusalem, 1970. Rome first edition, 1480. Reprint. Jerusalem, 1955. Constantinople 1509 edition with Commentaries. Reprint. Jerusalem, 1973.
Marshall	Marshall, I. Howard. *Last Supper and Lord's Supper*. Grand Rapids, Mich. 1981.
Martin	Martin, Joseph. *Symposion, die Geschichte einer Literarischen Form*. Studien zur Geschichte und Kultur des Altertums, vol. 17. Paderborn, 1931.
McKelvey	McKelvey, R. J. *The New Temple*. Oxford, 1969.
Meir Marim	Meir Marim of Kobrin. *Sefer Nir. Moʿed*. Vilna, 1890.

Meiri   Menahem Meiri, R. *Bet Habehira*. To whatever tractate
                 indicated. To: *Tractate Berakhot*. Edited by Shmuel
                 Daikman. Jerusalem, 1965. To: *Tractate Pesahim*.
                 Edited by Joseph Klein. 2d ed. Jerusalem, 1967.

Melito   See Hall and Perler.

Meyers   Meyers, Eric M. *Jewish Ossuaries: Reburial and Rebirth*.
                 Biblica et Orientalia, vol. 24. Rome, 1971.

Milgrom   Milgrom, Jacob. *Studies in Levitical Terminology*. Vol. 1.
                 Berkeley, 1970.

Milgrom   ———. "Profane Slaughter and a Formulaic Key to the
(1976).   Composition of Deuteronomy." *HUCA* 47 (1976):
                 1–17.

Montgomery   Montgomery, James A. *The Samaritans*. New York, 1968.

Morgenstern   Morgenstern, Julian. "The Bones of the Paschal Lamb."
                 JAOS 36 (1916):146–151.

Moshe Halavah   Moshe Halavah. *Commentary on Tractate Pesahim*. Jeru-
                 salem, 1873. Reprint. Jerusalem, 1972.

Muilenburg   Muilenburg, James. "A Liturgy on the Triumphs of
                 YAHWEH." In *Studia Biblica et Semitica Theodoro
                 Christiano Vriezen*, edited by W. C. Van Unnik, pp.
                 233–251. Wageningen, 1966.

Nahmanides   Nahmanides. Commentary on the Torah. *Perush HaRamban
                 ʿal HaTorah*. Edited by Haim Chavel. 2 vols.
                 Jerusalem, 1962–1963.

Neusner   Neusner, Jacob. *Development of a Legend*. Leiden, 1970.

Neusner   ———. *A History of the Jews in Babylonia*. 5 vols. Leiden,
(1966–1970)   1966–1970.

Neusner   ———. *Life of R. Yohanan b. Zakkai*. 2d ed. Leiden, 1970.
(1970)

Neusner   ———. "The Rabbinic Traditions about the Pharisees
(1971)   before 70: The Problem of Oral Transmission." *JJS* 22
                 (1971):1–18.

Neusner   ———. *Rabbinic Traditions about the Pharisees before 70*.
(1971)   3 vols. Leiden, 1971.
Pharisees

Neusner   ———. "Judaism in a Time of Crisis." *Judaism* 21
(1972)   (1972):313–327.

Neusner   ———. *Eliezer ben Hyrcanus, the Tradition and the Man.* 2
(1973)   vols. Leiden, 1973.

Neusner   ———. " 'Pharisaic-Rabbinic' Judaism: A Clarification."
(1973)   *HR* 12 (1973):250–270.
"Pharisaic"

Neusner   ———. *From Politics to Piety.* Englewood Cliffs, N.J.,
(1973)   1973.
"Politics"

Neusner   ———. *From Politics to Piety.* 2d ed. New York, 1979.
(1973, 1979)
Politics

Neusner   ———. *The Idea of Purity in Ancient Judaism.* Leiden,
(1973)   1973.
Purity

Neusner   ———. "The Written Tradition in Pharisaism before 70."
(1973)   *JSJ* 4 (1973):56–65.
"Written"

Neusner   ———. *A History of the Mishnaic Law of Purities.* 22 vols.
(1974–1977)   Leiden, 1974–1977.

Neusner   ———. "The Study of Religion as the Study of Tradition:
(1975)   Judaism." *HR* 14 (1975):191–206.

Neusner   ———. "The Formation of Rabbinic Judaism: Yavneh
(1979)   (Jamnia) from A.D. 70 to 100." *ANRW* 2.19.2
                        (1979):3–42.

Neusner   ———. "Map Without Territory: Mishnah's System of
(1979) "Map"   Sacrifice and Sanctuary." In *Method and Meaning in
                        Ancient Judaism.* Vol. 1, pp. 133–153. Missoula,
                        1979. [Reprinted from *HR* 1979.]

Neusner   ———. *Method and Meaning in Ancient Judaism.* Vol. 1.
(1979)   Missoula, 1979.
Method

Neusner   ———. *The Way of Torah.* 3d ed. North Scituate, Mass.,
(1979)   1979.
Torah

Neusner (1980)	———. *A History of the Mishnaic Law of Holy Things.* Vol. 6. Leiden, 1980.
Neusner (1981)	———. *Judaism: The Evidence of the Mishnah.* Chicago, 1981.
Nikiprowetzky	Nikiprowetzky, Valentin. "La Spiritualisation des sacrifices et le culte sacrificiel au Temple de Jérusalem chez Philon d'Alexandre." *Semitica* 17 (1967):97–116.
Nissim	Nissim b. Reuben Gerondi, Rabbenu. Commentary on Alfasi. In Vilna Editions of the BT.
Noth	Noth, Martin. *Exodus.* London, 1962.
Origen	Origen. *On Pascha.* See Guéraud and Nautin.
Ostow	Ostow, Mortimer. "The Jewish Response to Crisis." *Conservative Judaism* 33 (1980):3–25.
OxCD, "Athenaeus (1)"	*Oxford Classical Dictionary.* S.v. "Athenaeus (1)," by W. M. Edwards and Robert Browning.
OxCD, "Plutarch"	———. "Plutarch," by D. A. Russell.
OxCD, "Symposium"	———. "Symposium" by Michael Coffey.
OxCD, "Symposium Literature"	———. "Symposium Literature," by Michael Coffey.
Pagels	Pagels, Elaine H. "Origen and the Prophets of Israel: A Critique of Christian Typology." *Journal of the Ancient Near Eastern Society* 5 (1973):335–344.
Pardo	Pardo, David. *Ḥasde David on the Tosefta.* Vol. 1. Livorne, 1776. Reprint. Jerusalem, 1970.
Pelletier	Pelletier, André, ed. *Lettre D'Aristé A Philocrate.* Sources chrétiennes, vol. 89. Paris, 1962.
Perler	Perler, Othman, ed., trans., and commentator. *Meliton de Sardes Sur la Pâque.* Sources chrétiennes, vol. 123. Paris, 1966.
Petersen	Petersen, David L. *Late Israelite Prophecy: Studies in*

	Deutero-Prophetic Literature and in Chronicles. Missoula, 1977.
Petuchowski	Petuchowski, Jakob J. " 'Do This in Remembrance of Me' (I Cor. 11−24)." *JBL* 76 (1957):293−298.
Petuchowski (1980)	———. "Obscuring A Mishrah." *JRJ* 27, no. 4 (Fall 1980):72−74.
Philo	*Philo In Ten Volumes (And Two Supplementary Volumes).* Translated and edited by F. H. Colson, G. H. Whitaker, and Ralph Marcus. Loeb Classical Library. 1929−1962. *De Specialibus Legibus.* Vols. 1−2. Edited and translated by Suzanne Daniel. Paris, 1975. For *On the Contemplative Life*, see also the editions of Dauman and Miquel, Geoltrain, and Winston (1981).
Pines	Pines, S. " 'From Darkness to Light,' Parallels to Haggada Texts in Hellenistic Literature" [Hebrew]. In *Studies in Literature Presented to Simon Halkin*, edited by Ezra Fleischer, pp. 173−179. Jerusalem, 1973.
Plutarch	Plutarch. *Moralia: Table Talk.* Books 1−9. Translated and edited by Paul Clement, Herbert B. Hoffleidt, L. Minar, and F. H. Sanbach. Loeb Classical Library, vols. 8−9. London and Cambridge, 1961, 1969.
Porten	Porten, Bezalel. *Archives from Elephantine.* Berkeley, 1968.
Porton	Porton, Gary. "The Grape Cluster in Jewish Literature and Art of Late Antiquity." *JJS* 27 (1976):159−176.
Porton (1976−1982)	———. *The Traditions of R. Ishmael.* 4 vols. Leiden, 1976−1982.
Porton (1979)	———. "Midrash: Palestinian Judaism and the Hebrew Bible in the Greco-Roman Period." *ANRW* 2.19.2 (1979):103−138.
Rabin	Rabin, Chaim. *Qumran Studies.* New York, 1957, 1975.
Rabbinovicz	Rabbinovicz, Raphaelo. *Diqduqe Sofrim.* 12 vols. Reprint. New York, 1960. (Unless otherwise stipulated, to Tractate Pesaḥim.)
RAnC	*Reallexikon für Antike und Christentum.* S.v. "Eulogia," by A. Stuiber.

Raphael   Raphael, Chaim. *A Feast of History: The Drama of Passover Through the Ages*. London and Jerusalem, 1972.

Rashi   Solomon b. Isaac ("Rashi"). Commentary to the Babylonian Talmud. In editions of the BT.

Rashi (1905)   Solomon b. Isaac. *Sefer Ha-Orah*. Edited by S. Buber. Lemberg, 1905. Reprint, Jerusalem, 1967.

Ratner   Ratner, B. *Ahawath Zion We-Jeruscholaim. Tractate Pesaḥim*. Petrokow, 1908. Reprint. Jerusalem, 1967.

Reider   Reider, Jacob. *The Book of Wisdom*. New York, 1957.

Rice and   Rice, David G., and Stambaugh, John E. *Sources for the Study of Greek Religion*. Missoula, 1979.
Stambaugh

Richter   G. M. A. Richter. *Furniture of the Greeks, Etruscans, and Romans*. London, 1966.

Ringgren   Ringgren, Helmer. *Israelite Religion*. Philadelphia, 1966.

Rosenbaum   Rosenbaum, Jonathan. "Hezekiah's Reform and the Deuteronomistic Tradition." *HTR* 72 (1979):23−40.

Rosenstein   Rosenstein, Marc. "The Haggadah of Rabban Gamaliel." *CCARJ* 23, no. 2 (Spring 1975):28−32.

Safrai   Safrai, Shmuel. "He'erot Historiyot LeMishnah Pesaḥim Pereq Asiri." In *Bible and Jewish History. Studies in Dedication to the Memory of Jacob Levir*, edited by B. Uffenheimer, pp. 297−306. Tel Aviv, 1971.

Safrai (1965)   ———. *Pilgrimage at the Time of the Second Temple* [Hebrew]. Tel Aviv, 1965.

Safrai (1974)   ———. "Relations Between the Diaspora and the Land of Israel." In *The Jewish People in the First Century. Compendia Rerum Iudaicarum ad Novum Testamentum*, edited by S. Safrai et al., 1:184−215. Philadelphia, 1974.

Saldarini   Saldarini, Anthony J. "Apocalyptic and Rabbinic Literature." *CBQ* 37 (1975):348−358.

Sanders   Sanders, E. P. *Paul and Palestinian Judaism*. Philadelphia, 1977.

Sarfatti   Sarfatti, G. "Three Comments Regarding Some Tannaitic Sources" [Hebrew]. *Tarbiẓ* 32 (1963):136−142.

Sarfatti (1976)   ———. "Erev Pesaḥim." *Lešonenu* 41 (1976):21–28.

Sarna   Sarna, N. M. "The Psalm Superscriptions and the Guilds."
                   *Studies in Jewish Religious and Intellectual History
                   Presented to Alexander Altmann*, edited by Siegfried
                   Stein and Raphael Loewe, pp. 281–300. University,
                   Ala., 1980.

Schiffman   Schiffman, Lawrence H. *The Halakhah at Qumran*. Leiden,
                   1975.

Schiffman   ———. "Communal Meals at Qumran." *RQ* 10, no. 37
(1979)   (1979):45–56.

Scholem   Scholem, Gershom G. *On the Kabbalah and Its Symbolism*.
                   New York, 1965, 1969.

Scholem   ———. *The Messianic Idea in Judaism and Other Essays*.
(1971)   New York, 1971.

Schürer   Schürer, Emil. *The History of the Jewish People in the Age of
                   Jesus Christ. New Revised Edition*. Vols. 1–2. Revised
                   and edited by Fergus Millar and Geza Vermes. Edin-
                   burgh, 1973–1979.

Seeligman   Seeligman, J. A. "Jerusalem in Jewish-Hellenistic
                   Thought" [Hebrew]. In *Judah and Jerusalem*. Israel
                   Exploration Society. 12th Archaeological Convention,
                   pp. 192–208. Jerusalem, 1957.

Segal   Segal, J. B. *The Hebrew Passover*. Oxford, 1963.

Shalit   See Josephus.

Shanks   Shanks, Hershel. *Judaism in Stone*. New York, 1979.

Shinan   Shinan, Avigdor. "The Petiḥah to Midrash Exodus Rabbah"
                   [Hebrew]. In *Studies in Aggadah, Targum and Jewish
                   Liturgy in Memory of Joseph Heinemann*, edited by
                   J. J. Petuchowski and E. Fleischer et al., pp. 175–183.
                   Jerusalem, 1981.

Sibingar   Sibingar, Smit. "Melito of Sardis, the Artist and His Text."
                   Vigiliae Christianae 24 (1970):81–104.

Simon   Simon, Marcel. *Jewish Sects at the Time of Jesus*. Translated
                   by J. H. Farley. Philadelphia, 1967.

Sklare   Sklare, Marshall. *America's Jews*. New York, 1971.

Smallwood   Smallwood, E. Mary. *The Jews under Roman Rule*. Leiden, 1976.

Smith   Smith, Jonathan Z. "Native Cults in the Hellenistic Period." *HR* 11 (1971):236–249.

Smith (1980)   ———. "Fences and Neighbors: Some Contours of Early Judaism." In *Approaches to Ancient Judaism*, vol. 2, edited by W. S. Green, pp. 1–25. Chico, 1980.

Smith (1980) Bare   ———. "The Bare Facts of Ritual." *HR* 20 (1980): 112–27.

Smith, M.   Smith, Morton. "The Image of God." *Bulletin of the John Rylands Library* 40 (1958):473–512.

Smith, M. (1956)   ———. "Palestinian Judaism in the First Century." In *Israel: Its Role in Civilization*, edited by Moshe Davis, pp. 67–81. New York, 1956.

Smith, M. (1971)   ———. "The Dead Sea Sect in Relation to Ancient Judaism." *NTS* 7 (1971):347–360.

Smith, M. (1974)   ———. "On the Wine God in Palestine." In *Salo Wittamayer Baron Jubilee Volume*, edited by S. Lieberman, 2:815–829. New York, 1974.

Soleh   Soleh, M. Z. "On the Two Ancient Passover Customs" [Hebrew]. *Ha'arez* 14 Nisan 5735 (1975):13.

Solomon Haedani   Solomon Haedani. "Melekhet Shelomo." Commentary on the Mishnah in Romm edition of the Mishnah.

Stein   Stein, Siegfried. "The Influence of Symposia Literature on the Literary Form of the Pesah Haggadah." *JJS* 7 (1957):13–44.

Stone   Stone, Michael. *Scriptures, Sects and Visions*. Philadelphia, 1980.

Strange   Strange, J. F. "Archaeology and the Religion of Judaism in Palestine." *ANRW* 2.19.1 (1979):646–685.

Strashun   Strashun, Samuel b. Joseph. "Annotations." In back of Vilna editions of the BT.

Stylianopoulos   Stylianopoulos, Theodore. *Justin Martyr and the Mosaic Law*. Society of Biblical Literature Dissertation Series, no. 20. Missoula, 1975.

Sutcliffe　　　　　Sutcliffe, Edmund F. "Sacred Meals at Qumran." *Heythrop Journal* 1 (1960):48–65.

Tabory　　　　　　Tabory, Joseph. "The History of the Order of the Passover Eve" [Hebrew]. Ph.D. dissertation. Bar Ilan University. Ramat Gan, 1977.

Tabory (1977)　　　———. "The History of the First Dipping on Passover Eve in the Period of the Mishnah and Talmud." [Hebrew]. *BIA* 14–15 (1977):70–78.

Tabory
(1977–1978)　　　———. "On the Text of the Haggadah in the Time of the Temple." [Hebrew]. *Sinai* 82 (1977–78):97–108.

Tabory (1979)　　　———. "The Household Table in Rabbinic Times." *AJS* 4 (1979):211–215.

Tabory (1981)　　　———. "Towards a Characterization of the Passover Meal" [Hebrew]. *BIA* 18–19 (1981):68–78.

Talmon　　　　　　Talmon, Shemaryahu. "Divergences in Calender-Reckoning in Ephraim and Judah." *VT* 8 (1958):48–74.

Talmon (1960)　　　———. "The 'Manual of Benedictions' of the Sect of the Judean Desert." *RQ* 2 (1960):475–500.

Talmon (1977)　　　———. "The Samaritans." *Scientific American*, January 1977, pp. 100–108.

Talmon (1978)　　　———. "The Emergence of Institutionalized Prayer in Israel in the Light of the Qumran Literature." In *Qumran. Sa Piété, Theologie et son milieu*. Bibliotheca Ephemeridum theologicarum Lovaniensium, vol. 46, edited by M. Delcor, pp. 265–284. Louvain, 1978.

TDNT,
"Oinos"　　　　　*Theological Dictionary of the New Testament*. S.v. "Oinos," by H. Seeseman.

TDNT,
"Paska"　　　　　———. "Paska," by J. Jeremias.

TDNT,
"Zumē"　　　　　———. "Zumē," by Hans Windisch.

Temple Scroll　　See Yadin.

Thompson　　　　Thompson, James W. "Hebrews 9 and Hellenistic Concepts of Sacrifice." *JBL* 98 (1979):567–578.

Tigay   Tigay, Jeffrey H. "On Some Aspects of Prayer in the
        Bible." *AJS* 1 (1976):363−79.

Tosafot   Tosafot [Commentary on the Talmud]. In standard editions
        of the BT and in Venice first edition.

Tosefot   Heller, Yom Tov Lippman, R. "Tosefot Yom Ṭov." In
Yom Tov   standard editions of the Mishnah.

Townsend   Townsend, John T. "Changed Attitudes to the Jerusalem
        Temple After its Destruction." Unpublished MS.

Townsend   ———. "The Jerusalem Temple in the First Century." In
(1981)   *God and His Temple*, edited by Lawrence E. Frizzell,
        pp. 48−65. Seton Hall, N.J., 1981.

Turner   Turner, Victor. *The Ritual Process.* 1969. Ithaca, 1977,
        1979.

Turner (1974) ———. *Dramas, Fields, and Metaphors.* Ithaca, 1974.

Turner (1974) ———. "Pilgrimage as Social Process." In Turner (1974),
"Pilgrimage"   pp. 166−230.

Turner (1977) ———. "Sacrifice as Quintessential Process: Prophylaxis or
        Abandonment." *HR* 16 (1977):189−215.

Urbach   Urbach, Ephraim E. "The Derasha as a Basis of the Halakha
        and the Problem of the Soferim" [Hebrew]. *Tarbiẓ* 27
        (1958):166−182.

Urbach (1961) ———. Review of Goldschmidt's Haggadah [Hebrew]. *KS*
        36 (1961):148−160.

Urbach (1969) ———. *The Sages* [Hebrew]. Jerusalem, 1969.

Van der Ploeg Van der Ploeg, J. "The Meals of the Essenes." *JJS* 2
        (1957):163−175.

Vermes   Vermes, Geza. "The Impact of the Dead Sea Scrolls on the
        Study of the New Testament." *JJS* 27
        (1976):107−116.

Vermes (1973) ———. *Scripture and Tradition in Judaism.* 2d ed. Leiden,
        1973.

Vermes (1975) ———. *The Dead Sea Scrolls in English.* 2d ed. Middlesex,
        1975. Reprint. 1979.

Vermes 1976) ———. *Postbiblical Jewish Studies.* Leiden, 1976.

von Gall   von Gall, H. "Entwicklung und Gestalt des Thrones im
                Vorislamischen Iran." *Archaelogische Mitteilungen
                aus Iran* 4 (1971):207–235.

von Rad   von Rad, Gerhard. *The Problem of the Hexateuch and Other
                Essays.* Edinburgh, 1965, 1966.

Wach   Wach, Joachim. *Sociology of Religion.* Chicago, 1944,
                1971.

Wambacq   Wambacq, B. N. "Les Origines de la Pesaḥ israélite."
                Biblica 57 (1976):206–224, 301–326.

Wambacq   ———. "Les Maṣṣot." *Biblica* 61 (1980):31–54.
(1980)

Weinfeld   Weinfeld, Moshe. *Deuteronomy and the Deuteronomic
                School.* Oxford, 1972.

Weisberg   Weisberg, Steven E. "Journal of Confrontation." *CCARJ*
                23, no. 2 (Spring 1975):21–27.

Weiser   Weiser, Artur. *The Psalms, a Commentary.* Philadelphia,
                1962.

Wellesz   Wellesz, Egon. *A History of Byzantine Music and
                Hymnography.* 2d ed. Oxford, 1961.

Wellesz   ———. "Melito's Homily on the Passion." *JTS* 44
(1943)   (1943):41–52.

Werner   Werner, Eric. "Melito of Sardis." *HUCA* 37
                (1966):191–210.

Werner (1943)   ———. "Notes on the Attitude of the Early Church Fathers
                Towards Hebrew Psalmody." *Journal of Religion* 7
                (1943):339–352.

Werner (1957)   ———. "Musical Aspects of the Dead Sea Scrolls."
                Musical Quarterly 43 (1957):21–37.

Werner (1970)   ———. *The Sacred Bridge.* New York, 1970.

Werner (1976)   ———. "Communication." *CCARJ* 23, no. 1 (Winter,
                1976):12.

Wieder   Wieder, N. "The Old Palestinian Ritual: New Sources." *JJS*
                4 (1953):30–37, 65–73.

Williams   Williams, Sam K. *Jesus' Death as a Saving Event.* HTR,

	Harvard Dissertations in Religion, no. 2. Missoula, 1975.
Winston	Winston, David. *The Wisdom of Solomon*. A New Translation with Introduction and Commentary. New York, 1979.
Winston (1981)	———. Winston, David, trans. and intro. *Philo of Alexandria: The Contemplative Life, the Giants, and Selections*. New York, 1981.
Wisdom of Solomon	See Winston.
Wolfson	Wolfson, Harry A. *Philo*. 2 vols. Cambridge, 1947.
Yadin	Yadin, Yigael. *The Temple Scroll*. 3 vols. Jerusalem, 1977.
Yalkut HaMakhiri	Machir ben Abba Mari, R. *Jalkut Machiri: To Psalms*, edited by Salomon Buber. Berdyczew, 1899. Reprint. Jerusalem, 1964.
Ydit	Ydit, Meir. "An Obscure Mishnah and Haggadah Text." *JRJ* 27, no. 2 (Spring, 1980):76−80.
Zeitlin	Zeitlin, S. "The Liturgy of the First Night of Passover." *JQR* 38 (1948):435−460.
Zeitlin (1964)	———. *The Rise and Fall of the Judean State*. Vol. 1. Philadelphia, 1964.
Zeitlin (1973)	———. "The Mishnah in the Yerushalmi and the Mishnah in the Bavli" [Hebrew]. In *Zer li'Gevurot Zalman Shazar Jubilee Volume*, edited by B. Z. Luria, pp. 539−548. Jerusalem, 1973.
Zevulun and Olenik	Zevulun, Uza, and Olenik, Yael. *Function and Design in the Talmudic Period*. 2d ed. Haaretz Museum. Tel Aviv, 1979.
Zuntz	Zuntz, G. "Aristeas Studies I: 'The Seven Banquets.' " *JSS* 4 (1959):21−36.

INDEX

Note: This index lists primary sources where the context is significant and also lists the names of authors cited in the notes where their views are discussed.

BIBLICAL AND POSTBIBLICAL SOURCES

GENERAL INDEX

Designer:	UC Press Staff
Compositor:	Trend Western
Printer:	Thomson-Shore
Binder:	John H. Dekker & Sons
Text:	10/13 Times Roman
Display:	Times Roman